EUCHARIST AND CHURCH FELLOWSHIP
IN THE FIRST FOUR CENTURIES

EUCHARIST AND CHURCH FELLOWSHIP IN THE FIRST FOUR CENTURIES

by Werner Elert

TRANSLATED FROM THE GERMAN BY N. E. NAGEL

SAINT LOUIS

Concordia Publishing House Ltd., London, E. C. 1

Copyright © 1966 Concordia Publishing House
3558 S. Jefferson Avenue, St. Louis, MO 63118
Manufactured in the United States of America

Library of Congress Catalog Card No. 66-23212

Translated by permission from the original German *Abendmahl und Kirchengemeinschaft in der alten Kirche hauptsächlich des Ostens* published by Lutherisches Verlagshaus, Berlin

01 02 03 04 05 06 07 08 09 10   07 06 05 04 03 02 01 00 99 98

Translator's Preface

The desire to translate this book grew from a student's gratitude to its author. Hardly less than Elert's pastoral concern was his profound concern for healing the divisions among Christians. He was far too great a theologian to pretend they do not matter or to suppose they can be mended by a few sweeping gestures. So in this book he does not deal in generalities but rather with instances. His assessment is carefully built up bit by bit. The pieces have a way of embracing other pieces, particularly when their arms are as long and strong as *koinonia's*. The goal of this study may be said to be the true perception and practice of the *koinonia* of the one, holy, catholic, and apostolic church.

An apparently small matter which yet touches the nature of the church is the question when *c* in *church* shall be big or small. *Catholic* also has something in it which resists the imposition of a capital. It is, nevertheless, so used in this translation when a proper adjective, and so also *church* when a proper noun.

The question of *synod* or *council* is answered here by keeping *synod* for the East and *council* for the West, except when a synod is acknowledged by both East and West as ecumenical, for example, Synods of Antioch but the Council of Nicaea.

Elert's rather awesome bibliographies are sometimes reproduced more out of deference than for their accessible usefulness. They do, however, show the thoroughness with which the question has been examined. A few things have been added in the footnotes that may hopefully be useful to the English reader. When no *LCC* reference is available, one from *ACW* is given if possible, and *FC* is third man. A similar sequence has been followed with Stevenson, Bindley, Bright, and Watkins. Some local references may escape the English reader, but they also serve a purpose in showing that this study grew from earnest efforts to heal divi-

▼

sions. Here a man is often only as useful as he is specific, and Elert is specific beyond blessed relevance. There is something of a splendid catholic irrelevance here. He has no sectarian preoccupation with our little place in the centuries of the church and no new formula for licking it into shape. He points to the way things were first done in the family.

Elert is above all specific in examining pieces of evidence and letting them have their say whether that be to our comfort or not. His contribution is therefore perhaps not so comprehensive or neatly tailored as some, but if he does not say everything there is to be said, he nevertheless does let the early church answer his inquiry and have its say in the matter. And all this is pursued with that depth of churchly concern and humble, unsentimental clarity that were so evident to those who knew him and especially to those whose privilege it was to study under him.

An effort has been made to remove as much as possible from the text anything that might hinder the reader with little Latin and less Greek. A few useful terms remain. These he may shrewdly guess or pick up as he goes along. It may perhaps be helpful to give a little glossary here.

τῶν ἁγίων κοινωνία went into Latin as *sanctorum communio,* and we say "communion of saints."

οἱ ἅγιοι	= *sancti* (masculine nominative plural)	= the holy persons
		= the saints
τὰ ἅγια	= *sancta* (neuter nominative plural)	= the holy things
τῶν ἁγίων	= *sanctorum* (genitive of both the above)	
τοῖς ἁγίοις	= *sanctis* (dative of both the above)	

In the deacon's call τὰ ἅγια τοῖς ἁγίοις this dative is masculine, and we therefore translate "the holy things for the holy ones." In the discussion whether the above genitive is masculine or neuter we shall speak of a genitive of persons in contrast with a genitive of things.

ἐκκλησία = *ecclesia* = congregation = *Gemeinde*
                 church   = *Kirche*

Cambridge   N. E. NAGEL
Epiphany 1966

Author's Preface

The task of furnishing an account of the relation between altar fellowship and church fellowship in the history of the church was more easily accepted than carried out. In undertaking this task I felt sure that enough literature on the subject would be available to permit making a synopsis without difficulty. Such optimism was without foundation. A glance at the early church revealed that apart from occasional comments the historical literature consulted dealing with the church, its laws, dogmas, and liturgies, was practically unproductive. There was no exact account of what is meant by church fellowship *(communio ecclesiae* or *ecclesiastica),* although the expression appears often enough in the sources. Nor was there an answer to the questions whether and how church fellowship is essentially related to the understanding and practice of the Lord's Supper. There was nothing to do but to open a long-distance conversation with the early authors themselves.

Since the time for gathering, sifting, grouping, and evaluating the material was limited, various restrictions resulted. During the course of the work I also gained the impression that there was some justification in the material itself for limiting myself to the early church; not as though the early church took a stand peculiar to itself in this matter but rather because it anticipated almost every point of view, even those of today. The only person who might dispute this is the man for whom Christianity's confessional divisions are a phenomenon reserved for modern times. I believe the evidence adduced shows quite conclusively that this assumption, though widely held, is false. What is more, the early church also has the advantage of nearness to the apostolic age. This may appear at first to be only a chronological nearness, but this does not mean that it does not also enjoy a spiritual nearness such as the church of every age seeks to attain. In any case it is basic for the discussion of the main theme of our inquiry to know how the problem thus posed developed in the transition from the purely mission situation of the early Pauline age to the historical permanence to which the church was willy-nilly subjected.

The further restriction of our theme to the early church "chiefly of the East" I have dated from the fourth century on. From about that time the gradually deepening divergence between East and West also begins to affect our subject. From then on in the church of the West the motive of rulership gains the upper hand over the motive of fellowship, and in the understanding of the Eucharist the fellowship character also recedes into the background. In the process the basic presuppositions of the relation between altar fellowship and church fellowship drift so far apart — though the practice remains the same by and large — that a separate study would have to be made for the West.

Discussion of the meaning of the Eucharist was indispensable, but this, too, had to be limited if it was not to take us too far afield. No more could be attempted than registering the weight of those factors which are decisive and useful for our subject and are usually overlooked or at any rate neglected in presentations of the history of dogma. However, some vestiges remain from my originally more comprehensive plan. The purpose of comparing Luther with the early church is not to authenticate him in this way, still less the reverse, but rather that what we learn from the early church may stand out more clearly. The comparison of Schleiermacher and Luther at the beginning of the essay is justified on the ground of its usefulness for pointing out the ambiguities of the concept of fellowship in our theme. The further discussion of this concept in the context of the creedal formula *sanctorum communio* and the three excursuses reproduce, in part, my article on the origin of this formula in the *Theologische Literaturzeitung* (1949, cols. 577—586) with some correction of detail.

Erlangen
February 1954

Abbreviations

ACO	*Acta Conciliorum Oecumenicorum,* ed. E. Schwartz.
ACW	*Ancient Christian Writers,* ed. Johannes Quaston and J. C. Plampe. Westminster, Md.: Newman Press, 1946 ff.
AE	*Luther's Works, American Edition,* ed. Jaroslav Pelikan and Helmut Lehmann, St. Louis and Philadelphia, 1958—.
Ap. Can.	*Canones Apostolorum,* Apostolic Canons.
Ap. Const.	*Constitutiones Apostolorum,* Apostolic Constitutions.
Bindley	T. H. Bindley, *The Ecumenical Documents of the Faith,* 4th ed., London, 1950.
Bright	W. Bright, *The Canons of the First Four General Councils,* 2d ed., Oxford, 1892.
CCL	*Corpus Christianorum, Series Latina.*
CSCO	*Corpus Scriptorum Christianorum Orientalium.*
CSEL	*Corpus Scriptorum Ecclesiasticorum Latinorum.*
ET	English translation.
FC	*Fathers of the Church,* New York, 1947—.
Funk	F. X. Funk, *Didascalia et Constitutiones Apostolorum,* 2 vols., 1905.
GCS	*Die griechischen christlichen Schriftsteller der ersten drei Jahrhunderte.*
Hahn	A. Hahn, *Bibliothek der Symbole und Glaubensregeln der alten Kirche,* 3d ed., 1897.
Hefele	C. J. Hefele, *History of the Councils of the Church,* ET of 2d ed., London, 1882.
H. E.	*Historia Ecclesiastica,* Church History. That of Eusebius unless otherwise indicated.
JTS	*Journal of Theological Studies.*
Lauchert	F. Lauchert, *Die wichtigsten Kanones der altkirchlichen Konzilien,* 1896.

LCC   *Library of Christian Classics*, London, 1953—.

PG   *Patrologia Series Graeca*, ed. J. P. Migne, 1857—66.

PL   *Patrologia Series Latina*, ed. J. P. Migne, 1844—55.

PO   *Patrologia Orientalis*, ed. R. Graffin and F. Nau, 1907 ff.

Pitra   J. B. Pitra, *Iuris ecclesiastici Graecorum historia et monumenta*, 2 vols., 1864—68.

RE   *Realenzyklopaedie fuer protestantische Theologie und Kirche.*

RGG   *Religion in Geschichte und Gegenwart*, 2d ed., 1927—31.

Stevenson   J. Stevenson, *A New Eusebius*, London, 1957.

ThWb   *Theologisches Woerterbuch zum Neuen Testament*, ed. Gerhard Kittel and Gerhard Friedrich, 1933—.

WA   Weimar edition of the works of Martin Luther.

Watkins   O. D. Watkins, *A History of Penance*, 2 vols., London, 1920.

ZNTW   *Zeitschrift fuer neutestamentliche Wissenschaft.*

ZST   *Zeitschrift fuer systematische Theologie.*

CONTENTS

torium with the Arians (177). Personal responsibility of decision
(179). No free hand to manipulate altar fellowship (180). Confessional disunity to be removed first (180). Students' congregation in
Berytus (181). To receive the Sacrament in a church is to affirm its
confession (182).

1

COMMUNION

The early church had various names for the Lord's Supper. One of them was *koinonia,* in Latin, *communio.* Modern Catholics know *communio* as a current term for the reception of the Eucharist. It is also used in canon law *(sacra communio).* The derived terms "communicate" and "communicants" are found also in Protestant liturgies. There is already an interpretation of the rite in this term, not exhaustive, to be sure, and perhaps consciously one-sided from the receiver's point of view, but in any case one that expresses something still different than when "Last Supper" "Lord's Supper," "mystical sacrifice," "Eucharist," or some other expression is used. Here Paul is our guide. From him we have not only the oldest account of its institution but also its first interpretation. He calls it the "Lord's Table" (1 Cor. 10:21) or the "Lord's Supper" (11: 21). He also uses the expression *koinonia* for the cup and the bread. (10:16)

Koinonia went into Latin as *communio.* There was no alternative. Hence our Communion for the Lord's Supper. *Communio,* however, has more than one facet and therefore its setting is always crucial. In church usage we also find, for example, *communio ecclesiae* or *ecclesiastica.* This is church fellowship. In *communio,* then, we have a term which embraces both items of our study — the Lord's Supper and church fellowship. The German *Gemeinschaft* is similar. Luther so translated Paul's *koinonia.* German also has *Abendmahlsgemeinschaft* (altar fellowship). It would appear, therefore, that our first task is to discover the precise meaning of *communio,* or *Gemeinschaft,* and then to apply this to both the Lord's Supper and the factors involved in altar and church fellowship. This does not involve a departure from Greek usage, for *koinonia* is by no means reserved for the Lord's Supper. Κοινωνία τῆς ἐκκλησίας or ἐκκλησιαστική is as frequent as the corresponding *communio ecclesiae* or *ecclesiastica*.

Schleiermacher provides an instructive example of how the matter can be pursued in this way. For him the church is above all "a fellowship" *(Gemeinschaft)*. He says in his *Glaubenslehre* (§ 2, 2) that in order to know what the Christian church is one must first establish "the general concept of the church together with a right understanding of what is characteristically Christian." He goes on to say, "The general concept of the church, if there is to be such a thing, must be derived from ethics because the church at all events is a fellowship created by the voluntary actions of men, and only through these does it continue to exist." That certainly fixes the idea of fellowship. Since a fellowship arises through the voluntary actions of men and continues to exist only through such actions, the church, since it is a fellowship, arises in the same way, that is, only through "the voluntary actions of men etc." Pursuing this line we may go on to say that since the Lord's Supper is a fellowship *(koinonia)*, and since this term evidently includes both altar and church fellowship, they are both brought about "by the voluntary actions of men, and only through these can they continue to exist." [1] The concept of fellowship which is here said to characterize the church does not derive from the nature of the church, but the nature of the church is derived from the concept of fellowship. Wherever else this concept of fellowship may come from, it certainly does not have its source in the fact and character of the church.

It is not as if Schleiermacher here makes only an isolated slip. The statement is consistent with his understanding of the church. This permits him to regard the church as a special instance of the general category of fellowship. Behind this procedure lies the idealist conception of man and a view of the church which already has a long history with the English Independents and in the German Enlightenment. Such wide connections help to explain the popularity of his derivation of the church from the concept of fellowship, as also the role it has played and continues to play in theology and in much thinking and action regarding the church. His understanding of the church holds sway as far as does his concept of fellowship, and this still seems to grow rather than to decline in popularity in many parts of the world. It is nourished by democratic ideologies, as may be seen in North America and elsewhere. Social ideas and experiences slip imperceptibly into theological guise, and vice versa. When the German *Landeskirchen* (territorial churches) were to be reorganized after World War I, a *Freiwilligkeitskirche* (voluntary church) was proposed as a replacement for the *Volkskirche* (established church). *Volkskirche* referred to the situation encrusted with old orthodox ideas about church arrangements, while the *Freiwilligkeitskirche* was the thing for the future because, according to Schleiermacher, the church "can only continue to exist by the voluntary actions of men."

In European theology, at least, only a few stragglers still seriously cling to Schleiermacher's understanding of the church. His concept of fellowship is also in decline. This does not mean, however, that there is unanimity about what is to replace it, nor that Schleiermacher no longer has any influence in what goes on in church affairs. His persistent influence was evident in the recent discussions about altar and church fellowship which prompted this study. Much of what has been written on this theme suggests that altar and church fellowship are matters about which men are free to make their own arrangements. This means in effect that whether fellowship is granted or withheld depends on the good or ill will of those concerned. In harmony with such thinking we find altar fellowship arranged and practiced without full church agreement acknowledged by both sides. This can only be understood as a product of the view that Eucharistic *koinonia* is a "fellowship created by the voluntary actions of men, and only through these does it continue to exist." It is, then, a matter about which men are free to make their own arrangements.

As we shall see, there is no conceivable bridge between such a view and that of the early church. Historically, however, there does appear to be a point of contact that may help to explain the emergence of this utter contradiction. That is the *sanctorum communio* of the Apostles' Creed, or rather, the very constancy of this formula, which undoubtedly goes back to the early church. It also seems tolerant of that concept of fellowship of which we have been speaking. The Heidelberg Catechism translates the *communio* of the Creed with fellowship *(Gemeinschaft)*, and since this is understood, according to the word order, as qualifying the preceding *sancta ecclesia catholica,* nothing stands in the way of defining the church as a fellowship whose peculiarity is characterized only by the genitive *sanctorum.* That it is the *sancti* (saints) who create and continue the fellowship through the "voluntary actions of men," as Schleiermacher puts it, is not yet said, nor is it excluded. When this catechism further uses fellowship (Question 77), following Luther's translation of *koinonia* in 1 Cor. 10:16, the inclusion of both church and Lord's Supper in the concept of fellowship is apparently achieved. This would then parallel the Latin church usage of *communio.*

Luther proceeded differently. He was uneasy about the theological use of the word fellowship *(Gemeinschaft).* Even in translating 1 Cor. 10:16 he hesitated to use it. In his *Large Confession of the Lord's Supper* (1528) he traced the misunderstanding of his opponents partially to this word. "It is not the genuinely German equivalent as I would like to have it, for to have fellowship is ordinarily understood as meaning to have something to do with a person. Here (1 Cor. 10:16), however, it means, as I have explained earlier, many using, enjoying, or having part in a common thing. I have had to translate 'fellowship' because I simply could not find a better word" *(WA* 26, 493, 2; *AE* 37, 356). He is willing to use the expression "fellowship" of the Lord's Supper only if it is *not* taken according to the usage of the day, which understood it as "to have something to do with a person." This is not the meaning of *koinonia* in 1 Cor. 10:16, for there it means that many use, enjoy, or have part in a common thing.

This distinction shows what Luther considered vital. What links those who partake of the Lord's Supper is not that they have something to do with one another, their human relationship with each other, but that which they share together. This fellowship not only embraces still another ingredient besides the human participants but this other ingredient is not even produced by an act of man. It not only antedates the efforts of men, but fellowship *(koinonia)* means that this is the very element which unites the multitude. What Luther meant is, then, diametrically opposed to what Schleiermacher meant by fellowship when he spoke of the church. For Schleiermacher fellowship "is created by the voluntary actions of men." This is precisely what Luther rejected when he denied that fellowship means "to have something to do with a person."

Luther was set against applying such an idea of fellowship to the church. Least of all did he want "fellowship" as the translation of the Creed's *sanctorum communio.* He did indeed understand this as in apposition to *sancta ecclesia* but was nevertheless unwilling to translate *communio* with "fellowship." "No German language says or understands it that way." [2] *Communio* may not here be translated "fellowship" *(Gemeinschaft)* but must be translated "congregation" *(Gemeine).* Only in this way can the church be described as a *communio.* We see here how intent he was to make a clear distinction between *Gemeinschaft* and *Gemeine.* In Latin he used *communio* both of the church and of the Sacrament — of the Sacrament because it was ancient usage rooted in the Latin translation of *koinonia* in 1 Cor. 10:16, of the church because he took it in the Creed as an appositive to the church. When he translated into German, however, he felt impelled to differentiate in each context, for there is no German word which matches the various senses of *communio.* It can mean *Gemeinschaft* as well as *Gemeine:* the one with the Sacrament, the other with the church, and there is to be no indiscriminate exchange. Unlike Schleiermacher, Luther did not get an idea of fellowship from somewhere or other and then derive the nature of the church from the nature of fellowship. He first asked what is the church, and what is the Sacrament, and then sought to determine in what way each might be called a *communio.* This idea of fellowship has no importance in his understanding of the church. He was unwilling to apply it to the church at all.

By taking *sanctorum communio* in apposition to *sancta ecclesia* Luther followed a long tradition. He knew of course that the phrase was not always in the Creed (Large Catechism, II, 47). This he concluded from Rufinus' *Commentary on the Apostles' Creed,* which lacks the phrase (*WA*, 2, 190, 22). Although it cannot therefore rank as "apostolic," he regarded it as coming from the early church. Most expositions of the Creed before him understood the phrase as in apposition to *sancta ecclesia,* and this tradition has not lost ground since. There may be some explanation for it in the likely time and place of the phrase's origin and reception into the Creed.

Until the turn of the century it was held that the phrase, as well as the final form of the Creed, appeared first in Faustus of Riez (c. 450). It was therefore concluded that if it did not originate in Gaul, then certainly it was first received there. If Rufinus did not know it, then it might be supposed that it gained its place through Augustine's enormous influence. In Augustine, however, it is, strictly speaking, not to be found. It appears once when he quotes a Donatist source. It appears also in a Donatist document. Augustine does indeed once use the phrase *communio sanctorum,* but this cannot be the phrase of the Creed, for there the word order as we know it is always *sanctorum communio.*[3] From this fact alone that the creed as handed down to us always has *sanctorum communio* and never *communio sanctorum* Kattenbusch concluded that it must come from a single source. Obviously it could not have come from the writings of Augustine, although for later generations it did have an Augustinian ring. Taken in apposition to *sancta ecclesia,* it appeared to be an interpretation of the concept "church," which was the subject of dispute between Augustine and the Donatists, and so it seemed to preserve the fruit of that great controversy. Augustine described the church as *congregatio sanctorum,* as *societas sanctorum,* and as *populus sanctorum.* He was plainly not overmeticulous in his terms of association. Since he also spoke of the *communio ecclesiae* as the *communio fidelium,* it remained only to take up the idea of the *sancti* from here and combine it with the *communio* of his other statements in order to see Augustine as the originator of the phrase *sanctorum communio.* Even if this were so, we would still not have the answers to the questions when, where, and how the phrase came into the Creed.[4]

If one follows these Augustinian lines, the church appears as a *com-*

munio of *sancti,* that is, of persons. This view produced many similar formulations throughout the Middle Ages down to Luther — *congregatio sanctorum* (Gregory I), *fidelium* (Thomas), *praedestinatorum* (Wycliffe); *collectio catholicorum* (Nicholas I), *fidelium* (Richard of Middleton); *multitudo fidelium* (Hugh of St. Victor); *communio fidelium* (Duns Scotus), *sanctorum* (Wessel); *respublica fidelium* (Roger Bacon); *consortium sanctorum* (William of Auvergne); *universitas christianorum* (Hugh), *fidelium* (Scotus), *praedestinatorum* (Wycliffe). Occam has a particularly prolific selection: *multitudo christianorum* or *populi christiani, communitas fidelium, congregatio fidelium* or *christianorum, communitas tota christianorum,* etc.[5] Each was understood as variously as the various conceptions of the church which ranged from outspoken hierarchicalism to extreme enthusiasm. *Sanctorum communio* of the Creed is taken as either the same as *sancta ecclesia* or as an attribute which adds a new thought. The *sancti* are now saints in the narrow sense, now all the baptized, now only the living, now also including the dead, now the true believers excluding the hypocrites, now the elect, now the whole lot all together. In every case, however, *sanctorum communio* is a *communio* of persons. *Sanctorum* is taken as the genitive of *sancti,* that is in the masculine, of persons.

Here *sanctorum communio* was only one term in a great pile from which a man can select one or another according to his need. It did, however, enjoy some precedence because of its place in the Creed. This gave it ecclesiastical approval and authority and made it theologically unimpeachable. All sorts of ideas about the church could sally forth under this aegis. What was to stop Schleiermacher's "those born again" from being the *sancti,* and the *communio* "a fellowship created by the voluntary actions of men"? *Sanctorum communio* does not forbid this, and since it is in the Creed, it can appear to afford original sanction for such a view. Whoever has a different understanding of *sanctorum communio,* as Luther did in translating *Gemeine* and not *Gemeinschaft,* has to prove that here *communio* does not mean either Schleiermacher's *Gemeinschaft* "created by the voluntary actions of men" or that rejected by Luther, "to have something to do with a person." Such proof can only come from a thorough understanding of the *sancta ecclesia catholica* developed from the sources, for all attempts to interpret *sanctorum communio* stumble over the ambiguity of *communio*. (Excursus I)

The history of the interpretation of *sanctorum communio* is the history of the Western interpretation of the church. There is no parallel for this in the East. The reason for this is that the Apostles' Creed was never ecclesiastically accepted there. The West, too, got along without the formula *sanctorum communio* in the Creed for 400 years. This is not to say that it arose in Augustine's day. It is actually much older than used to be supposed. It appears in the report of the Council of Nimes in 396 and roughly at the same time in an exposition of the Creed by a Bishop Niceta of Remesiana, which was in what we now call Serbia. This suggests that the phrase may have originated not in the West but in the East. If there is other evidence of this, the phrase is to be understood according to its Greek and not its Latin form.

There is such evidence. The first appearance of the phrase is not in Nimes, as Kattenbusch and others supposed. It appears already eight years earlier in an imperial rescript directed against the Apollinarians in the year 388. The order, however, is *communio sanctorum*. It appears also in a still earlier confession that comes to us under the name of Jerome and is probably the one required of him during his stay in the desert of Chalcis (Syria) 374—379. It contains some very archaic features and some which clearly distinguish it from Western confessions and so must have its origin in the East. This confession already contains the formula in question, and it appears in the following setting: *credo remissionem peccatorum in sancta ecclesia catholica, sanctorum communionem, carnis resurrectionem ad vitam aeternam.* (Excursus II)

If this confession originated in the East, then the formula *sanctorum communio* did too. Its first appearance in the West comes at least 20 years later. The whole character of the confession both in style and content demonstrates that it was not derived from the West. The single manuscript we have of the Latin text is a translation. The original Greek would then read τῶν ἁγίων κοινωνίαν.[6] Its setting here gives an important clue for its interpretation. The accusative of *sanctorum communionem* cannot stand in apposition to the preceding ablative of *in sancta ecclesia catholica*. Consequently the phrase can be neither an attribute nor an explication of the concept "church." It is an independent item syntactically parallel with *remissionem* and *resurrectionem*. These three blessings — *remissio, communio, resurrectio* — are listed as content of the faith. In Greek: πιστεύω ἄφεσιν ἁμαρτιῶν ἐν τῇ ἁγίᾳ ἐκκλησίᾳ καθολικῇ, τῶν ἁγίων κοινωνίαν, σαρκὸς ἀνάστασιν.

But what is meant by *sanctorum communio* (τῶν ἁγίων κοινωνία) if not the church? The usual Western interpretation as we have seen is a communion of holy persons. *Sanctorum* is then the genitive of *sancti*. To be in harmony with this, τῶν ἁγίων must be the genitive of οἱ ἅγιοι. This, however, is most unlikely since it stands parallel with and between remission of sins and resurrection and since both of these are coupled with a genitive of things. Further, since there is no grammatical connection between *sanctorum communio* and *sancta ecclesia,* we would be forced to conceive of a communion of holy persons alongside the church. Such a thought is utterly foreign to the whole early church. That *sanctorum communio* stands as an independent item immediately following *ecclesia* can only be explained if it means something other than the church, that is, other than persons. *Sanctorum* is, then, the genitive not of *sancti* but of *sancta,* and τῶν ἁγίων the genitive not of οἱ ἅγιοι but of τὰ ἅγια.

Modern research has often suggested this but so long as the Latin is regarded as original, it will be no more than a suggestion. In Latin there are many apparent or actual synonyms of *communio,* all of which are used with a genitive of persons. In Greek, however, things are different. Here the combination of *koinonia* with a genitive of persons is a rare exception, the combination with a genitive of things the rule. The only question is whether there is a satisfactory explanation for τὰ ἅγια as the form from which the genitive τῶν ἁγίων is derived. This, however, is no more than a rhetorical question. Before the distribution at every Eucharist every early Eastern Christian heard the call τὰ ἅγια τοῖς ἁγίοις and knew exactly what was meant. Τὰ ἅγια is not a plural but a dual form referring to the consecrated elements. Accordingly the *koinonia* means the *koinonia* of the Eucharist, and the whole phrase refers to the

Lord's Supper. In Latin, therefore, the *sancta* of the phrase *sanctorum communio* do not refer, as some scholars have suggested, to the sacraments but to the consecrated elements, and the whole phrase to the Sacrament of the Altar. The reference of the phrase is sacramental. That a sacrament should also be mentioned in the Creed is not extraordinary. In other Eastern confessions Baptism is mentioned at this point.[7] We shall have to pursue this Eastern understanding of τῶν ἁγίων κοινωνία further, for it is basic to our study of Eucharist and church fellowship in the early Eastern Church. (Excursus III)

There is corresponding evidence also in the West. A 7th-century manuscript from northern Ireland (Monasterium Benchorense) has a confession which after *Credo et in spiritum sanctum* reads *sanctam esse ecclesiam catholicam, abremissa peccatorum, sanctorum communionem, carnis resurrectionem* (Hahn, pp. 84 f.). The grammatical explanation of *abremissa* is doubtful, but the forgiveness of sins is obviously meant, and by this phrase *ecclesiam catholicam* and *sanctorum communionem* are so separated as to make it impossible to understand *sanctorum communio* as in apposition to *sancta ecclesia*. This corresponds to what we saw in the confession of Jerome, and since the phrase is an independent item in the Creed here too, we may draw the same conclusion.

The Middle Ages provide further evidence for this sacramental interpretation. A Norman French translation of the Apostles' Creed gives the Third Article as follows: *Jeo crei el Seint Espirit; seinte eglise catholica; la communiun des seintes choses; remissium des pecchiez; resurrectiun de charn; vie pardurable.* Our only manuscript of this is dated by C. A. Heurtley, its discoverer and editor, about 1125.[8] *Sanctorum* is translated by *seintes choses* and so beyond all doubt it is thought of as referring not to persons but to things. Since the manuscript includes also the psalter and a number of hymns, we may assume that this text of the Creed was in actual liturgical use. Abelard (d. 1142) may well have known it, for it comes from the linguistic area where he spent his youth and a part of his later life. He also knew and allowed the possibility of *sanctorum's* being the genitive of *sancta* as well as of *sancti*.[9] We may conclude, then, that the understanding of *sanctorum* as from *sancta* was known throughout a considerable part of western France. The interim between the phrase's reception into the Creed and Abelard's day is long, but it is conceivable that the Norman French manuscript follows a tradition that goes back to the time of the adoption of the phrase in the West. This is at least more likely than that the genitive of persons, which meanwhile became the generally accepted interpretation in the West, should later have lost some ground to the genitive of things.

It is sufficient for our purpose to note that the original Eastern understanding of the phrase persisted also in the text of several Western creeds. The "holy things" of the Norman manuscript can only have a sacramental meaning. Abelard correctly refers the *sancta* to the Eucharist, and the ancient Irish text scarcely permits any other interpretation, for there, too, the phrase is not connected with the church.[10] Those who understand persons can still make an indirect connection with the sacraments. The phrase is then, as usual, taken as in apposition to *ecclesia* into whose communion the *sancti* are joined and sustained by the sacraments. This thought is common to both West and East but in the West the phrase's connection with the church draws it into the whole problem of the understanding of the concept "church," whereas in the East it is confined to considerations of the Eucharistic *koinonia*.[11]

We are here brought to the boundary between the early church of the East and the West. The West received the phrase from the East, but when the Greek precision was replaced by the Latin ambiguity, room was given for it to be understood of persons. This finally led to a merely social understanding of *communio* as a fellowship among men constituted by their relation to one another and as such applied also to the Lord's Supper. Thus τῶν ἁγίων κοινωνία arrived at a complete contradiction of its original meaning. The East had indeed more than one use for *koinonia* and used it of the fellowship of the church, but it kept intact its sacramental understanding of the Eucharistic *koinonia*. In the history of the phrase's interpretation in the West we have the portrayal not only of the problems inherent in the Western understanding of the church but also, since the end of the age of orthodoxy, its progressive secularization.

Notes to Chapter 1

1. For Schleiermacher this means philosophical ethics. In his *Glaubenslehre* he speaks of another concept of fellowship (*Lebensgemeinschaft mit dem Erloeser, Gemeinschaft mit Christo,* and this also in connection with the Lord's Supper), but in discussing the church he holds unwaveringly to the concept derived from philosophical ethics: "The Christian church is formed by the coming together of regenerated individuals for ordered interaction and cooperation." (§ 115)

2. Large Catechism, II, 49. Cf. *WA* 2, 190, 18; 279, 16; 6, 293, 1, et passim.

3. *Sanctorum communio* in Augustine's condemnation of the Donatists, *enarr. in Ps.* 36, *sermo* II, 20 (*t.* IV; *PL,* 36, 379) and in the Donatists' letter to Flavius Marcellinus, c. 3 (Appendix to Augustine's *op. t.* IX; *PL,* 43, 835). Augustine himself, *sermo* 52, c. III, 6 (*t.* V; *PL,* 38, 357): *removit istos (scil. Patripassianos) ecclesia catholica a communione sanctorum.* These passages can be found in G. von Zezschwitz's *System der christlichen Katechetik,* II (1864), 119, and are reproduced in F. Kattenbusch's *Das apostolische Symbol,* II (1900), 930 ff.

4. For these last formulations of Augustine see R. Seeberg, *Dogmengeschichte,* II (3d ed.), 465 f. Seeberg himself adopts the interpretation of our phrase which is in harmony with these Augustinian formulations.

5. For most of these see R. Seeberg, *Dogmengeschichte,* III, 42, 280, 507, et passim; Occam, *Dial. de pot. imp. et pap.;* Goldast, *Monarchia,* II, 392 ff.

6. Thus later Greek translators of the Latin Apostles' Creed. Hahn, p. 31. Two omit the article: ἁγίων κοινωνίαν (pp. 30, 34). One translates meaninglessly: ἁγίαν κενονίαν. (P. 32)

7. In the Nicaeno-Constantinopolitan Creed, Armenian confessions, Cyril of Jerusalem, Epiphanius, Pseudo-Athanasius, and Nestorius; usually with the addition of εἰς ἄφεσιν ἁμαρτιῶν. Hahn, pp. 134, 135, 137, 138, 146, 151 (No. 426), 153, 165.

8. C. A. Heurtley, *Harmonia Symbolica* (Oxford, 1858), pp. 91 ff., reproduced in Hahn, pp. 82 f.

9. He gives the following definition: "*Sanctorum communio,* that is those things by which the *sancti* are made (*efficiuntur*) or strengthened (*confirmantur*) in holiness, that is, by participation in the divine Sacrament; or the common faith of the church or the unity of love (*caritas*)." But then he goes on, "*Possumus et sanctorum dicere* neutraliter, *id est sanctificati panis et vini in sacramentum altaris.*" *Expositio symboli quod dicitur Apostolorum, PL,* 178, 629.

10. The medieval expositions of the received text which regularly take our phrase as in apposition to *sancta ecclesia* were likely encouraged by the legend that the Creed was made up by a contribution from each apostle. Accordingly the Creed was dissected into 12 pieces, and both *sanctam ecclesiam* and *sanctorum communionem* were drawn from the mouth of one and the same apostle, e. g., Pseudo-Augustine's *Sermo* 240 (Hahn, p. 52); otherwise in the Vienna manuscript of the 15th century (p. 54). In the *Catechismus Romanus* we can clearly see how the interpretation is determined by putting the two phrases together in the 9th Article (*p. I, cap. X, qu.* 21 ff.). Aquinas, incidentally, divides the Creed up into 14 articles, not 12. (*Summa theologica*, II, 2, *qu.* 1, *art.* 8)

11. E. g., Ivo of Chartres, Abelard's older contemporary. Some feel he favored a genitive of things, but this seems to go beyond the evidence. *De symbolo apostolorum sermo* XXIII (2), *PL,* 162, 606. Hjalmar Lindroth has recently drawn attention to Thomas Aquinas' explanation of the Creed in "Das fruehchristliche Bekenntnis," *Buch von der Kirche* (1951), p. 206. This is the 1951 German translation of the book translated from the Swedish *En Bok om Kyrkan* (1943) into English as *This Is the Church.* The section on Aquinas does not appear in the English translation. Here is Aquinas' explanation from *Compendium Theologiae,* cap. 147 (ed. Fr. Albert [1896], p. 244). *Convenienter effectus divinae providentiae circa personam Spiritus sancti ponuntur. Quantum autem ad effectum supernaturalis cognitionis, quam per fidem in hominibus Deus facit, dicitur: "Sanctam ecclesiam catholicam," nam ecclesia congregatio fidelium est. Quantum vero ad gratiam, quam hominibus communicat, dicitur: "Sanctorum communionem." Quantum vero ad remissionem culpae, dicitur: "Peccatorum remissionem."* Luther also says in his explanation of the phrase: "I am also a part and member of it, partaking and sharing in all its possessions through the Holy Ghost, who has brought me to it and incorporated me, etc" (*Large Catechism,* II, 52). Cf. II, 54: "Forgiveness of sins which comes through the holy sacraments and absolution . . . and holiness made of the Holy Ghost through the Word of God in the fellowship (*Vereinigung*) of the Christian church." Cf. also *Catechismus Romanus* at this point.

Bibliography for Chapter 1

Althaus, Paul. *Communio Sanctorum. Die Gemeinde im lutherischen Kirchengedanken,* 1929.

———. *Grundrisz der Ethik,* 2d ed., 1953, pp. 89 ff.

Barth, Karl. *Gemeinschaft in der Kirche,* 1943.

Bonhoeffer, Dietrich. *Sanctorum Communio. Eine dogmatische Untersuchung zur Soziologie der Kirche,* 1930.

Brunner, Emil. *The Divine Imperative,* trans. O. Wyon (London, 1937), pp. 300 ff.

Cordes, Cord. *Der Gemeinschaftsbegriff im deutschen Katholizismus und Protestantismus der Gegenwart* (Leipzig phil. diss.), 1931.

Grob, Rudolf. *Aufbau der Gemeinschaft. Grundzuege einer reformierten Sozialethik,* 1940.

Kelly, John N. *Early Christian Creeds,* 2d ed. (London, 1960), pp. 388 ff.

Linton, O. *Das Problem der Urkirche in der neueren Forschung,* 1932.

Lohmeyer, Ernst. *Der Begriff der religioesen Gemeinschaft,* 1925.

Odeberg, Hugo. "The Individualism of Today and the Concept of the Church in the New Testament," *This Is the Church,* ed. A. Nygren, trans. C. Rasmussen (Philadelphia, 1952), pp. 62 ff.

Olsson, Herbert. "The Church's Visibility and Invisibility According to Luther," *This Is the Church,* pp. 226 ff.

Siegfried, Theodor. *Das protestantische Prinzip in Kirche und Welt,* 1939, pp. 192 ff.

2

KOINONIA AS PARTAKING *(METALEPSIS)*

The Creed's *sanctorum communio* in its original Greek form meant the Lord's Supper. This in itself expresses a particular understanding of the Sacrament held in the early church at least in the East. However, since there is no explicit discussion of it even in the East, the question regarding the extent of its theological implications still remains unanswered. For the pursuit of these a comparison with other terms may prove useful, for in the East, too, there were obviously other terms used of the Sacrament. A comprehensive presentation of the ancient understanding of the Eucharist is of course not our purpose. It must suffice to investigate only what relates to the question of Eucharist and church fellowship.

Koinonia, the principal word of our phrase, appears in combinations of considerable variety. Already in the New Testament, especially if we take into account its verbal forms, we find various possibilities for its combination with a genitive of things. It is clear at the outset that its combination with τὰ ἅγια does not mean the extending of sympathy, liberality, or benevolence, as is usually the case in contexts of charity.[1] The phrase cannot mean to confess that we extend the *sancta* to others. What is meant by fellowship nowadays is most closely approached by such expressions as *koinonia* of life, love, or faith (Excursus III). If our phrase were understood in harmony with these, we would then have to take it as a fellowship of common relation to the *sancta,* that is, the Sacrament of the Lord's Supper. This thought is certainly not to be rejected, for the concept of a fellowship brought about by the Sacrament among those who participate in it is indeed found in the early church. To derive this immediately from τῶν ἁγίων κοινωνία would, however, be to skip some crucial evidence.

Of decisive importance is Paul's usage of *koinonia* in his statement of the Lord's Supper in 1 Cor. 10:16: The cup which we bless — the *koinonia* of the blood; the bread which we break — the *koinonia* of the body of Christ. Two genitives of things are coupled with *koinonia* which match the meaning of the liturgical τὰ ἅγια τοῖς ἁγίοις and the creedal τῶν ἁγίων κοινωνία. The *koinonia* of the blood and the *koinonia* of the body of which Paul speaks separately are combined in the Creed in what is then a dual form to be understood in accordance with Paul's statement.

There are modern exegetes who have understood Paul as speaking of "a fellowship which is first of all among those who go to the Lord's Supper together," or of "a comradeship of the body and blood of Christ." [2] We may defer for a moment the question whether that is in fact what Paul means. He is quite certainly not so understood in early Greek theology. *Koinonia* is never understood in this modern sense of comradeship, nor does *communio* in the West ever mean a company or mere society (Excursus I). The ancient understanding is shown in that when speaking of the Sacrament they use κοινωνεῖν τινὸς (to partake of something), and not κοινωνεῖν τινὶ (to have fellowship with somebody). *Koinonia* of the body and blood of Christ is used of the single communicant without any reference sidewards to those who communicate with him. So we read in Cyril of Jerusalem: μετὰ τὸ κοινωνῆσαί σε τοῦ σώματος Χριστοῦ προσέρχου καὶ τῷ ποτηρίῳ τοῦ αἵματος . . . καὶ ἐκ τοῦ αἵματος μεταλαμβάνων Χριστοῦ ("After you partake of the body of Christ, proceed also to the cup of the blood . . . also receiving from the blood your share of Christ"). Here there is no mention whatever of a relation to other participants. We note further that κοινωνεῖν τινὸς and μεταλαμβάνειν ("partake") are interchangeable. [3] If there can still be any doubt what these synonyms mean, it is removed by the *Euchologion* of Serapion in which the same terms are also used interchangeably. [4] In the Postcommunion we read, after mention has been made of the *koinonia* of the body and blood, ποίησον ἡμᾶς μέρος ἔχειν μετὰ τοῦ σώματος καὶ τοῦ αἵματος κτλ ("Make us to have a share in the body and the blood, etc."). [5] If the *koinonia* of the body and blood is that of 1 Cor. 10:16, then the alternative expressions show conclusively that the *koinonia* was understood as a partaking of the body and blood. These are expressions of sharing, receiving, and partaking: μετάληψις, μετοχή, μεταλαμβάνειν, μετέχειν, μέρος ἔχειν. Μετέχειν ("to have a share in") comes naturally enough as *koinonia's* synonym, for Paul uses it in the same context, 1 Cor. 10:17, 21 ("partake of"). Understanding the Sacrament as a partaking of the body and blood of Christ is as old as the theological interpretation of the Sarcament itself.[6]

The body and blood of Christ, or the consecrated elements, are also combined in the expression τὰ μυστήρια ("the mysteries") as in the creedal τὰ ἅγια, and both terms are coupled now with *koinonia* and now with *metalepsis*. When Basil speaks of μεταλαμβάνειν τῶν ἁγίων he reproduces exactly what is meant by the creedal τῶν ἁγίων.[7] It is admittedly possible that more than one sacrament are meant by "the mysteries." In Serapion, however, τὰ μυστήρια τὰ παρόντα ("the present mysteries") mean quite clearly the consecrated elements, and in this sense he speaks of their *koinonia* and *metalepsis*.[8] The identity of these two is even more clearly shown by the use of μεταλαμβάνειν with no need of adding anything to convey the meaning of communicate.[9] The Sacrament is called indeed "the holy *metalepsis*."[10] By its equation with this term *koinonia* is unmistakably interpreted as relating to the Sacrament.

The Sacrament had indeed a variety of names. Eucharist was long the most favored. Besides *metalepsis* there were the Pauline Lord's Supper, Lord's Table, and derivatives (τράπεζα δεσποτική, μυστική, φρικτή, ἱερὰ etc.) There were also sacrificial terms (προσφορά, θυσία), *synaxis*, and still others. Yet in the fourth century we find the *koinonia* as the simple term for the Sacrament, as *communio* was in the West. At the same time *koinonia* was used of the duly constituted church fellowship which was safeguarded by the bishops and had its boundaries and criteria established by synodical decisions. It is not always possible to determine from the context which of these two meanings is intended. When Athanasius, for example, deals with the question whether Arius died "having had *koinonia* with the church" (κοινωνήσας τῇ ἐκκλησίᾳ), it is not immediately clear how this *koinonia* presumably was expressed."[11] Athanasius records that Bishop Alexander of Constantinople denied Arius readmission on the ground that a father of heresy may not be ad-

mitted to the Communion (εἰς κοινωνίαν δεχθῆναι). The Latin translation makes this *in ecclesiam recipi* ("be received into the church"). But
a reference to the Eucharist is surely more likely, for otherwise *koinonia*
would normally be qualified by ἐκκλησιαστικὴ or τῆς ἐκκλησίας. On the
eve of Arius' death the Eusebians announced that he would take part
in their *synaxis* (25,688 b. συναχθήσεται μεθ' ἡμῶν ἐν τῇ ἐκκλησίᾳ ταύτῃ).
Arius, however, died during the night and so was robbed of "*koinonia*
and of life" (688 c. τῆς τε κοινωνίας καὶ τοῦ ζῆν). Since *koinonia* is here,
too, used without qualification, it evidently also refers to the Sacrament.
Bishop Alexander rejoiced that the *synaxis* could now be celebrated "in
the fear of God and orthodoxy," that is, without Arius (688 d). What
exactly, however, was this *synaxis*? It could be every divine service, and
it could according to later settled usage be the Sacrament. When Athanasius concludes that the Lord Himself has here judged the Arian heresy
"in that he showed that it was unworthy of the *koinonia* of the church"
(689 a), this can be understood as the general, duly constituted fellowship. The word *unworthy* (ἀνάξιος), however, may well be an echo of
1 Cor. 11:27 and so point to the Sacrament.[12]

The *Euchologion* of Bishop Serapion of Thmuis, to whom Athanasius'
account is addressed, twice has the *koinonia* with Paul's qualification (of
the body etc.),[13] and once without it, but in this last instance it is used
plainly parallel with *metalepsis*.[14] Even if this were here only a chance
abbreviation, the general usage shows that the *koinonia* without qualification became the fixed and popular term for the Sacrament. Basil declares
that whoever does not understand the meaning of the *metalepsis* of the
body and blood of Christ and "comes to the *koinonia*" receives no benefit
from it.[15] A man possessed ought not "to be admitted to the *koinonia*."[16]
Chrysostom speaks of the "time of *koinonia*" (καιρὸς κοινωνίας) and
says, "You are about to receive the King through the *koinonia*."[17] Basil
even says that in the distress of persecution when there is no priest or
liturgist, one may "take the *koinonia* into one's own hand." He reports
that in Alexandria and Egypt every one has the *koinonia* in his house and
partakes of it (μεταλαμβάνει) when he wishes.[18] Here the term is so
objectivized that strictly understood it refers not to the action but simply
to the consecrated elements. Since Basil says this in a short letter to

a woman inquirer, we must conclude that he was following popular usage.

This is confirmed by the formal definition which Isidore, Abbot of Pelusium, gives "concerning the *koinonia*" (περὶ τῆς κοινωνίας). "*Koinonia* is the name for the reception of the divine mysteries, for thereby we receive the gift of being made one with Christ and partakers of His kingdom." [19] This definition takes us back to the time when *sanctorum communio* first appeared in a creed. Isidore was a younger contemporary of Chrysostom. His definition is carefully weighed, perfectly clear, and in harmony with the usage of its day. It reads like an answer to the question we began with, a question which could also concern a thoughtful inquirer at that time: what is meant by *sanctorum communio* (τῶν ἁγίων κοινωνία) in Jerome's creed from the Antiochene circle? [20]

The men of whom we have been speaking were of course not ignorant of the saints (ἅγιοι). Chrysostom speaks of their graves (θῆκαι) and relics,[21] and *koinonia* can mean various things. But after the term had become so closely linked with the Lord's Supper that *koinonia* and *eucharistia* became virtual synonyms, even Isidore, asked about the meaning, could define it only as in fact he did. *Koinonia* is *metalepsis, participatio* in the mysteries. "The divine mysteries" (τὰ θεῖα μυστήρια) is a dual term for the consecrated elements in the Eucharist. That they were called τὰ ἅγια in the liturgy was as well known to the Egyptian Abbot Isidore as to Antiochene Chrysostom, and they are also so named by Basil of Cappadocia. We see therefore beyond all doubt that the *sanctorum communio* of Jerome's creed was understood in the sense of Isidore's definition. This agrees with the theological understanding of the Lord's Supper insofar as it is defined as *metalepsis* through the concept *koinonia*.[22]

Notes to Chapter 2

1. Rom. 15:26; 2 Cor. 9:13. Cf. the relevant κοινωνεῖν of Gal. 6:6; Phil. 4:15; *Didache*, 4, 7: *LCC*, I, 173; *Ap. Const.*, II, 25, 3; 36, 8; and so also frequently in Clement of Alexandria, Origen, and Chrysostom.
2. Thus Ed. von Dobschuetz in "Sakrament und Symbol im Urchristentum," *Theol. Stud. und Krit.*, 1905, pp. 12, 28 f. W. Heitmueller, *RGG*, 1st ed., I, 35: ". . . the means of enacting inmost brotherhood and fellowship. Inmost

fellowship with one another. But then also with Jesus. Actualization of the fellowship of the disciples with one another is the basic thought of the action. However, the other fellowship is then also immediately present. Since Jesus is the bond in the fellowship of the disciples, the fellowship with Him is then also indirectly (sic!) there."

3. Catecheses mystagogicae, V, 22; cf. I, 4: Χριστὸς αἵματος μοὶ καὶ σαρκὸς κοινωνήσας. In St. Cyril of Jerusalem's Lectures on the Christian Sacraments, ed. F. L. Cross (London, 1951), pp. 38 f., 79; cf. pp. 14, 55. Dionysius of Alexandria says of a repentant heretic τοῦ σώματος καὶ τοῦ αἵματος . . . μετασχόντα (H. E., VII, 9, 4). Here also μετέχειν in the same sense, synonymous with μεταλαμβάνειν/κοινωνεῖν, is used of the partaking individual. When the repentant man is encouraged τῇ μετοχῇ τῶν ἁγίων προσιέναι, we have τῶν ἁγίων meaning exactly the same as the Creed's τῶν ἁγίων κοινωνία.

4. XIV, 1, 2; XIII, 11; XVIII, 1, 2: Funk, pp. 176, 23—178, 3; 174, 8; 180, 10—13. In The Sacramentary of Serapion of Thmuis, ed. F. E. Brightman, JTS, 1899—1900, pp. 107, 6—9; 105, 28; 108, 14—17.

5. XVI, 2, 3: Funk, p. 178, 18—21; Brightman, p. 107, 30—33; G. Dix, The Shape of the Liturgy (Westminster, 1945), p. 512.

6. Irenaeus, Haer., V, 2, 2 f.: LCC, I, 388. Pseudo-Athanasius, PG, 26, 1012b: μεταλαμβάνειν, μετάληψις τοῦ σώματος. Cyril of Jerusalem, Cat. myst., IV, 3; V, 1, 21: Cross, pp. 27, 68; 30, 71; 38, 79. Basil, PG, 31, 757; 32, 484. Chrysostom, PG, 49, 345; 59, 261: μετέχειν. Cf. Justin, Apology, I, 67, 5: μετάληψις ἀπὸ τῶν εὐχαρισθέντων; 65, 5: LCC, I, 286 f. Irenaeus, Haer., IV, 18, 5: τῆς εὐχαριστίας, LCC, I, 287. Clement of Alexandria, Paed., II, 19, 4.

7. PG, 31, 74. Cf. Eutychius of Constantinople, PG, 86, 2396a: μετὰ τῶν ἁγίων μετάληψιν.

8. Euchologion, XV, 1 (post fractionem clericis distributam): Funk, p. 179, 5; Brightman, p. 107, 16. Cyril of Jerusalem, Cat. myst., V, 20: Cross, pp. 38, 79. Chrysostom, PG, 49, 373; 50, 653. John Moschus, Pratum spirituale, 121: PG, 87, 2988 d. In Chrysostom also τῆς μυστικῆς τραπέζης, PG, 49, 345; 61, 235. Theodoret, Ep. 77: Schultze, IV, 1130. Socrates, H. E., V, 21; PG, 67, 621 c. Gregory of Nyssa, PG, 45, 23: μεταληψόμεθα τοῦ πάσχα. Eutychius of Constantinople even has τὰ κοινωνικὰ μυστήρια, Serm. de pasch., PG, 86, 2399a.

9. For κοινωνεῖν meaning to communicate cf. ὡς λαικὸς κοινωνείτω (of the cleric who remains in another parish without episcopal approval), Ap. Const., VIII, 47, 15: Funk, p. 568, 14; Ap. Can., 15. Cornelius of Rome in H. E., VI, 43, 10. Lex Canonica S. Apost., 4—5: Funk, II, 150. Serapion, Euchologion, XIII, 15: οἱ κοινωνοῦντες = the communicants: Funk, II, 176, 3;

Brightman, p. 106, 16. For μεταλαμβάνειν meaning to communicate cf. *Ap. Const.*, XVIII, 13, 14: μεταλαμβανέτω ὁ ἐπίσκοπος; in 15 the same is said of all the rest. Funk, p. 516, 22.

10. *Ap. Const.*, VIII, 47, 9: Funk, p. 566, 13.

11. *Ep. ad Serap. de morte Arii: PG*, 25, 685 a. Cf. J. W. C. Wand, *Doctors and Councils* (London, 1962), pp. 26 f.

12. Cf. also the shorter report in *Ep. ad Episc. Aeg. et Lib.: PG*, 25, 581 ff.

13. XVI, 2; XVIII, 1: Funk, II, 178, 19; 180, 11; Brightman, pp. 107, 31; 108, 15.

14. XIV, 1, 2: Funk, II, 176 f.; Brightman, p. 107.

15. *Moralia*, c. 2: *PG*, 31, 759.

16. *Ap. Const.*, VIII, 32, 6; cf. 47, 33: Funk, pp. 534, 20; 572, 27.

17. *De consubst.: PG*, 48, 755 f.

18. *Ep.* 93: *PG*, 32, 484.

19. *Ep.*, I, 228 (*PG*, 78, 325): κοινωνία κέκληται ἡ τῶν θείων μυστηρίων μετάληψις διὰ τὸ τὴν πρὸς Χριστὸν ἡμῖν χαρίζεσθαι ἕνωσιν καὶ κοινωνοὺς ἡμᾶς τῆς αὐτοῦ ποιεῖν βασιλείας.

20. Jerome was ordained presbyter by Bishop Paulinus in Antioch c. 379. There also, in his native city, Chrysostom was ordained deacon in 381 by the counter-bishop Meletius, whose successor ordained him presbyter in 386. Cf. D. Attwater, *St. John Chrysostom* (London, 1959), pp. 24, 38. In his letters Isidore of Pelusium gives frequent expression of his veneration for Chrysostom.

21. *PG*, 49, 595 f.; 647.

22. In the light of Seesemann's convincing expositions and those of numerous recent exegetes who adduce compelling evidence in their elucidation of the *koinonia* of 1 Cor. 10:16 as *metalepsis*, it is really astonishing to find that the men who took part in the 1947 discussions in Frankfurt on the Lord's Supper could not come to agreement about it. See the reports of Julius Schniewind and Ernst Sommerlath in *Abendmahlsgespraech*, ed. E. Schlink, 1952, p. 14. Sommerlath at least comes out clearly for this interpretation. When the view that *koinonia* means partaking is described as "widespread," it is perhaps not out of place to mention that those who made it so include all the interpreters of the early church, as also, for example, Thomas Aquinas (*Comm. in omnes S. Pauli ep.*, ed. Taurin., 1891, I, 318) and Luther (see above, p. 4).

Bibliography for Chapter 2

Arnold, A. *Der Ursprung des christlichen Abendmahls im Lichte der neusten liturgiegeschichtlichen Forschung*, 2d ed., 1939.

Bachmann, Philipp. *Der erste Brief des Paulus an die Korinther,* 1921.

Cullmann, O. *La signification de la Sainte Cène dans le Christianisme primitif,* 1936.

Gaugler, E. *Das Abendmahl im Neuen Testament,* 1943.

Goppelt, L. "Kirchengemeinschaft und Abendmahlsgemeinschaft nach dem Neuen Testament," *Koinonia,* ed. F. Huebner, 1957, pp. 24 ff.

Hauck, Friedrich. Κοινός, *ThWb,* III, 789 ff.

Jeremias, J. *The Eucharistic Words of Jesus,* trans. A. Ehrhardt, 1955.

Kaesemann, E. *Leib und Leib Christi,* 1933.

———. "Das Abendmahl im Neuen Testament," *Abendmahlsgemeinschaft?* ed. Edmund Schlink, 2d ed., 1938.

———. "Anliegen und Eigenart der paulinischen Abendmahlslehre," *Evangelische Theologie,* 1947—48, pp. 263 ff.

Krause, W. von. "Was sagt uns das Neue Testament zur Frage der Kirchen- und Abendmahlsgemeinschaft?" *Koinonia,* pp. 34 ff.

Lietzmann, Hans. *Messe und Herrenmahl,* 1926.

———. *An die Korinther,* 2 vols., 4th ed., ed. W. Kuemmel, 1949.

Lohmeyer, Ernst. "Vom urchristlichen Abendmahl," *Theologische Rundschau,* 1937, pp. 168 ff., 195 ff.; 1938, pp. 81 ff.

Marxsen, W. "Die Einsetzungsberichte zum Abendmahl," 1951 (microfilm).

Mascall, E. L. *Corpus Christi. Studies in the Church and the Eucharist* (London, 1953).

Percy, E. "Der Leib Christi," (1942), *Lund Univ. Arsskr.,* 1, 38, 1.

Robinson, J. A. T. *The Body. A Study in Pauline Theology* (London, 1952).

Sasse, Hermann. "Das Abendmahl im Neuen Testament," *Vom Sakrament des Altars,* 1941, pp. 26 ff.

Schmidt, Traugott. *Der Leib Christi,* 1919.

Seesemann, Heinrich. *Der Begriff Koinonia im Neuen Testament,* 1933. This exposition of *koinonia* as *participation* and *partaking* in the New Testament harmonizes perfectly with the way it was understood in the early church. Pp. 31—86.

Steitz, G. E. "Die Abendmahlslehre der griechischen Kirche," *Jahrbuch fuer deutsche Theologie,* IX—XIII (1864—68). The only comprehensive presentation of its subject — altogether about 500 pages. However, since its essential orientation is to questions raised by the Reformation, it is of little use to us here.

Wendland, H. D. *Das Neue Testament Deutsch,* Vol. VII: *Die Briefe an die Korinther,* 5th ed., 1948.

For further bibliography see Peter Brunner, *Leiturgia,* 1952, I, 84 ff.

3

THE SACRAMENT AS FELLOWSHIP

The interpretation of *koinonia* grew out of 1 Cor. 10:16. Accordingly "to communicate" means to partake of the body and blood of Christ. By this, as Cyril of Jerusalem puts it, the communicant is one body and one blood (σύσσωμος καὶ σύναιμος) with Christ.[1] He points to 2 Peter 1: 4 to show that we are to "have a share in the divine nature *(physis)*." The reference to this text, so frequent in Greek theology, betrays the "physical" understanding of salvation which is customarily ascribed to that theology. This is not altogether unjust, only one may not imagine that they understood the term materially as we do today or that it was an ethically inactive term. For them the essential criterion of the "divine nature" was immortality. Failure to appreciate these facts often lies behind modern strictures upon Ignatius, especially when he speaks of the bread of the Sacrament as "medicine of immortality." The emphasis here lies on the second term and not on the first. This particular expression of Ignatius is very similar to a statement of Clement of Alexandria, who is indeed given to extreme spiritualizing. He says that to drink the blood of Christ is "to partake of the immortality of the Lord."[2] As regards the ethical implications, every catechumen learned before his baptism that eternal life is bound up with his "being dead to sin."[3]

However materially they may have spoken of the body and blood of Christ and of sharing the divine "nature," the paramount conviction was their certainty of being personally made one with the exalted Christ. After speaking of being one body with Christ *(concorporalis)*, Cyril of Jerusalem declares, "Thus we become carriers of Christ *(Christophori)*." Here another relation is developed, one based on Johannine and Pauline origins. In the Postcommunion of Serapion already quoted the μέρος ἔχειν in place of the customary μεταλαμβάνειν [4] is an obvious echo of the "have part in" of John 13:8. Then, too, Cyril of Jerusalem's "of one body and one blood with Christ" reminds us of the expression of "the same body" (σύσσωμα) of Eph. 3:6 and in this context also of "conformed to his image" (σύμμορφος) of Rom. 8:29 and Phil. 3:10, 21. The theme of "being made into the likeness" of Christ had a rich development not only as an "imitation" (1 Cor. 11:1) but also as a *koinonia* (Phil. 3:10). The martyrs particularly were regarded as "brothers of the Lord" because they were made worthy of showing forth His sufferings, of the *koinonia* of His blood, and of being fashioned according to the death of Christ.[5] All Christians indeed have "put on Christ" through Baptism, as Cyril of Jerusalem, following Paul, points out in his instructions for Baptism. Since all Christians are baptized into the death of Christ, they are taken into the likeness of His death and also of His resurrection. They are therefore conformed to the image (σύμμορφοι) of His death.[6]

The interpretation of the Eucharistic *koinonia* that we saw in Isidore of Pelusium rests therefore not on an isolated exegesis of 1 Cor. 10:16. It is rather an integral part of an understanding of salvation which has its center in the personal relationship of the Christian with Christ and so is in complete harmony with Paul. It is consequently not only understandable but necessary that communicating be understood as Christians having part in the body and blood of Christ. This is true also for the individual communicant. The *koinonia* of the sufferings of Christ (Phil. 3:10) provides a parallel *koinonia,* and one most clearly shown in the case of the martyrs, for partaking and participation is an individual event both in Baptism and the Lord's Supper.

This does not deny or diminish the fellowship of the Holy Communion. The question is only in what it consists and how it fits with 1 Cor. 10:16. Already in Athanasius we come upon the term *synaxis,* which, like *koinonia,* gradually became a name for the Holy Communion.[7] In early Christian usage the verb (συνάγεσθαι, συνέρχεσθαι) meant the congregation's gathering together or the being gathered together, usually for worship. The editor of the *Apostolic Constitutions* still understands *synaxis* in this general way.[8] If *synaxis* derives its content from this usage, then it is the action or the result of men coming together. If the word were later used of the Holy Communion only in this sense it would indeed express the fellowship of the Sacrament, but a fellowship that exists already independent of the Sacrament itself. The "coming together (συνηγμένων) to break bread" of Acts 20:7 cannot be adduced to the contrary.[9] We would then have a Sacrament which is a fellowship because a number of Christians agree to celebrate it together and by their coming together carry out their agreement.

However, already in the Eucharistic sections of the *Didache* a much deeper connection is indicated. "As this bread was scattered (διεσκορπισμένον) on the hills and by being gathered together (συναχθὲν, scil. of the grains) was made one, so may Thy church be gathered together (συναχθήτω) from the ends of the earth into Thy kingdom." [10] Here the same verb is used, but the being gathered together derives not from the decision of the participants but from God Himself. The prayer which follows asks Him, "Gather it (σύναξον, *scil.* Thy church, *deine Gemeinde*), the sanctified, from the four winds into Thy kingdom, which Thou hast prepared for it" (10, 5). Here a complete shift of viewpoint from the middle to the passive voice is involved. The being gathered together, it is true, extends beyond participation in the Eucharist. Perhaps there is also an echo of John 11:52, where it is said of Jesus that He "should gather together in one the children of God that were scattered abroad" (διεσκορπισμένα). The reference to the gathering of the grains into one bread indicates, however, that it is in the Eucharist itself that the congregation experiences the being gathered together which they ask of God. The connection between the Eucharist and the unity of the congregation is admittedly not very closely drawn as yet. Even though the prayers of the *Didache* remained in later liturgical use and were made soteriologically more explicit and theologically more profound,[11] it is still difficult to say whether the subsequent use of the term "synaxis" for the Eucharist always reflected the original sense of σύναξον. Melanchthon is doubtless correct when in the Apology he says of the "old term *synaxis*" that it "shows that the Mass was formerly the communion of many" (XXIV, 79). Taken by itself, however, the term *synaxis* does allow the possibility that the fellowship of the Sacrament derives from the mere coming together.

For Ignatius the unity of the church which he so strongly emphasizes finds expression in their coming together for the Sacrament and in breaking the one bread.[12] But he does not think merely of human activity. "Zealously use the one Eucharist, for it is the one flesh of our Lord Jesus Christ and the one cup for being made one (ἕνωσις) by His blood, one sacrifice, as one bishop is together with his presbytery and deacons." The connection between 1 Cor. 10:16 and 17 rings through when he greets all members of the congregation in Smyrna: "Be all united (κοινῇ) man for man, in the name of Jesus Christ and in His flesh and blood, suffering and resurrection, in fleshly and spiritual unity of God with you." [13] Fleshly and spiritual unity particularly echo Paul, even though Paul writes body and not flesh. Ignatius, to be sure, gives pride of place to the unity of episcopal polity which he enjoins upon all congregations rather than to the unity which according to Paul is brought about by the eating of the one bread. Only that Eucharist is trustworthy which takes place under the bishop or his deputies.[14] Here a direct dependence on Paul is not discernable. There is agreement, however, in this that for both Ignatius and Paul the fellowship of the Sacrament did not derive from the coming together of the participants but from the fact that the Eucharist is "the one flesh of our Lord . . . and one cup for being made one by His blood."

There is a direct reference to 1 Cor. 10:16 in the works of Irenaeus, for he uses the text against the Gnostic denial of the immortality of the flesh.[15] The flesh receives permanency and becomes immortal through the partaking of the body and blood of Christ in the Eucharist. Irenaeus, with Paul, clearly understands koinonia as partaking of the body and blood of Christ. His emphasis is on the effect on the individual: our bodies are nourished in the Eucharist so that they may not suffer corruption.[16] But he does not fail to express the thought that through the Eucharist we become members of the body of Christ and that thus all who partake are made one body. In support of this Irenaeus does not quote 1 Cor. 10:17, which would be most natural after having used v. 16.

He refers instead to Eph. 5:30.[17] He turns to the epistle from which he derived the most characteristic concept of his whole theology, the idea of "recapitulation," that gathering of the new humanity under Christ its Head. He seems to have been unaware of Paul's clear connection between 1 Cor. 10:16 and 17. In the *Dialog* of Adamantius (c. 300), which also quotes 1 Cor. 10:16, only the ethical lesson is drawn that the *koinonia* of the body and blood of Christ does not accord with an inclination toward evil.[18] At any rate, Irenaeus, too, was far from deriving the fellowship of the Sacrament merely from the coming together of the participants.

Feeling for the Sacrament as fellowship declined with the gradual decline of the original conception of a sacrifice which the congregation offered with its prayers and the gifts it placed on the altar, and with its replacement by a sacrifice performed by a priest at the altar. Awareness of the fellowship of the Sacrament was, however, never lost in the early church. Even if we do not build too much on the term *synaxis*, there is still the significant connection between exclusion from the Sacrament and exclusion from the congregation. We shall look more closely at this later. Theologically the Sacrament was always understood as binding its participants together.[19]

In Chrysostom we have the most careful working out of the connection between 1 Cor. 10:16 and 17. He raises the question why in v. 16 Paul does not use "partaking" (μετοχή) but *koinonia*.[20] He answers that communicating (κοινωνεῖν) involves not only partaking (μετέχειν and μεταλαμβάνειν) but also being made one (ἑνοῦσθαι), for as the body is united with Christ, so are we made one with Him through this bread. Here Chrysostom is not, as might appear at first glance, speaking against "partaking" as such as a meaning of *koinonia*. He himself frequently uses the term μετάληψις in the same connection.[21] His desire here is not to show that this passage says something contrary but to point out that it carries even more meaning. The additional content is the concept of the *"koinonia of the body"* (κοινωνία τοῦ σώματος):

> What makes the *koinonia* (τὸ κοινωνοῦν) is not the same as that with which the koinonia is made (οὗ κοινωνεῖ). Even this apparently trifling

difference he [Paul] sets aside. By speaking of the "koinonia of the body" he strives for an even closer description, and so adds, "Because it is one bread, we many are one body." [Here he goes over to v. 17.] "What do I mean with *koinonia?*" he says. "We are that selfsame body." For what is the bread? The body of Christ. What do they become who partake of it (μεταλαμβάνοντες)? The body of Christ: not many bodies but one body. Many grains are made into one bread so that the grains appear no more at all, though they are still there. In their joined state (συναφεία) their diversity is no longer discernible. In the same way we are also bound up (συναπτόμεθα) with one another and with Christ. You are not nourished from one body and the next man from a different body, but all from one and the same body. For this reason he adds, "We have all partaken of one bread. If of one and the same bread, then we are all become the same thing."

Who could improve on this interpretation of the connection between 1 Cor. 10:16 and 17? The *koinonia* as partaking, which is first individual, remains clear, but by its very nature the many become one whole. Those who participate in eating the same bread are together the body of Christ. They do not produce this body. The body of Christ is there before they are and before what they do. They are rather drawn into it so they become its members. The fellowship-nature of the Sacrament is in this that Christ incorporates into Himself those who partake of it.

In the further discussion Chrysostom also makes use of the term *physis*. The old *physis* of the flesh was through sin given over to death and so remote from life. Christ, however, has "given His flesh for all to partake of. It is the same flesh as ours except that it is free of sin and full of life. By it we are nourished and in putting off the former, the dead, we are fitted for immortal life (ἀνακερασθῶμεν) by this Supper." Ethical consequences flow from this apparently very "physical" statement. Chrysostom points out how all quarreling and ill will are a contradiction of this fellowship.

If we eat of the same bread and so become the same, why then do we not show the same love and in this also become one? So it was with our forefathers for "the multitude of believers were of one heart and one soul." You who were so far from Him Christ has united with Himself, while you scorn uniting with the brother in due concern. You put yourself apart after you have received such abundant love and life from the Lord.[22]

Antiochene Chrysostom is not alone here. In Alexandria, Cyril, despite their other differences, has the same understanding of the fellowship-nature of the Sacrament. As we would expect, the Incarnation looms large when he speaks of the unification of the new humanity in Christ, its Lord. "We are all in Him, and all that is humanity (τὸ κοινὸν τῆς ἀνθρωπότητος πρόσωπον) lives again in Him." [23] The new humanity as a whole is already comprehended in the second Adam. The Holy Ghost makes this unification effective for the individual. The new unity is just as much a *koinonia* of the Spirit as it is a partaking of the divine nature of Christ.[24] This is how it is also in the Eucharist. The believers' being made one with Christ is both spiritual and bodily. Christ calls His flesh spirit (on John 6:63), and this He says not because He would deny that it is flesh, but because the life-giving and sanctifying power of the Spirit is united with it.[25]

This all echoes in part Irenaeus and in part Ignatius, who also had already spoken of a "fleshly and spiritual unity." What has been said about the spiritual side of this unity has its echo also in Chrysostom at least as far as it is Biblical. It would be wrong to regard Cyril's understanding of the Sacrament as more spiritual. As little as for Paul or Luther, did "spiritual" (πνευματικὸς) for Cyril mean something confined to the mind. He declares that the apparent absence of Christ for which He had prepared His disciples must not prompt us to reduce His holy body to nothing (ἐν τῷ μηδενὶ τιθέντες). In the "mystical eulogy" this body is powerful (ἐνεργὸν) to implant in us His own holiness.[26] As we are made one spiritually by the Holy Spirit, so are we made one bodily by Sacramental partaking (μυστικὴ μετάληψις) of the body of Christ.[27] Thereby we become one body with Christ (σύσσωμοι). The same expression we found used by Cyril of Jerusalem. While he does not, however, go beyond the bond between the communicant and Christ, for Cyril of Alexandria this also includes the relationship of the communicants with one another. "We are all one body together in Christ." [28] "We are, so to speak, divided up into individual persons. One is Peter or John, Thomas or Matthew. In Christ, however, we are become one body (σύσσωμοι) nourished from the one flesh, our unity sealed by the Holy

Ghost. If Christ is indivisible, then in no circumstances whatsoever will He let Himself be divided. In Him we are all one." [29] Cyril of Alexandria also finds his ground for this in 1 Cor. 10:17. "If we all partake of the one bread, we are all become together one body. It is impossible that Christ be divided. For this reason the church is also called the body of Christ, and we, according to Paul, are members as parts" (ἀνὰ μέρος, cf. ἐκ μέρους, 1 Cor. 12:27).[30] This looks almost inescapably as though Cyril of Alexandria found the origin of the church's description as the body of Christ in 1 Cor. 10:17. What he says further about oneness and unity derives rather from Ephesians, but there also we meet "of one body" (σύσσωμα, Eph. 3:6) and "one body and one spirit" (Eph. 4:4). "We many are one in Christ and in the Holy Ghost, bodily and spiritually." [31] The Eucharist makes us bodily one. It unites all with Christ but also all with one another. The Pauline admonition to mutual love and peace follows naturally in Cyril as also in Chrysostom.[32]

Notes to Chapter 3

1. *Cat. myst.*, IV, 3: Cross, pp. 27, 68.

2. *Paed.*, II, 19, 4.

3. *Ap. Const.*, VII, 39, 4.

4. *Euchologion*, XVI, 3: Funk, II, 178, 20; Brightman, p. 107, 32; Dix, p. 512.

5. *Ap. Const.*, V, 2; cf. VIII, 13, 6. Cf. *Martyrdom of Polycarp*, 6, 2: Χριστοῦ κοινωνὸς γενόμενος (*LCC*, I, 151); 17, 3 (*LCC*, I, 155). H. von Campenhausen, *Die Idee des Martyriums in der alten Kirche* (1936), pp. 56 ff.

6. *Cat. myst.*, II, 4—III, 1: Cross, pp. 19—22, 60—64. Gal. 3:27; Rom. 6:3 ff.; Col. 2:12.

7. Later quite unequivocally Dionysius the Pseudo-Areopagite wrote, *Hier. eccl.*, III, 2: μυστήριον συνάξεως εἴτουν κοινωνίας; Maximus Confessor, *PG*, 90, 657 ff.: μυσταγωγία . . . ἐπὶ τῆς συνάξεως; Anastasius Sinaita, as the title of a sermon on the Eucharist, *PG*, 89, 825 ff.: περὶ τῆς ἁγίας συνάξεως. Cf. Dix, pp. 36 f.

8. Acts 4:31; 11:26; 15:6; 13:44 (here of the "whole city"); 1 Cor. 5:4. 1 Clem. 34, 7: ἐπὶ τὸ αὐτὸ συναχθέντες. Cf. James 2:2: συναγωγή; Heb. 10:25: ἐπισυναγωγή. Justin, *Apol.*, I, 67, 7, says instead ἐπίλευσις. *Ap. Const.*, II, 39, 6 (according to Funk, I, 129, 7, an editorial interpo-

lation). Perhaps also still in Cyril of Jerusalem, *Cat. myst.*, V, 1 (Cross, pp. 30, 71), and Theodoret, *Ep.* 160 (Schultze, IV, 1330) et passim.

9. The quite fearful "Gather for the great supper of God" in Rev. 19:17 provides at most a merely formal parallel.

10. *Didache*, 9, 4: *LCC*, I, 175. The evidence of the *Didache* cannot be ruled out of court here even though its Eucharist is supposed to be different from the Supper in Paul. See Lietzmann, pp. 230 ff. He regards it as related to Serapion's *Euchologion*.

11. *Ap. Const.*, VII, 25 f.

12. *Eph.*, 20, 2: *LCC*, I, 93.

13. *Smyrn.*, 12, 2: *LCC*, 1, 116.

14. *Smyrn.*, 9, 1: *LCC*, I, 115.

15. *Haer.*, V, 2, 2: *LCC*, I, 387 f.

16. Cf. *Haer.*, IV, 18, 5; Justin, *Apology*, I, 66, 2: *LCC*, I, 286.

17. *Haer.*, V, 2, 3: *LCC*, I, 388.

18. *GCS*, p. 108, 19 ff.

19. No account is taken here of the West. I find it impossible to understand how R. Seeberg (*Dogmengeschichte*, 3d ed., I, 463) can find a reference to 1 Cor. 10:17 in Tertullian, *De Orat.*, 6. Cf. Ernest Evans, ed., *Tertullian's Tract on the Prayer* (London, 1953), pp. 10 f. On the other hand, there are undeniable references to the Pauline passage in Augustine, *In Joh.*, 26, 13 ff. (on John 6:53): *Op.*, IIIb, 1613 f. (*vinculum charitatis, societas sanctorum* etc.). Cf. *Sermo* 272, *Op.*, Va, 1247. Cyprian, *Ep.* 63, 13; 69, 5: *LCC*, V, 153; 168: T. A. Lacey, *Select Epistles of St. Cyprian* (London, 1922), pp. 130, 169. Lacey numbers the paragraphs differently. *Didache*, 9, 4: *LCC*, I, 175.

20. *Homilies on 1 Cor.*, 24, 4: *PG*, 61, 200 f.; ET, Cornish and Medley, p. 327.

21. *PG*, 45, 345; 49, 380, 391, et passim. There is hardly another exegete who has been at such pains as Chrysostom to ascertain and differentiate the various meanings of *koinonia* in the New Testament. For example, he refers Phil. 2:1 to the relationship of the Philippians to the apostle. He therefore paraphrases κοινωνία πνεύματος with εἰ ἔστιν ὑμῖν κοινωνῆσαι ἐν πνεύματι and adds εἰ ἔστι κοινωνῆσαι ὑμῖν ἐν κυρίῳ (*PG*, 62, 213). *Koinonia* is here understood as the fellowship between the apostle and his readers in their relationship to the Spirit and to the Lord. On the other hand, his comment on ἐκοινώνησεν of Phil. 4:14 is κοινωνία γὰρ τὸ πρᾶγμά ἐστιν. The giving and receiving of which Paul speaks are related to one another as buying is to selling: τοῦτο γὰρ ἐστιν κοινωνία (*PG*, 62, 290). Here

koinonia is a reciprocal relationship among the parties. This is the same understanding of the word as given by Luther's definition of fellowship *(Gemeinschaft):* "to have to do with somebody" (above p. 4). The *koinonia* of Acts 2:42 Chrysostom also takes as an activity, but here not a reciprocal relationship but an activity together (πάντα κοινῇ ἐποίουν), that is, something in common and yet not the common relationship to a third party as in Phil. 2:1, but the relationship of both parties to one another (*Homilies on Acts,* VII: *PG,* 60, 64).

22. *PG,* 61, 200 f.
23. On John 1:14: *PG,* 73, 161 c.
24. Thes. 34 on Eph. 1:13 f.: *PG,* 75, 612 a; *Dial. de Trin.,* 4, p. 905 a.
25. *PG,* 73, 604; 74, 528 (on John 17:13).
26. *PG,* 74, 528 ab.
27. *PG,* 74, 560 b; 561: κατὰ μέθεξιν. Cyril also understands Paul's κοινωνία τοῦ πνεύματος as a partaking of the Spirit.
28. *PG,* 74, 560 d.
29. *Dial. de Trin.: PG,* 75, 697 b.
30. *PG,* 74, 560 b.
31. *PG,* 75, 697 c.
32. Eph. 4:2: *PG,* 74, 561 b.

Bibliography for Chapter 3

See Chapter 2.
Dibelius, M. "Die Mahlgebete der Didache," *ZNTW,* 1938, p. 37.
Giertz, Bo. "Koinonia," *Buch von der Kirche,* pp. 405 ff. Not in ET.
Sjoeberg, E. "The Church and the Cultus in the New Testament," *This Is the Church,* pp. 75 ff.
von Soden, H. "Sakrament und Ethik bei Paulus (on 1 Cor. 8—10), *Urchristentum und Geschichte,* II (1951), 239 ff.

4

"THE LORD'S SUPPER,
NOT THE CHRISTIANS' SUPPER"

For the early church the Lord's Supper was always a fellowship. Only in the course of time did this receive theological definition. Isidore of Pelusium's definition of *koinonia* centered entirely in being made one with Christ, although he did move beyond a purely individual understanding in pointing out that thereby we become "partakers of His kingdom" (p. 19). Nevertheless, no specific consideration was given to this lateral fellowship. This theme which we saw developing in Chrysostom and Cyril of Alexandria has its first definitive statement in John of Damascus. "We say *koinonia*, and so it is, for through it we have *koinonia* with Christ and partake of His flesh and deity, but through it we also have *koinonia* [among ourselves] and are united with one another. Since we receive of one bread, we all become one body of Christ and one blood, and members one of another. We are united in one body with Christ." [1] Here the *koinonia* of the communicants with one another is the corollary of the *koinonia* with Christ. That they are understood not merely as two things externally side by side is shown by the use of Paul's statement in 1 Cor. 10:17 as documentation.

This passage flows into the general stream of Paul's thoughts about the body of Christ, whose members are the Christians. [2] Perhaps it is even the source of the whole stream. [3] Its contribution must doubtless be ranked high. What otherwise might be taken as metaphor or analogy this passage establishes as solid fact. We eat one bread and by that, by that eating, we become one body. The "bodily unity" of which ancient Greek theology is always speaking, or the "fleshly unity," as Ignatius puts it, is not meant metaphorically but literally. We cannot but go on with Chrysostom, "Because it is one bread, we many are one body. . . .

We are that selfsame body. For what is the bread? The body of Christ. What do they who partake of it become? The body of Christ" (p. 27). Any further comment on 1 Cor. 10:16—17 seems superfluous. From the more detailed context which we considered earlier we saw that Chrysostom understood Paul correctly and brought his message home to his readers. No modern exegete has done better. Thus, and only thus, also the fellowship of the Sacrament is understood in harmony with the apostle. "The many" are made into a unity. There is a lateral fellowship, one man is bound to another, but this result is achieved not by them but by that which articulates and incorporates them. It includes them but is not brought into being by them.

The exposition of Cyril of Alexandria is salutary in showing the connection of the Sacrament with the church and in emphasizing the *koinonia* of the Spirit or the spiritual unity. He refers to 1 Cor. 12:13 ("We are all made to drink of one Spirit") and to John's sacramental chapter with its statement that it is the Spirit who makes us alive. He does not overlook that Jesus here identifies His words with the Spirit (John 6:63). Without the *koinonia* of the Spirit (for Cyril that is partaking of the Spirit) there cannot be the self-examination which Paul enjoins before receiving the Sacrament, nor the discerning of the Lord's body (1 Cor. 11: 28 f. Cf. 2:12 f.), nor the ethical fruits which are emphasized by them all. It was essential to speak of the unity in the Holy Ghost when the body of Christ, as used in 1 Cor. 10:17, was brought together with the church as the body of Christ. This Cyril does in good Pauline fashion. Paul himself, however, while he indeed speaks of a "spiritual food" and a "spiritual drink" of the Old Testament fathers (1 Cor. 10:3 f.), does not so much as mention the Spirit in his discussion of the Sacrament. The only possible explanation is that what concerns Paul here is precisely the bodily unity; otherwise 1 Cor. 10:17 quite loses its point.

John of Damascus states the two things: the unity of the communicants with Christ and the unity of the communicants with one another. The first accords with the sacramental words of Jesus in John, "He that eats My flesh and drinks My blood dwells in Me, and I in him" (6:56); the second with Paul's conclusion in 1 Cor. 10:17. While the first is not foreign to Paul, it may facilitate our discussion to speak simply of the Johannine and the Pauline lines of Eucharistic interpretation. It would appear that the Pauline has its most radical expression in the term *synaxis*. This beyond all doubt speaks of the lateral relationship of the communicants with one another. *Synaxis* as the coming together of Christians for their common observances is given a description though not a basis in Tertullian's terms *coetus, congregatio,* and *conventus* (*Apology,* 39). This is not alien to Paul, who also speaks of this coming together (συνέρχεσθαι ἐπὶ τὸ αὐτό, 1 Cor. 11:17, 20; 14:23, 26). However, what he says of the Corinthians' coming together in 1 Cor. 11:17 ff., that is, we may say, of their *synaxis*, sheds no light on the *koinonia* of which he was speaking earlier (10:16-17). It is rather the contradiction between the two that is disclosed. What they conduct is no Lord's Supper. Everyone eats what he has brought along by himself. A man can eat his fill at home (11:20 f.). And then comes the account of what the apostle had "received from the Lord," the institution of the Lord's Supper.

Naturally if the Lord's Supper is to be celebrated, the Christians must come together. The Corinthian improprieties can, to be sure, be avoided, and there need be no discord between the *synaxis* and *koinonia* of the Eucharist. That these improprieties were possible at all, and are always possible in some form or other, demonstrates the difference between the two both in fact and concept. The difference disappears only when *synaxis* is understood in that other sense of the prayers of the *Didache* and John 11:52: the *synaxis* is made not by men's joining themselves together but by God Himself. God gathers together His church from the four winds, or Christ gathers together the scattered children of God. This other understanding of the *synaxis* is not to be confined to the Eucharist, but when it is used of the Sacrament, as became the settled usage in the East, it certainly is at least no hindrance to the right understanding of this *koinonia*. Indeed it supports it at a crucial point. Christ is the host of the Sacrament not only because He instituted it, but also because He is active at every repetition of it. In the foreground we see the coming together of the communicants, but behind it all is the Lord, who is like the man who arranges a great feast and calls together his guests (Luke 14:16 f.) or who knocks at the door that He may come in and sup with him who opens the door. (Rev. 3:20)

The picture in Luke is thoroughly Pauline, that in Revelation Johannine. Both, however, converge in the same point. In both the initiative lies with the Lord. When He does what according to both John and Paul He promised to do, He is present with His body and blood in the Sacrament as the exalted Lord. When Ignatius says that the Eucharist is the "one flesh of our Lord Jesus Christ and the one cup for being made one by His blood," and when Luther writes in the Small Catechism, "What is the Sacrament of the Altar? It is the true body and blood of our Lord Jesus Christ," these are not arbitrary abbreviations but completely factual definitions. The contention of Ignatius that only that Eucharist is trustworthy which takes place "under the bishop" we may pass over here, for neither John nor Paul knows anything of it. The objection that these definitions are inadequate because the communicants are essential to the Sacrament is quite misleading. Even Luther's further words, "for us Christians to eat and drink," are in this connection inessential. The communicants do indeed belong to it, but when the Sacrament is celebrated according to its institution, that is, when they eat of this bread and drink of this cup, they can, with Chrysostom, say, "We are that selfsame body." 1 Cor. 10:16 permits no other interpretation. The Sacrament is a fellowship of the communicants because, as these definitions rightly say, it *is* the body of Christ. In receiving the Sacrament they are together this body and are united in it.

Greek theology understood the *koinonia* of 1 Cor. 10:16 as *metalepsis*, as partaking, and we can see now how right this is and how much depends on it. This interpretation combines the Pauline and the Johannine. The individual communicant is included as is all that John 6 says concerning the eating of the bread, which is Christ and His flesh (6:51), as it applies to the individual who receives it. Giving heed to John 6 does not at all mean an antithesis to the Pauline being made one through the *koinonia* (that is, *metalepsis*, "partaking") of the communicants. The man who wrote in 1 John 1:6-7 that the fellowship with Christ is impossible without fellowship with one another cannot be setting himself in opposition to Paul, even though in this passage he is not speaking of the Sacrament and *koinonia* has another significance. (μετ' αὐτοῦ)

The understanding of *koinonia* as *metalepsis* stands implacably against the misunderstanding, yes, the false teaching, that the Sacrament is what it is by the action together of Christians. Even if the Sacrament is a fellowship, it certainly is not so because men "have something to do with one another." Here Luther is absolutely right. The *koinonia* of the participants with one another arises much rather from this, and in the Eucharist solely from this, that each through the eating and drinking has *koinonia* with Christ. Kaesemann, indebted to Lohmeyer, expresses it beautifully. The Sacrament "is not constituted horizontally by men being gathered together, but much rather by a higher authority independent of them, that is, vertically." [4] "Horizontal" and "vertical" vividly illustrate that the fellowship is in another dimension than that of a human friendly association. Sommerlath says the same. "It is just the Lord's Supper which gives this fellowship (that of Christians with one another) its profound depth." [5] Not the coming together, nor the common prayer, nor the *anamnesis* or *epiklesis,* nor even the faith of the communicants is what makes the Sacrament a fellowship. All these lie in the foreground, in the dimension of time and space, while the body and blood of Christ, to which measurements of time and space cannot be applied, are not confinable in this dimension but transcend all earthly existence.

This distinction of dimensions is relevant also to the question of the relationship between the body and blood of Christ in the Sacrament and the bread and wine, and of that between the bodily eating and drinking and the *koinonia* with Christ. The problem of this distinction was the starting point of the sacramental controversies in the early Middle Ages and also at the time of the Reformation. It evoked in part metaphysical and in part Christological statements. These cannot, at least at their outset, be declared inadmissible, for the question of the Real Presence of the body and blood of the exalted Christ in the temporal and local event of the Sacrament, in bread and wine, in eating and drinking, can be put both metaphysically and Christologically. When the question is put metaphysically or Christologically, one cannot deny theology the privilege of giving an answer from the same viewpoints.

Even Luther did not evade this type of question. We quote him here because he focused the problem of fellowship for us at the beginning of our inquiry, and also because there is hardly another who has so keenly drawn the boundaries of all theological argument regarding the Lord's Supper. His controversies first with Carlstadt and then with the Swiss followed in part a philosophical and metaphysical course. Patristic Christology entered the discussion to play its role, while Biblical arguments were naturally employed by both sides. We can follow all this vividly in the reports of the Marburg Colloquy — down to that dramatic moment, recorded by Osiander, when Luther drew back the velvet tablecloth and pointed to the words he had earlier chalked on the table: "This is My body." [6] These words were for him more than another quotation of Scripture. They called a halt to any further dialectic.

Of all that the Bible says about the Sacrament, 1 Cor. 10:16 made the deepest impression on Luther. "I have extolled this text and do extol it as the joy and crown of my heart." [7] But the words of Christ, "This is My body," meant even more. There may be no disputing about these words. This was the conviction that prompted him that moment in Marburg. They are not words *about* the Sacrament. They are not words of Scripture like other words of Scripture. They may not be subjected to exegetical discourses as the words of John or Paul may. They are the creative words of Christ Himself. They are without analogy and are therefore not to be explained by means of other examples.[8] They do not describe the Sacrament; they constitute it. They speak personally to each communicant. They claim faith, and yet unbelief cannot frustrate them.

Here the flights and disputings of theology are called back to a point from which there may be no departure. This point was not theologically or systematically defined by Luther, just as Paul was not concerned to discuss the connection between the Sacrament and his doctrine of Justification, or the Atonement, Election, Sanctification, or Baptism. Luther had rather the actual Sacrament always before his eyes. He knew that he was a partaker in the *koinonia* not because of some theological reflections, but because he knew himself to be put into a personal bond by the, so to speak, quite untheological words of his Lord. These did not permit him to discuss the matter as if he were merely a spectator or engaged in a theological discussion. When he did discuss the *est* in our Lord's words, his endeavor was not to replace an explanation which he regarded as false with one that he held to be right; it was his purpose to repudiate every attempt at explanation. What Luther taught of the Sacrament can be summed up as "The Lord means what He says."

In this living relationship to the Sacrament Luther was most close to the Eucharistic theology of the early church. He shared with the early exegetes the same conscientious pursuit of understanding all that the Bible says about the Sacrament. His opposition to the medieval doctrine of transubstantiation and the interpretation of the Sacrament as a sacrifice men offer separated him from many a teacher of the ancient church in whom these doctrines were already forming. This, however, is all far outweighed by that which united him with the early church. He was at one with the early church in agreeing that the fellowship of the Sacrament is determined by the *koinonia,* which is not an association of men but a *metalepsis,* a partaking of the body of Christ (*WA* 26, 490, 19; *AE* 37, 353); that the fellowship of the communicants with one another is constituted not by the will of man nor the common "faith in the heart" (490, 31) but by the body of Christ; that he who eats the one bread eats the body of Christ; that the eating and drinking is a bodily eating and drinking which through the words of Christ is also a "spiritual" eating and drinking and does not thereby cease to be bodily; that from this eating and drinking a bodily fellowship arises (492, 17) in which the "unworthy" also participate though it be to their judgment (493, 3); in short, that the Sacrament "rests not on the faith or unbelief of men but on God's Word and ordinance" (506, 24). All this united Luther with the early church as it unites both with Paul.

This unity was not more or less a thing of chance. As we saw, Luther always had the actual Sacrament before his eyes. It was for him as for the whole Christian church since the days of the apostles an essential part of the spiritual life. The divergence in the doctrine of the Sacrament could never have had such decisive consequences for his church conduct if it had had no more than a dogmatically theoretical significance. What the Bible says did not speak to him of what happened once in Corinth or Jerusalem, but of what he himself experienced under the constituting words of His Lord at every celebration of the Sacrament.

It is the same living in the Sacrament which shaped the Eucharistic theology of the early church, or perhaps it would be better to say, her theology of the Sacrament interpreted her liturgy of the Sacrament. The liturgy was not constructed according to theological insights, but rather these grew out of the liturgy.[9] This was proper as long as the church did not stray from the liturgical usage of the early church, in which provincial variations were of course not ruled out. On this basis the church saw that it not only could but must acknowledge the Sacrament as a fact basic to its existence. It was decisive not only for her interpreting theology but for the whole life of the church.[10] Only when we appreciate that for the early church this fact stood above all possibility of discussion, do we understand the way it dealt with the relation between the Lord's Supper and church fellowship. Beyond doubt the Sacrament is a *koinonia,* but this *koinonia* is not the product of men's decisions and dealings but an objective fact according to which church fellowship also must be ordered.

"We know that it is and is called the Lord's Supper, not the Christians' supper." [11] To this criterion of Luther's the whole mass of conflicting concepts regarding fellowship may well be referred. In the early church this truth stood unchallenged. In Luther's time it was already no longer so, and in our day it is not at all so. Even today it is not openly attacked, but it has not escaped the attention of those theologians who understand how to make every "either or" into an "as well as." Even using the English term "Lord's Supper" does not guarantee that people will also act according to the meaning of the term. That is shown when people reveal how far they are prepared to limit their own right to arrange and manage things.

Notes to Chapter 4

1. *De fide orth.*, IV, 13: *PG*, 94, 1153a: κοινωνία δὲ λέγεταί τε καὶ ἔστιν ἀληθῶς διὰ τὸ κοινωνεῖν ἡμᾶς δι' αὐτῆς τῷ Χριστῷ καὶ μετέχειν αὐτοῦ τῆς σαρκός τε καὶ τῆς θεότητος· κοινωνεῖν δὲ καὶ ἐνοῦσθαι ἀλλήλοις δι' αὐτῆς· ἐπεὶ γὰρ ἐξ ἑνὸς ἄρτου μεταλαμβάνομεν οἱ πάντες ἓν σῶμα Χριστοῦ καὶ ἓν αἷμα καὶ ἀλλήλων μέλη γινόμεθα σύσσωμοι Χριστοῦ χρηματίζοντες.

2. Rom. 12:5; 1 Cor. 6:15; 12:12 ff.; 12:27; also Eph. 1:23; 4:4, 16; 5:23, 30; Col. 1:18; 3:15.

3. Thus F. Kattenbusch. "Paul's calling the church the body of Christ had its roots in what was said of the bread: 'This is my body.'" *Theol. Stud. u. Krit.*, 1922, p. 114. E. Lohmeyer comments, "Unfortunately this statement has no more cogency than that of a suggestion." *Theol. Rundschau*, 1937, p. 223. His "unfortunately" at least indicates that Lohmeyer regards the connection as possible. We have seen that Cyril of Alexandria already held it to be so ("For this reason the church is also called the body of Christ."). We need not here pursue the apparent shift in meaning in Ephesians (Christ the Head). Cf. H. Schlier, *Christus und die Kirche im Epheserbrief*, 1930; Goesta Lindeskog, "Gottes Reich und Kirche im Neuen Testament," *Buch von der Kirche*, pp. 145 f.

4. "Abendmahlsgemeinschaft?" Supplement 3 to *Evang. Theologie*, 1937, p. 77.

5. *Abendmahlsgespraech*, ed. E. Schlink, 1952, p. 51.

6. *WA* 30 III, 147, 15; cf. the anonymous report, 137, 9; Hermann Sasse, *This Is My Body* (1959), p. 257.

7. *WA* 26, 487, 12; *AE* 37, 348.

8. Luther here adduced the universal principle: *quemque articulum fidei sui ipsius principium esse, nec opus esse exemplo simili probari* ("Every article of faith is its own foundation. It has no need of proof by a similar example"). *WA* 30 III, 141, 12. Sasse, p. 261.

9. Wilhelm Maurer, *Bekenntnis und Sakrament*, I (1939), 11 ff. Hermann Sasse, *Vom Sakrament des Altars* (1941), pp. 84 ff.

10. Erik Sjoeberg, "The Church and the Cultus in the New Testament," *This Is the Church*, p. 99. "A personal Christianity, apart from its foundations in the cultus, is something which does not enter into consideration. The new life is never without the bond of the cultic fellowship around the living Lord."

11. *WA* 23, 271, 8; *AE* 37, 142.

Bibliography for Chapter 4

Andersen, Wilhelm. "Das Herrenmahl als Opfer," *Evangelisch-lutherische Kirchenzeitung*, 4 (1950), pp. 41 ff.

Asmussen, Hans. *Abendmahl und Messe*, 1949.

Bring, Ragnar. "On the Lutheran Concept of the Sacrament," *World Lutheranism Today*, Festschrift for Anders Nygren, ed. Y. Brilioth (Oxford, 1950), pp. 36 ff.

Josefson, Ruben. "The Lutheran View of the Lord's Supper," *This Is the Church*, pp. 255 ff.

Knolle, Th. "Luthers Reform der Abendmahlsfeier in ihrer konstitutiven Bedeutung," in Herntrich and Knolle's *Schrift und Bekenntnis*, 1950, pp. 88 ff.

Lindeskog, Goesta. "The Kingdom of God and the Church in the New Testament," *This Is the Church*, pp. 136 ff.

Maurer, Wilhelm. *Bekenntnis und Sakrament*, I (1939).

Nygren, Anders. "Corpus Christi," ibid., pp. 3 ff.

Schmidt, Wilhelm F. "Repraesentatio," *ELKZ*, 4 (1950), pp. 24 f. See also Eduard Ellwein, ibid., p. 148.

Schweitzer, E. "Das Abendmahl eine Vergegenwaertigung des Todes Jesu oder ein eschatologisches Freudenmahl," *Theol. Zeitschrift*, Basle, 1946, pp. 81 ff.

Vajta, Vilmos. *Die Theologie des Gottesdienstes bei Luther*, 1952; trans. U. S. Leupold, *Luther on Worship*. Philadelphia, 1958.

5

UNITY AND FELLOWSHIP

This inquiry into the connection between the Eucharist and church fellowship has been called for by contemporary church conditions and events. It may appear doubtful therefore whether the question can fairly be put to the early church. Present answers about the granting or refusing of fellowship are in such terms as "intercommunion," "intercelebration," and "open" or "closed Communion." These presuppose divisions in the church. Since when have there been these divisions? Hans Asmussen, speaking for many, sees their origin in the "confessional churches" which arose from the Reformation. "The division at the Lord's Table as we have it today has a history of four hundred years." [1] According to the context of this statement it is clear that in his view such divisions first arose 400 years ago. This is more than a little slip of a year or two. Half a millenium before the Reformation there was the division between the Western Church and the Orthodox of the East, and a thousand years before that there were the divisions with the Monophysites and the Nestorians. These churches did not designate themselves as confessional churches, and yet anyone for whom "confessional" is a word of honor and not of abuse certainly cannot withhold it from them.

The division at the Lord's Table, about which Asmussen justly grieves, is in fact much older than that. In the Codex Theodosianus of 428 we observe a respectable number of Christian confessions existing beside one another. All but one are pronounced heretical and punishable in civil law, but this may not lead us to suppose that they are thereby excluded from Christendom. None of them, except the Manichaeans, would have denied that "Jesus Christ is the Lord," a statement which in our day has been taken as sufficient to qualify a church as Christian.

None of these heretics was united at the Lord's Table with the others or with the majority church. They go back in part into the second century. Already at the beginning of that century the bishop of Antioch, Ignatius, was at pains to warn against heresies the congregations to which he wrote, in which, however, he could not deny that "Jesus Christ is interwoven." [2] This was the evening of the apostolic age. In the New Testament itself we read of divisions and false doctrine, nor are these referred to first in the pastoral epistles. However current the contrary notion may be nowadays, the divisions of the church did not begin with the Reformation. The church has always and from its beginning suffered such divisions. Since the days of the apostles the church has faced the question how these divisions affect altar fellowship.

The hymn of the unity of the church in Ephesians gives the other side of the picture (4:4-6). It does not speak of divisions. Does it, however, express what is believed or what is a discernable statistical fact, or both? Without doubt it is the former, for the church spoken of here is the church which has Christ as its head and "which is His body, the fullness of Him that fills all in all" (1:22 f). This church whose fullness is beyond every dimension (1:21) is certainly not a statistical thing. It has its origin in God's choice before the foundation of the world (1:4), and its riches will first be revealed in the ages to come (2:7). This church in Ephesians is the church as seen by God. He knows more than we are able to perceive. It is "the church of the living God, the pillar and ground of truth," as another hymn of the early church puts it. There we read also "preached to the Gentiles, believed on in the world" (1 Tim. 3:15 f.). What the Epistle to the Ephesians says of the church is a confession of faith, not a conclusion based on visible evidence.

The palpable presence of the church is not here contested or minimized. On the contrary, the readers are addressed as belonging together in the same house and building "built upon the foundation of the apostles and prophets" (2:20). The apostles were persons as real as the readers themselves. The admonitions of the epistle are for their conduct in this world, not in the next. The church as a "building" is therefore a matter not only of faith but also of experience — exactly like the kingdom of God or of heaven, the coming of which the incarnate Jesus proclaims in the synoptic gospels. How the Kingdom and the church are otherwise related need not be gone into here.[3] No one will deny that they are bound up together. The important fact here is that as there is only one kingdom there is also one church, for there is only one Christ, and that this oneness is both believed and experienced. The body of Christ is at the same time heavenly and earthly. It is earthly, for apostles, prophets, evangelists, pastors, and teachers serve in building it up (4:11 f.), and all other members have their part in this also (4:16). If we consider, too, that among the criteria of the unity of the church — one body, one Spirit, one hope, one Lord, one faith — we find also one Baptism (4:4 f.), we may even come to the conclusion that the church of Ephesians is also a statistical thing, for why should those baptized not be counted?

It is difficult to escape the impression that the church of Ephesians despite its transcending all perceptible dimensions was already set in a certain form that is absent from Paul's earlier letters. This has not been the least of the reasons why the Pauline authorship has been denied. Paul preached "Christ crucified" (1 Cor. 1:22), and where there was a division into parties as in Corinth, all are called back to the one foundation that is laid, which is Jesus Christ (3:11). Here we are in the first stage of his great mission, which has its task not in building up the church but in proclaiming the crucified and risen Christ. These are certainly not mutually exclusive, but in the mission stage the preaching of Christ and the church are related not as means and goal but rather as cause and effect.

The first church in Jerusalem was different, for it was not in the mission stage in which Paul found himself. It was there and needed only to grow. Where Paul came as a missionary there was nothing. Word and Spirit produced, so to speak, a church out of nothing — not *the* church, for apart from Ephesians and Colossians Paul usually speaks of a church qualified only by a place name (Corinth, Thessalonica), and so he speaks also of "the churches" in the plural.[4] In First Corinthians he speaks of the unity of the body of Christ (12:12). This is self-evident, for there is only one Christ. Here we find almost exactly the same criteria as in Ephesians. It is almost as if he had transcribed: one body and one Spirit, one Lord, one Baptism (12:4 ff., 13). What occupies Paul here is the internal situation in the congregation to which he is writing. Things have not settled down there. Factions must unite. False apostles are causing confusion (2 Cor. 11). Members who are called brother must be put out (1 Cor. 5:11-13). The church at Corinth is indeed not "invisible," but its unity is. Inasmuch as it is the body of Christ, it is one; but as a church it has still to become that unity.

Other congregations such as that at Philippi did not cause the apostle so much trouble. This cannot be said of the original congregations of his mission in Galatia. Here his opponents were such as to exclude the thought of unity from the outset. There is no mention of unity in his whole letter to them, although it is of course what he is striving for through it all. Unity can only be established or reestablished if the congregations hold fast to the pure Gospel and if they set their anathema against every other gospel and against every man who preaches another gospel. Unity between these congregations and the apostle is possible only if they completely abjure all others. What is discernible in the letters to Corinth is here quite clear: the unity of the body of Christ which is there by the very nature of that body and which no disorders of man can destroy needs, if it is to appear in the visible church, an uncompromising declaration of its stand and loyalty.

While Paul was still living, the congregations he founded had already grown beyond the mission situation of their beginning. In the later parts of the New Testament it is possible to trace a general settling of the way the church was ordered. An essential cause, if one considers only its obvious consequences, was the delay in the Second Coming of the Lord. What we learn, for example, from the first Epistle of Clement concerning the congregation in Corinth is largely conditioned by the simple fact that 50 years have elapsed since the beginning of the congregation. The founding generation had grown old and was in part already replaced by a younger generation. The death of all the apostles, of all "witnesses" of the birth of the church, had the same effects as the delay of the Second Coming, or rather made people feel the effects of that delay most keenly. As long as Paul was alive, he managed the critical touchstones of the unity of the church. He decided who was to be put out of the church. He drew the line between true and false prophets. He did this on the basis of his own apostolic authority, but this authority was unique and not capable of being repeated, for it was personally given him by the Lord in quite exceptional circumstances. His passing and that of the other apostles were of decisive significance for the constitutional history of the early church.

In the present context our only question is whether at the death of the apostles the church stood in unity? If we take the church as the body of Christ in accordance with Ephesians, then certainly. If we think of churches in the plural, in accordance with Paul's earlier letters and the first three chapters of Revelation, then certainly not. This plurality does not of itself exclude the unity. Whether the churches in the plural exhibit the criteria of the church in the singular can only be discovered by an examination of the facts in each case. Such an examination of the seven churches in Revelation produces such diverse findings that no one could maintain that they present a picture which matches the unity of the body of Christ. Even in Ephesians the hymn of unity is preceded by an admonition to be zealous in keeping the unity of the Spirit (4:3). In view of the actual conditions it could not by any means be taken for granted. Although the church is spoken of in the singular in Colossians, admonitions and warnings are prompted by very concrete dangers that injure and disrupt the church. In the later writings of the New Testament [5] we see the battle of "sound doctrine" and "good confession" against "false doctrine," "myths," "what is falsely called knowledge," "heresy," and "apostasy from the faith." It is a battle which has never ceased from then until now. It is not avowedly waged for unity, but rather for those conditions in which alone unity can exist.

In the later literature of the church of the majority there is from the very beginning a hard and fast borderline between those within the church and those without. One can hardly challenge such a line of demarcation or the conviction that within the church is the truth and outside it error, that within are the orthodox and without the heretics. These are statements of faith which, however, are not readily demonstrable from the historical evidence. Later antiheretical writers seem nevertheless to know exactly about each personage in the past whether he was orthodox or heretical. From their vantage point in time they look back and see men as outside the church because the balance has come down against them and their case is decided. Yet in their own time the contentions of these men were in controversy *within* the church. In effect such writers accept the verdict of the victorious party, which was of course scarcely ever acknowledged by the vanquished. Hegesippus, for example, declares that the church in Corinth "remained in the right doctrine" until Primus was bishop.[6] To be quite exact he should have remarked first "after Paul had succeeded in disposing of the false apostles of Christ whom he denounces in Second Corinthians." From the apostle's warning we must conclude that the false apostles had established themselves *in* the congregation. They certainly claimed to be as much *in* the church as Paul, for they gave themselves out to be apostles of Christ. This claim is characteristic of all heresy. The line between truth and error is indeed forever unchangeable, but it must first be discovered in the case of each teacher and his teaching. There is usually some element of truth resident even in the doctrine of false teachers. Walter Bauer claims to show that what was once heretical was later incorporated as orthodox (Edessa, Egypt). Martin Werner has good evidence to show that the border between the Gnostics and the church of the majority was fluid and not firmly demarcated, as the later ecclesiastical accounts maintain. In the final analysis we must agree when Schoeps maintains that the Ebionites of the second century, the question of whose heresy was later regarded as settled, "had as much right as the emergent Catholic Church to regard the first congregation as their common mother." [7] Marcion of course declared that the church he organized was *the* Christian church and his doctrine orthodox. Apocryphal gospels, acts of apostles, and apocalypses were long read unchallenged in the church before they were pronounced heretical. Tertullian, who strove to render every heretic utterly defenseless, was himself entangled in the Montanist heresy, which later never failed to appear in the catalog of heresies.

The unity of the church is the presupposition of church fellowship. Whatever the early church meant by church fellowship (κοινωνία τῆς ἐκκλησίας or ἐκκλησιαστική), it had to do with fellowship of or in one and the same church. This takes for granted that there is only one church. This oneness is expressed in the Eastern creeds where "one" usually comes before "holy church." [8] The admonition in Ephesians "to keep the unity (ἑνότης) of the Spirit in the bond of peace" (4:3) enlarges the meaning of unity beyond this numerical oneness. Here the opposite of unity is not plurality but discord and disunity. The unity of the church consequently means being at one together, or rather this is essential to that unity. Nobody, not even the heretics, ever doubted the unity of the church in the sense that there is only one church. What was of great moment was the unity of the church in the sense of agreeing and being at one together. This was a problem at least from the time when Paul identified true and false apostles of Jesus Christ and pronounced the anathema upon those who preached a gospel differing from his. If the unity of the church involves being at one and church fellowship presupposes such unity, then the question of church fellowship arises whenever Christians are not at one, and this question of church fellowship then calls for a practical decision.

Paul made such decisions on the basis of his apostolic authority. He also acknowledged the decisions of the congregation under the guidance of the Holy Spirit.[9] Acts 15 describes a synod making such a decision. After the time of the apostles the disagreements which disturbed Christian unity did not grow less but greater, and then there was no apostle. These disagreements could not be settled on paper. They made their way into the divine service, into the preaching, and into the sacraments — the Gnostics also celebrated their mysteries. Every congregation declared what it stood for in its liturgy, its selection of lections, and in its prayers and hymns. Marcion rejected the whole Old Testament. When there was disagreement in any place, the burden of decision rested on each member.

We see from the warnings of Ignatius how close together the false teachers and the faithful lived. He described the doctrine and practice of dangerous neighbors. He will not name them; everybody knows them. He warns his readers not to associate with them and not even to speak of them publicly or privately.[10] They are to hold to their bishop. Here the faithful are given a clear direction which is seemingly as convincing as it is simple, but unfortunately it did not work. It did not fulfill what Ignatius and his congregations expected of it. One hundred and fifty years later the bishop of Antioch was the archheretic Paul of Samosata. What would have happened if the Christians of Antioch had followed Ignatius' directive? Another century later we find three, and for a time even four, bishops opposing one another for decades in Antioch. These pronounced one another heterodox or schismatic. All claimed the Antiochene apostolic succession which would make them the legitimate successors of Ignatius. This was the time of the Meletian schism. Every Christian in Antioch who remembered Ignatius' admonition to obey the bishop [11] could not help asking, "Which one? With which one am I to be in fellowship?" (συνήθεια, Eph., 5, 1)

We may suppose that the possibility of a schism in one and the same congregation did not occur to Ignatius. How was it among the bishops? The area was limited in which this seemingly sure directive operated; each was to hold to *his* bishop. There were, however, many bishops, and a man could hardly know whether they were all as reliable as those in the congregations to which Ignatius wrote.[12] A man as conscientious as Ignatius could only obligate a congregation to be obedient to their bishop "as to Jesus Christ" [13] if he were convinced of the orthodoxy and blamelessness of that bishop. This could only be known from case to case. Hegesippus a generation later put each case to the test. On his journey from the East to Rome he visited "very many" bishops. He happily found the same doctrine among them all.[14] Before he began his journey he was certainly not sure of this, otherwise he need not have bothered to make the test. Moreover, it is very doubtful how far the polity of monarchic bishops which Ignatius posits had spread into other parts of the church at his time. In his letter to the church in Rome, which he knows so well and praises quite extravagantly, he does not so much as mention the bishop, as he always does in his letters to the churches in Asia Minor.

There was always communication between the various parts of the church from the days of the apostles. There was much traveling, and a good deal of it was to Rome. The *Didache* gives settled instructions about receiving "prophets," "apostles," and others who came "in the name of the Lord." [15] This was necessary, for there were also "false prophets." We observe also a lively exchange of letters.[16] The various writings of the New Testament and many others had been passed about the East and the West by the end of the second century. Accounts of martyrs were exchanged. May we not see in this lively intercourse evidence of the unity of the church? Not really. Of the 25 "notable Christians" whom Harnack selected from the records up to the middle of the third century about half are heretics. The literary works of the Gnostics were not automatically offensive to informed, "Catholic" Christians. The Holy Scriptures were acknowledged in them also. Gnostic writings probably had a wider circulation than those which enjoyed the approval of the ecclesiastical majority. The same may be said of the writings of the Montanists.[17] All this personal and literary communication unfortunately provides no proof of the unity of the church. It could do either, help or hinder, prove or disprove that unity.

This state of affairs could neither be merely accepted by the church as unavoidable nor be set aside by some single stroke. The extent of the intercourse between the various local churches and of the growing intercommunication through travelers, letters, and literature was also the extent of the Gnostic propaganda. It sought to establish itself throughout whole provinces, indeed through all Christendom. Even Montanism, which was quite provincial in its origin, flowed over into the West. It was no longer so simple for each local congregation to decide by itself matters of church unity which at the same time were matters of church fellowship. How were they effectively to decide the boundaries and practice of church fellowship? In the early days when the Second Coming was momently expected, it was perhaps possible. The longer that Advent was in coming, however, the more keenly they felt the pressures of time and place in which they still found themselves. Time meant earthly continuance, and that demanded some continuing arrangements. Place put them into a context of other local congregations. They were in communication with these. Some arrangements had to be made about church fellowship.

In the course of the second century the church drew firm and indeed narrow lines as the boundaries of church fellowship. Could they not have been more charitable, more liberal, more tolerant? Nowadays the advice would certainly be given that the unity of the church is established and the foundation for the practice of church fellowship provided by the common recognition of "Jesus Christ as Lord and Savior." Nothing more would be asked. Thus advised, the early church would have been able to regard as unexceptionable Marcion's denial of the authority of the Old Testament, Valentinus' unevangelical aeon Christology, and the Montanists' claim to represent the Paraclete. It would then not have been necessary to insist that the God and Father of Jesus Christ, and not another god, is the Creator of the world, as the Apostles' Creed declares. Nothing would then have stood in the way of intercommunion with Marcion, Valentinus, and Montanus. Thus confessional isolation would have been avoided. The church would not have insisted on binding all members to baptismal creeds which were narrowed by the addition of more and more formulas, and so it would have avoided developing into a confessional church, that is, a church with a clear and loyally held confession.

The early church lacked the benefit of such advice and followed another course. It inquired what decisions the apostles had already made and sought direction from them as crises arose. The classical historians of doctrine (F. C. Baur, von Harnack, R. Seeberg, Loofs) are in general agreed that this inquiry led to the establishment of three norms which had authority in the later formulation of doctrine: the episcopate, the canon of the New Testament, and the Rule of Faith (regula fidei). With these norms the early church believed it was heeding the apostles. Church fellowship was also determined by the same norms. They were the three strong walls which were expected to prevent divisions in the church in the future. No one can maintain that they succeeded in fulfilling their promise. They certainly did not prevent further divisions. Yet success and failure were not the same with each of the three.

As Ignatius had done, so also Cyprian in the middle of the third century directed every Christian to his bishop.[18] While for Ignatius each individual bishop with his congregation represented "the catholic church," [19] for Cyprian all the bishops together made up the episcopate which represented and guaranteed the unity of the church.[20] He understandably did not count the "unbelievers" who, since no one gave them the episcopate, had simply appropriated the name.[21] For him the true bishop was distinguished by the apostolic succession.[22] Cyprian's episcopate thus defined and seemingly sure was, however, by no means evident in fact. Even the episcopal sees which because of their apostolic foundation and unbroken succession enjoyed special rank [23] (Constantinople with some legendary assistance was also thus esteemed) proved themselves faulty pillars. Irenaeus regarded Ephesus as one of the guarantors of the apostolic tradition,[24] yet we already find Victor of Rome excluding "all congregations of Asia and neighboring regions" from church fellowship because the Bishop of Ephesus, Polycrates, supported a date for the Easter festival contrary to that of Rome.[25] The Ephesian succession had obviously not held good. Again, how was Hippolytus' schism in Rome possible when he himself claimed the succession, although this was not the only contention between him and the bishop there? [26] How could there be a Donatist schism which divided the African bishops in half? [27] How many legitimate occupants of the see of Antioch fell under the anathema of victorious ecclesiastical majorities! The Sixth Ecumenical Council posthumously excommunicated no less than five occupants of patriarchal sees and at least deposed Macarios of Antioch while he was still living. And that no man may have whereof to glory, he who sat on the Roman cathedra of Peter, Honorius I, was added to those condemned for false doctrine, and Pope Leo II expressly confirmed this sentence. If the unity of the church rested on the bishops and their apostolic succession, it rested rather insecurely.

It is different with the second wall of the New Testament canon. Here it is not the successors of the apostles but they themselves who speak, and through them the Lord Himself. What is here addressed to the church stands sure for all time. We may add to this the Old Testament, whose authority was no more called in question after the exclusion of Marcion. The unity of the church on earth can only be conceived, if we are to witness it at all, as being there where nothing in the church contradicts the will of Christ and His apostles. Divisions can consequently only be overcome by all being submissively recalled to this incontrovertible authority. This authority, however, was not acknowledged by the "catholic" church alone. Already Tertullian records that all the heretics base themselves on it also,[28] and Vincent of Lérins has vividly described this state of affairs. Read the works of the heretics, he avers, "there you have innumerable examples and find scarcely a page without the decoration and color of passages from the New and Old Testaments." [29] Exactly as today. The early church drew the conclusion from this that they must distinguish between the Holy Scripture and what men have made out of it. This is indeed true but this basic principle must be applied not only to the heretics but also to their Catholic opponents. At any rate, what is nowadays called "hearkening to the Word of God" has not in fact prevented divisions, even though all parties claim to be hearkening to the Word of God.

There remains the third wall which the early Catholic Church erected to safeguard its unity, the Rule of Faith (regula fidei or regula veritatis, κανὼν τῆς πίστεως or ἀληθείας). What exactly the writers of the second and third century understood by this term and the related traditio apostolorum (παράδοσις ἀποστολική) is disputed by scholars.[30] The usage in polemics against heretics indicates that what is meant is the baptismal creed together with its theological interpretation. Roman Catholic scholars seek to maintain a special role for the baptismal creed (symbolum) alongside the regula fidei. However, what the baptismal creeds at that time already presumably contained by way of formulas is also found without exception in the actual references to the Rule of Faith. We need pursue the question no further since we are here concerned only with the function which was ascribed to the Rule of Faith, or that which it in fact performed.[31]

This function was first to accredit the apostolic succession of the bishops. The succession could be a weapon against heresy only if it had a solid and clearly defined doctrine or order to be safeguarded as apostolic. The doctrine to be safeguarded is the Rule of Faith. This conjunction of succession and doctrine has on the face of it the consequence that the Rule of Faith suffers loss when the episcopate fails to safeguard it. Such a failure was perhaps not to be foreseen at the time of Cyprian. The following centuries, as we have seen, did nevertheless witness it. Now despite the conjunction of bishop and Rule of Faith they did not stand or fall together. The name Rule of Faith and similar expressions declined in use but not the formulas which express their basic content and which are the same as the baptismal creeds. These persisted with astonishing constancy. In the West the Apostles' Creed remained vital through the divisions of the Reformation period. In the East the whole development of doctrine is associated with a basic stock of formulas derived from the baptismal creeds. In the continuing doctrinal discussions and debates these formulas were enlarged, made more explicit, and strengthened with antiheretical additions, but the basic content remained always the same. The Nicaeno-Constantinopolitan Creed had the same constancy in the East as the Apostles' Creed in the West. It still provides a bridge with the West. The original conjunction of bishop and doctrine, with the bishop attesting the doctrine, came to have almost the reverse operation. Even though the synods which made doctrinal decisions were composed of bishops, the orthodox doctrine, once formulated, from the fourth century on had such weight of its own that bishops were judged by it and patriarchs who did not meet its standards were excommunicated.

The Rule of Faith had a further function toward the Bible. The connection between them appears at first very loose. Irenaeus speaks of "barbarians" who without the Scriptures have a Christian faith which can be stated in a few sentences and which he acknowledges as quite sufficient.[32] Is Scripture then actually superfluous? That is certainly not his meaning. Tertullian, too, speaks of the Rule of Faith as being so distinct from the Scripture that he first calls for its acceptance before one may appeal to, or indeed even read, the Scripture.[33] Clement of Alexandria would have the Bible expounded according to the "canon of the truth."[34] Tertullian is of the same mind. Here the connection is very close. The Rule of Faith provides a rule for the right understanding of Scripture. When we put it this way, the authority of Scripture seems to be depreciated. In applying this principle, we might come to the conclusion that Scripture played only a subordinate role in the development of the doctrine of the Rule of Faith. We find, in fact, quite the reverse. The same Clement of Alexandria also defends the principle that every proof passage of Scripture is to be reinforced by Scripture itself.[35] This comes close to the Lutheran principle *scriptura scripturae interpres* (Scripture is its own interpreter). From Hippolytus and Origen on, the early church produced massive exegetical works. Such Scriptural activity was indeed in harmony with the Rule of Faith but in no way derived its validity from it. In the great controversies from the fourth century on, what Tertullian observed as characteristic of the heretics was true of the great men of all parties — they were armed to the teeth with Scripture passages. Athanasius indeed often appealed to the "church doctrine," to "the tradition of the fathers," to the doctrine "given by the Lord, proclaimed by the apostles, and preserved by the fathers." Yet he wrote: "The true faith in the Lord [as it was confessed at Nicaea] is open to all, for it grows out of the knowledge of the Holy Scriptures, and any reader may find it there." The basic proclamation of the church is written in Matt. 28:19. How much direct Scriptural proof not dependent on any tradition for its legitimacy is there not in Leo the Great's *Tome,* which prevailed in the Christological controversy at Chalcedon.[36]

If the dogma of the early church was a development of the Rule of Faith,[37] Scripture was not on that account pushed into the background, but on the contrary given expression. It is possible to see the whole development of doctrine as an endeavor for unity in the right understanding of Scripture. We naturally ask whether this was successful. Had there been success here, then the third wall would have achieved what the other two failed to achieve: the establishment of a schism-free unity of the church on earth. For a great part of the church there was such success, although it was certainly not complete, for we cannot deny that the Donatists, Nestorians, Monophysites, and Armenians were in the church of Christ. Even though the goal was not attained, it was not therefore wrong to strive for it. On the contrary, that goal had to be

striven for, for the dogma and its precursor, the Rule of Faith, had yet
a final function.

When modern presentations of the doctrinal development are given
the title "doctrinal controversies," they are not untrue but still one-sided,
and when nothing else is shown, they are misleading. The dogma and
already the Rule of Faith naturally want to be understood as teaching
(*doctrina*, διδασκαλία). The debates do indeed at times give the impression of controversies among scholars whose meaning is known only to
them. The protagonists often accuse one another of mere fighting about
words (λογομαχία) or of useless babbling (περιεργάζεσθαι) not to mention the calling in of the police. The doctrinal development, however,
does not take place in a vacuum, and a faulty method does not allow us to
draw conclusions regarding the motive or the result. Irenaeus describes
doctrine as *kerygma*, which like the sun — the same for the whole world
— should shine on all men who desire to come to the knowledge of the
truth. In the service of its kerygmatic purpose it is stated in such
a way that nothing needs to be added but also that nothing may be
omitted for brevity's sake.[38] For Origen doctrine is comprehended in
the term "apostolic teaching" [39] and Athanasius speaks also of the dogma
of Nicaea as *kerygma*.[40] Rule of Faith and dogma are witness. They
are designed to fulfill the task of the church to be a witness to the world
of the truth.

Tertullian calls this witness "confessing" *(profiteri)*.[41] In him we
see the connection with the baptismal "confession," and the New Testament source of this final function of the Rule of Faith becomes evident.
Confessing is a duty incumbent on each Christian, particularly before
baptism. The New Testament shows clearly that for this purpose settled
forms were in use from the beginning. It could scarcely have been otherwise. The formulas do not declare, "I believe what my bishop believes,"
also not, "I believe in the Holy Scriptures." They all point back to the
confession of Peter [42] and soon underwent expansion. [43] The early church
never forgot that dogma is confession. In the statements of synods as
in individual confessions the expression "we confess (ὁμολογοῦμεν) is
often replaced by "we believe" or "we teach" or similar expressions.[44]
Even where we have only the customary "we believe," the doctrine is

confession. The confessors vouch for their confession with themselves. It is particularly striking that most of the Western baptismal creeds, and also some of those in the East, begin with the singular "I believe." On the other hand when "we" was used, each one knew himself to be linked with all believers and confessors. The subject of "we believe" is "the church which reaches to the ends of the world. . . . The churches in Germany believe and hand down nothing but what is taught also in the churches among the Iberians and Celts, in Egypt and Libya, and at the center of the world." That "we" begins with the apostles and extends without break to the present.[45] The baptismal creed, the Rule of Faith, and the dogma are confession, and in their consonance the unity of the church expresses itself as unanimity. This gives indication also of the scope of church fellowship as practiced in the early church.

Notes to Chapter 5

1. *Abendmahlsgemeinschaft?* 1937, p. 5. Cf. S. L. Greenslade, *Schism in the Early Church* (London, 1953), pp. 15 f.; E. L. Mascall, *The Recovery of Unity* (London, 1958), p. 94.

2. *Trall.,* 6, 2: *LCC,* I, 100.

3. Anton Fridrichsen, "The New Testament Congregation," *This Is the Church,* pp. 40 ff.; also Goesta Lindeskog, ibid., pp. 136 ff., and the cited investigations of Gloege, Sommerlath, Cullmann, W. Bieder, Bo Giertz, and O. Michel. For these, reference must be made to the original Swedish *En Bok om Kyrkan,* 1943, or the German translation, *Buch von der Kirche,* 1951.

4. In Galatia, Macedonia, Asia, and Judaea. 1 Cor. 16:1, 19; 2 Cor. 8:1; Gal. 1:2, 22; 1 Thess. 2:14; also Rom. 16:4, 16; 1 Cor. 4:17; 11:16; 14:33 f.; 2 Cor. 8:18 f., 23 f.; 11:8, 28; 12:13; 1 Thess. 2:14; etc.

5. Pastoral Epistles, 1 and 2 John, 2 Peter, Jude, Revelation.

6. *H. E.,* IV, 22, 2: Stevenson, p. 73.

7. Walter Bauer, *Rechtglaeubigkeit und Ketzerei im aeltesten Christentum,* 1934. Martin Werner, *Die Entstehung des christlichen Dogmas* (1941), p. 131. The sentence is omitted in S. G. F. Brandon's ET, *The Formation of Christian Dogma* (London, 1957). H. J. Schoeps, *Theologie und Geschichte des Judenchristentums* (1949), p. 257.

8. Clement of Alexandria has a similar understanding of the hymn of unity in Ephesians. *Strom.,* VII, 107, 3 ff. We all know that the received text of

the Apostles' Creed did not take in an *"una"* before *"sancta ecclesia,"* although it was smuggled in from time to time.

9. Otto Michel, *Das Zeugnis des NT von der Gemeinde,* p. 67. H. von Campenhausen, *Kirchliches Amt,* pp. 58 ff.

10. *Smyrn.,* 5, 3; 7, 2: *LCC,* I, 114.

11. *Eph.,* 20, 2; *Trall.,* 2, 1; *Polyc.,* 6, 1: *LCC,* I, 93; 98; 119.

12. Indeed he may perhaps have known the opposite. W. Bauer has made a comparison between the seven churches of Asia Minor in John's Revelation and the churches to which Ignatius wrote. Only three (Ephesus, Smyrna, Philadelphia) are common to both. "Is it propounding too much," Bauer asks (p. 83), "to draw the following conclusion from what Ignatius does and does not say? For the sake of his people in Antioch he already strives to extend the boundaries of his influence as far as possible. In view of what is said in Revelation, was there nothing more for him to hope for from the Christian groups in Pergamum, Thyatira, Sardis, and Laodicea because there was no point of contact for him there, no *bishop* to whom he could turn because the heretics had either remained or become dominant?" This deduction of Bauer's is certainly not compelling, but it is altogether possible that the last-named churches had succumbed in the meantime to the dangers against which the writer of Revelation had warned them, that they were in fact without any bishop, and that therefore Ignatius was at a loss what directions to give them for their recovery.

13. *Trall.,* 2, 1; *Eph.,* 6, 1: *LCC,* I, 98; 89.

14. *H. E.,* IV, 22, 1: Stevenson, p. 73.

15. *Didache,* 11, 12: *LCC,* I, 176 f.

16. Th. Zahn, *Weltverkehr und Kirche waehrend der ersten drei Jahrhunderte, Skizze aus dem Leben der alten Kirche,* 3d ed., 1908. The source material of the first three centuries on travel, letters, and literary exchanges is given by A. Harnack in *Mission und Ausbreitung des Christentums in den ersten drei Jahrhunderten,* 4th ed. (1924), pp. 379 ff. ET by J. Moffat, *The Mission and Expansion of Christianity in the First Three Centuries* (1908), I, 369 ff.

17. Irenaeus, *Haer.,* III, 12; Hippolytus, *Refut.,* 8, 19: Stevenson, p. 114.

18. *Ep.,* 66, 6: Lacey, p. 109.

19. *Smyrn.,* 8, 2: *LCC,* I, 115. Cf. *Mart. Pol.,* 16, 2: *LCC,* I, 155.

20. *De unit.,* 5: *LCC,* V, 126 f.

21. *De unit.,* 10: *LCC,* V, 130.

22. *De unit.,* 4: *LCC,* V, 126.

23. Tertullian, *De praescr.,* 20, 32, 36: *LCC,* V, 43 f., 52 f., 56 ff.

24. *Haer.*, III, 3, 4: *LCC*, I, 374.

25. *H. E.*, V, 24, 9: Stevenson, p. 149.

26. Adolf Hamel, *Kirche bei Hippolyt von Rom* (1951), pp. 163 ff.

27. In the year 411: 279 Donatists to 286 Catholics. Cf. W. H. C. Frend, *The Donatist Church* (Oxford, 1952), p. 284.

28. *De praescr.*, 15 ff.: *LCC*, V, 41.

29. *Commonitorium*, ch. 25 (35): Moxon, p. 103, 5; *FC*, VII, 315 f.

30. The most important witnesses are Dionysius of Corinth, Irenaeus, Clement of Alexandria, Tertullian, Hippolytus, and Novatian. For the reconstruction of the content see also the sources (Justin, Origen, etc.) in the first section of Hahn's *Symbole,* as also the earliest liturgical tradition. Kelly, pp. 2, 29, 76 ff.

31. The literature on the historical problem of the Rule of Faith is included in the composite account given by de Ghellinck, "Les recherches sur l'origine du symbole depuis XXV années," *Rev. d'Hist. Ecclés.*, 1942, pp. 97 ff., 361 ff.

32. *Haer.*, III, 4, 2: *LCC*, I, 374 f.

33. *De praescr.*, 13 ff., 37: *LCC*, V, 39 ff., 58.

34. *Strom.*, VI, 124, 5; 125, 2; VII, 94 ff.

35. *Strom.*, VII, 96, 4: *LCC*, II, 155 f.

36. Hahn, pp. 321—330. Athanasius, *Ad Serap.*, I, 28: *PG*, 26, 593 d, 596 c; C. R. B. Shapland, *The Letters of St. Athanasius* (London, 1951), pp. 133 to 136. *Ad Jovian.*, c. 1: *PG*, 26, 816 a.

37. Loofs: "Where the Rule was acknowledged, there was dogma."

38. *Haer.*, I, 10, 2: *LCC*, I, 361.

39. *De princ.*, I, *Praef.* 4: G. W. Butterworth, *Origen on First Principles* (London, 1936), pp. 2 f.

40. See above, n. 36.

41. *De praescr.*, 13: *CCL*, I, 197.

42. Matt. 16:16. Cf. John 6:69.

43. Phil. 2:11; 1 Cor. 12:3; Acts 8:37 (E); 1 John 4:15; Rom. 10:9; 1 Cor. 15:3 f.; Heb. 10:22 f.; cf. Eph. 4:5: "one faith, one Baptism"; 1 Tim. 6:12. O. Cullmann, *Les premières confessions de foi chrétienne*, 2d ed., 1948. Hermann Diem, *Theologie als kirchliche* Wissenschaft, 1951, pp. 124 ff. Hjalmar Lindroth, "Das fruehchristliche Bekenntnis," *Buch von der Kirche*, pp. 202 ff. Not in ET. Kelly, pp. 15 ff.

44. *Ap. Const.*, VI, 7, 9. ὁμολογοῦμεν also in (page numbers according to Hahn) the Nicaeno-Constantinopolitan before ἓν βάπτισμα (p. 165);

Sardican formula (p. 188); Acacians at Seleucia (p. 207); Apollinaris (p. 266); Pseudo-Athanasius (p. 266); at the beginning of the Christological section (28) of the Athanasian Creed: *ut credamus et confiteamur* (p. 176); Basil (p. 269); Antioch, 433 (p. 215); Lateran, 649 (p. 238); Toledo VI, 638 (p. 236); Toledo XI, 675 (p. 242); Milan, 680 (p. 248). In anathemas: εἴ τις οὐχ ὁμολογεῖ, Constantinople, 553 (p. 168), et passim. In the dogma of Chalcedon where the subject of the confession is not the Christology but Christ Himself: ἕνα καὶ τὸν αὐτὸν ὁμολογεῖν υἱὸν τὸν κύριον ἡμῶν Ἰησοῦν Χριστὸν (p. 166); similarly Constantinople, 680 f. (p. 172).

45. Irenaeus, *Haer.*, I, 10, 3: *LCC,* I, 360. Eusebius, Preface of the Caesarean confession presented at Nicaea. Hahn, p. 257 f.; *PG,* 20, 1,537; *LCC,* III, 337.

Bibliography for Chapter 5

Altendorf, E. *Einheit und Heiligkeit der Kirche, Entwicklung des Kirchenbegriffs im Abendland* (Tertullian, Cyprian, Augustine), 1932.

Asmussen, Hans. *Der Brief des Paulus an die Epheser,* 1950.

Bauer, Walter. *Rechtglaeubigkeit und Ketzerei im aeltesten Christentum,* 1934.

Bieder, W. *Ekklesia und Polis im Neuen Testament und in der alten Kirche.* Basle Dissertation, 1941.

Bring, Ragnar. "The Subjective and the Objective in the Concept of the Church," *This Is the Church,* pp. 205 ff.

Brun, Lyder. "Der kirchliche Einheitsgedanke im Urchristentum," *ZST,* 14 (1937), 86 ff.

Bultmann, Rudolf. *Theology of the New Testament,* trans. K. Grobel, 1952—55, II, 95 ff., 127 ff.

Butterworth, G. W. *Origen on First Principles.* London, 1936.

Campenhausen, H. von. "Recht und Gehorsam in der aeltesten Kirche," *Theol. Bl.,* 20 (1941), 279 ff.

———. *Kirchliches Amt und geistliche Vollmacht in den ersten drei Jahrhunderten,* 1953.

Cullmann, O. *Les primières confessions de foi chrétienne.* 2d ed., 1948.

Dahl, N. A. *Das Volk Gottes,* 1941.

Diem, Hermann. *Theologie als Kirchliche Wissenschaft,* 1951.

Frend, W. H. C. *The Donatist Church.* Oxford, 1952.

Fridrichsen, A. "Église et Sacrement dans le Nouveau Testament," *Rev. d'Hist. et de Phil. rel.,* 1937, pp. 337 ff.

———. "The New Testament Congregation," *This Is the Church,* pp. 40 ff.

Goguel, Maurice. *L'Église primitive,* 1947.

Greenslade, S. L. *Schism in the Early Church.* London, 1953.

Hamel, Adolph. *Kirche bei Hippolyt von Rom,* 1951.

Harnack, A. von. *Mission und Ausbreitung des Christentums in den ersten drei Jahrhunderten.* 4th ed., 1924.

Johansson, Nils. "Who Belonged to the Early Christian Church?" *This Is the Church,* pp. 148 ff.

Kattenbusch, Ferdinand. 'Der Quellort der Kirchenidee," *Festgabe fuer A. von Harnack,* 1921, pp. 143 ff.

Lietzman, H. "Die Anfaenge des Glaubensbekenntnisses," ibid., pp. 226 ff.

———. "Symbolstudien," *ZNTW,* 1922—23, pp. 21 f.

Lindroth, Hjalmar. "The Dogma Concerning the Church," *This Is the Church,* pp. 205 ff.

———. "Das fruehchristliche Bekenntnis," *Buch von der Kirche,* pp. 202 ff. Not in *This Is the Church.*

Linton, O. *Das Problem der Urkirche in der neueren Forschung,* 1932.

Mascall, E. L. *The Recovery of Unity.* London, 1958.

Michel, Otto. *Das Zeugnis des Neuen Testaments von der Gemeinde,* 1941.

Moffat, J. *The Mission and Expansion of Christianity in the First Three Centuries,* 1908. ET of A. v. Harnack, *Mission und Ausbreitung.*

Oepke, A. *Das neue Gottesvolk,* 1950.

Rawlinson, A. E. J. "Corpus Christi," *Mysterium Christi,* ed. G. K. A. Bell and A. Deissmann. London, 1930.

Rengstorf, K. H. *Die Auferstehung Jesu,* 1952, pp. 78 ff.

Schnorr von Carolsfeld, L. *Geschichte der juristischen Person,* 1933, I, 168 ff.

Schoeps, H. J. *Theologie und Geschichte des Judenchristentums,* 1949.

Shapland, C. R. B. *The Letters of St. Athanasius.* London, 1951.

Staehlin, Leonhard. *Christus praesens,* 1940.

Stauffer, Ethelbert. *New Testament Theology,* trans. John Marsh. New York: Macmillan, 1955.

Wikenhauser, A. *Die Kirche als der mystische Leib Christi nach dem Apostel Paulus,* 1937.

Zahn, Theodor. *Weltverkehr und Kirche waehrend der ersten drei Jahrhunderte,* 3d ed., 1908.

A synopsis of the discussions of the ecumenical conferences is given in *Intercommunion, Report of the Theological Commission Appointed by the Continuation Committee of the World Conference on Faith and Order,* ed. Donald Baillie and John Marsh, London, 1952. The contributions come from various churches. That of G. Florovsky, "Terms of Communion in the Undivided Church," pp. 47 to 57, deals with the early church. The concluding sentence of his short presentation ("Communion and an integral unity were exact correlatives") agrees with the results of our investigation.

6

CHURCH FELLOWSHIP
IN THE LOCAL CONGREGATION

Church fellowship was a problem already in the postapostolic age. Fitness of fellowship was decided from case to case (Hegesippus), and Bishop Victor of Rome quite formally withdrew fellowship from the church of Asia Minor. The problem was full-grown after the great divisions of the fourth century. Adherents of conflicting parties replaced each other in one and the same bishopric, and so the question who was in fellowship with whom was an ever-present and practical one. Indeed, it was already so in the time of the apostles. At the end of a critical discussion "the hand of fellowship" *(koinonia)* was given by the "pillars" of Jerusalem (Gal. 2:9) to Paul and Barnabas, the apostles of the Gentiles.

Here *koinonia* has another meaning than that in Paul's discussion of the Sacrament (1 Cor. 10:16). There the derivation is to be made from κοινωνεῖν τινὸς, and the meaning is *metalepsis,* "having a share in something." Here it is a close binding together of persons (κοινωνία πρός [εἰς, μετά] τινα) as in 1 John 1:3, 6-7. The verb in the background here is κοινωνεῖν with the dative of the person. This can indeed also mean to let a person participate in something, to give a part in. However, when Justin says of the Gnostics ὧν οὐδενὶ κοινωνοῦμεν ("with none of whom we are in communion"), or when what he says of the exclusion of a heretic or an illegitimate bishop applies also to πάντες οἱ κοινωνοῦντες αὐτῷ ("all who are in communion with him"), or when Athanasius reports that Arsenius wished κοινωνεῖν ἡμῖν ("to be in communion with us"), there is no doubt that in each case the meaning is to have fellowship with someone.[1] In this sense κοινωνεῖν is also used with the dative τῇ ἐκκλησίᾳ ("the church") and correspondingly also with τῇ αἱρέσει ("heresy"). The oath of the imperial ministers under Justinian contains the formula κοινωνικός εἰμι τῇ ἁγίᾳ τοῦ θεοῦ καθολικῇ καὶ ἀποστολικῇ ἐκκλησίᾳ ("I am in fellowship with God's holy, catholic, and apostolic church"). κοινωνικὸς is one who is included in the fellowship; ἀκοινώνητος is one excluded.[2]

Koinonia never means merely being in company with one another and therefore never describes the church as a body of persons, nor even a single congregation. This would be in harmony with the later understanding of *sanctorum communio*. The *koinonia* is not the aggregate of members or parts of the church, but a relationship existing within the church and mediated by it, a relationship of members and parts with one another or a relationship of members and parts with the whole church. The unity of the church is there as a datum before the *koinonia*. It is objectively there as the common thing (κοινὸν) in which all belonging to the fellowship (κοινωνικοὶ) participate. But *koinonia* is only what results fellowship-wise (κοινῇ) for the actual life of the congregation and the church.[3] What does this mean?

We must first distinguish between local congregations and the whole church. Primitively this distinction was without meaning, for the churches in Corinth and Thessalonica were not separate parts of a superior organization. As Rudolf Sohm has rightly put it, in each congregation in each town *the* church of God or of Christ is present in indivisible completeness.[4] In theology or faith this has never changed. The church of Christ is the body of Christ and therefore similarly indivisible. Where the body of Christ is, there it is fully, and hence the church, too, is always fully there. The fact of the local church is not dependent on the construction of what would later be called a legitimate and ordered polity. It was there from the beginning. Paul already speaks of churches in the plural. He compares them with one another (2 Cor. 12:13; Phil. 4:15), as do Acts and Revelation (1—3). We observe the simple fact of Christians living together in one place. They form a local unity there as they participate in their meetings, agapes, and other arrangements. It is all quite localized, and the *koinonia* we are looking for is experienced most immediately within these boundaries. We shall accordingly speak of local congregations, or simply of congregations.

In the early church this phenomenon of the local congregation, like all that belongs to it — worship, organization, and discipline — went through many developments which we cannot pursue here. We must confine ourselves to the general categories in which its fellowship was exercised, insofar as there was some consistency. It is generally accepted that from the beginning worship was the preeminent category. This does not assume liturgical uniformity, but one cannot conceive of a Christian congregation which does not meet to celebrate the Holy Supper and for common prayer. These are exactly what make a congregation out of a cluster of believers, what Luther calls a *Gemeine*. There are obvious differences between the Jerusalem congregation as depicted in Acts and that at Corinth. The rowdy competition in exercising the charismatic gifts of the Spirit could scarcely have happened in Jerusalem. It may well be that in Jerusalem the expectation of the returning Lord was at first stronger than the certainty of the presence of the risen Lord. It is quite improbable that when the writer of Acts uses *koinonia* in his description of the life of the congregation in Jerusalem he means the same as Paul does when he speaks of the *koinonia* of the body of Christ.[5] The *koinonia* of 1 Cor. 10:16 f., however, does not exclude the *koinonia* of Christians among themselves but much rather includes it (p. 26). In every case the congregation celebrating the Sacrament is gathering about its Lord, whether in Jerusalem or in Corinth. The common celebration of the Sacrament in every local congregation is the basic criterion of its church fellowship, and yet not this by itself.

The *koinonia* of the Eucharist in the local congregation is, as we shall see, exclusive. Not everyone is admitted, and a man once admitted can later be excluded. Exclusion is ordinarily imposed for offenses against the other principles which regulate the *koinonia* of the congregation. We must examine these in order to understand this exclusion. There are naturally considerable differences. The Jewish Christian congregation in Jerusalem at first displayed criteria of fellowship which did not spread through the rest of Christendom. Its social and corporate sense was so strong as to extend even to a fellowship of property and consumers' cooperative. We hear very little of this going on later [6] and in ordinary congregations not at all, although it is still found in the cloisters. Paul calls instead for joyous giving by the well-to-do for the poor. In this the early church showed such action and proof of its *koinonia,* the congregation in Rome above all others, that the apologists of the second century could proudly point to this characteristically Christian feeling of belonging to one another. And yet Paul had to complain of greed often enough, and things did not improve later. Even the maximum social *koinonia* in Jerusalem was not proof against fraud (Acts 5:1 ff.). If church fellowship is gauged by the charitable aid it provides, it may indeed appear rather insecure.

The motive that underlies and prompts the foregoing is *agape* or more specifically "brotherly love" (Rom. 12:10; 1 Thess. 4:9; Heb. 13:1). The *koinonia* is not merely being with one another, but also for one another, for all the members of the congregation. It is brotherhood (1 Peter 2:17; 5:9). The brother is not to be harmed (Rom. 14:10; 1 Cor. 8:13), not to be taken advantage of in business (1 Thess. 4:6), nor to be allowed to suffer want (James 2:15), let alone to be hated (1 John 2:9). "Brothers" and "saints" are interchangeable names for the Christians.[7] They greet one another with the holy kiss. The strength of their ties with one another is matched by the strength of the boundary they draw to the outside. In business dealings with one another they do not choose an unbeliever to arbitrate; they transact their business "before the saints" and between "brother and brother" (1 Cor. 6:1, 5). One is to throw in one's lot with those who fear the Lord, consider their common good,[8] and daily visit the saints face to face.[9]

Despite all this the *koinonia* as brotherhood is not so secure as may at first appear. A complete exclusion of "those outside" cannot be achieved. The Christians of the Jerusalem congregation wished as Christians to remain Jews. They lived in the old fellowship of their people according to the old law. Like all Jews they prayed in the temple. They had sacrifices offered for them. Their leader James, the brother of the Lord, enjoyed high esteem among their non-Christian compatriots.[10] Paul instructed the Corinthians that in marriages between Christians and non-Christians they were to maintain the closest natural fellowship (1 Cor. 7: 12 ff.). The congregation in Rome felt itself so closely connected with its civil environment that it speaks of the Roman soldiers as "our soldiers." [11] A few decades later Hermas took it amiss that wealthy Christians preferred to associate with heathen rather than with the "righteous." Of a few of these he concedes that they still remain in the faith, although they do not act according to it. Others who have gone too far must be accounted heathen.[12] Where was the line to be drawn? Those of whom Hermas speaks apparently regarded social intercourse beyond the circle of the Christian brotherhood as less harmful than Hermas himself, who had been successively slave, freedman, wealthy, and then again impoverished. After Constantine things changed radically with the influx of the masses. This did not prosper the Christian brotherhood. If we can believe only half of what Salvian says, there was not much left of it a hundred years later in many parts of western Christendom.

The boundary to the outside is not the only problem to disconcert the brotherhood. Deceit can subvert the name of brother to ulterior designs. In Jerusalem itself, where according to Acts we may find the shining example of all Christian *koinonia*, Paul came upon "false brothers" (Gal. 2:4), and elsewhere it was "false brothers" who brought him into personal peril (2 Cor. 11:26). It is understandable then that the brothers should be very carefully scrutinized. The Thessalonians were to withdraw from a brother who walked disorderly and not according to the teaching received from the apostle (2 Thess. 3:6). To be sure, they should not treat him as an enemy but rather admonish him as a brother (3:15). From this it would appear that the same man is referred to as in v. 6. Paul wrote to Corinth that there are Christians who claim the name of brother with whom one is not to eat. This applies to the immoral, the greedy, the idolater, the reviler, the drunkard, or the robber (1 Cor. 5:11). As he expressly emphasized, Paul was not thinking of men outside the congregation but precisely of those who accept the name of brother. This went on *within* the congregation. We shall postpone for the moment the discussion of what Paul meant by not eating together. Presumably it means the same as the concluding sentence taken from Deuteronomy: "Put away from among you that wicked person."

The brotherhood of the early Christian congregation was doubtless to be more than an association for mutual helpfulness. Its greater purpose cannot be merely the principle and action of brotherly love, for if this were so, then its denial would be the single ground for exclusion. We hear nothing of this. Unbrotherliness and behavior that injures the brotherhood are often censured, but these do not prompt exclusion. Paul wants the gross sinners excluded. He requires a congregational discipline whose standards are largely those of the Decalog.[13] This is observed throughout early Christendom, although there are some additional ascetic requirements. The church is to be a chaste virgin (2 Cor. 11:2), the bride of Christ (Rev. 21:2, 9), His body, whose members may not be defiled. Where there is such defilement it must be "cut out."[14] If gross sinners are to be excluded, then logically this can only be done by those not thus guilty. Church fellowship has clearly also ethical features which do not simply derive from brotherly love.

The strongest thrust in the campaign of the apologists of the second century is the morality of the Christian congregations. This is effective in disproving slander, for it is something that can be seen by those outside, but it is often so put as to suggest that they regarded this as their best means for winning men over. Thus the church, to put it crudely, appears validated by its moral purpose and the completeness with which this its ideal is realized. There are gathered the righteous, the good, the men "of good will." The apologists naturally had other things to speak of as well, but the elevation of ethical achievement betrays a more fundamental change in the understanding of salvation. The *Didache*, which styles itself the *Teaching of the Twelve Apostles*, gives as the content of that teaching long catalogs of prescriptions and prohibitions as if *these* were the Gospel. The *Didache* does not stand alone in this view of the apostolic teaching, and its influence went far beyond the circle which produced it. This understanding is the basis of later church codes which all agree in claiming that their clearly defined congregational discipline, as a whole and in detail, derives from the apostles themselves.

This development may not be overlooked, because it provided principles for excommunication and so for exclusion from church fellowship and because we may draw conclusions from it as to what was meant by church fellowship. The early Catholic Church did in fact become a disciplinary institution, and one of the reasons for this is undoubtedly the moralizing way of its understanding of salvation. However, the assessment of church membership by ethical standards alone was rejected. Some modern critics, who see in this moralization, and we believe rightly, a depravation of the Gospel, yet regard the rejection of its rigorous consequences (Montanism and Novatianism) as a culpable decline from the rigor of early Christendom. A laxer view plainly did displace a stricter one, but that is only one side of the matter.[15]

When Paul wanted the gross sinners excluded, he gave the reason that "the unrighteous shall not inherit the kingdom of God" (1 Cor. 6: 9 f.). Only the saints shall judge the world (6:2). Paul here sees the end of all things not as distant but as imminent, indeed, in a way, already begun. He is not thinking of the church as an abiding institution which must perenially decide who belongs to it and who not. He looks to the imminent fulfillment of the kingdom of Christ. Putting out the unrighteous man is an item that has to be attended to because the Lord is at hand. That the Corinthian congregation has a thousand years of history before it lies beyond his horizon. The church has since then had to possess its soul in patience. Nothing shows more strikingly the acceptance of this present age's continuance than the prescription of penitential periods of 10 or 20 or even more years before full readmission into the *koinonia*.[16] What would Paul or the writer of Revelation have said to such long periods in church discipline? And yet we must not be too quick to judge the ancient church for making the practical adjustments in congregational discipline occasioned by the Parousia's delay.

Never did it regard itself as *only* a disciplinary institution or evaluate church fellowship *only* by ethical standards. The prompting of Paul's concern for presenting to Christ a chaste virgin is not prompted by any general ethical dangers but by those of the false teachers who threaten the Corinthian congregation (2 Cor. 11:2 ff.). The same thought is still present in Hegesippus' use of the picture of the church as a virgin.[17] That Paul was not more indulgent toward false prophets than gross sinners is clear from his pronouncing them servants of Satan. This matches the messages to the congregations in Asia Minor which we read in Revelation. Here the synagog of Satan is not characterized merely by bad morals (2:9). The exhortation is to hate not only the works of the Nicolaitans but also their doctrine (2:15). One is not to receive into one's house a man who does not come with the true doctrine of Christ (2 John 10). Aged John left the baths in Ephesus with all speed when he descried a heretic there.[18] How heresy affects church fellowship is a problem for the whole church, but we can see here how from the very beginning it was of direct concern to the local congregation.

Already in the Pastoral Epistles we find discrimination between true and false doctrine as a responsibility of the holder of spiritual office.[19] In Ignatius it is the bishop. We can observe the beginning of a development which could lead to the total disenfranchisement of the laity for whom there would then be nothing left but blind faith in another's authority. There are indeed portents of this already in the early church. This, however, was not the intention of Ignatius. He directs the congregations to "the word of Jesus" and to the dogmas of the Lord and the apostles. He provides objective criteria for distinguishing the right doctrine from the false.[20] These are of such a nature that every baptized Christian must not only know but also confess them. That is at least the view of Ignatius. There is no reason to doubt but, on the contrary, very much to confirm that these criteria reproduce the content of the baptismal confession used in Ignatius' circle. They are in a measure verbally parallel to the later settled and written baptismal confessions: one God, Jesus Christ God's Son, born of Mary, suffered under Pontius Pilate,[21] crucified, died, and rose from the dead. This can of course be called faith in an authority, but the authority on which the right doctrine to be confessed bases itself is not the bishop but the witness of the apostles. We have seen how Athanasius thought similarly.

Those walls which later were to define and demarcate the unity of the whole church on earth were first evident in brief in the local congregation. The New Testament Scriptures do not as yet come into question as they are not yet united in the canon. The bishop, however, is already there and the Rule of Faith in substance if not in name. The competence of the bishop gradually extended itself. He guaranteed the faithful transmission of the doctrine. He assumed the right to make vital decisions in doctrine, and he excluded heretics by virtue of his office. Never, however, did he presume to produce new dogmas. Much rather did he maintain the basic principle that only that is pure doctrine which the apostles taught. How far this basic principle was faithfully carried out is another question. Of first importance for us is the fact that the right doctrine expressed in the baptismal confession or the Rule of Faith was not a mere appendage of hierarchial management but something that maintained its independent function in the local congregation.

This is most clear in its confessional character. The Christians are of one body and one Spirit. The unity of the Spirit is of one piece with the unity of the faith (Eph. 4:3-5); the *koinonia* of the Spirit (2 Cor. 13: 13; Phil. 2:1) with the *koinonia* of the faith (Philemon 6). The unity of faith is not merely some shared sentiment. Paul had already made clear not only that there is no faith without *kerygma,* but also that believing with the heart is coupled with confessing with the mouth (Rom. 10: 8 ff.). In this passage he gives a formulation of the faith which is later substantially never lacking in any baptismal confession: that God raised Jesus from the dead. Fellowship is possible only on the basis of the confessed faith. Such confession of the formulated content of faith was required by the early church of every full member (p. 57). That this was no pious fiction is plain from the high level and the content of the careful instruction given to catechumens. This instruction was part of the activity of the local congregation by which its life was sustained. It by no means consisted of mere mental appropriation of doctrinal material. In Justin already we read how the candidates for Baptism were tested before admission as to whether what was taught them was a matter of conviction and whether they were ready to demonstrate what they confessed in a corresponding manner of life.[22] The baptismal confession was in part so arranged that separate statements were put to the candidate to each of which he was to reply "I believe." [23] From the *Catecheses* of Cyril of Jerusalem, which were partly for candidates and partly for the newly baptized, we can see how much theology was expected of every baptized Christian. He makes a clear distinction between believing and what is believed and then explains the whole confession of faith point by point.[24] These *Catecheses* are from the middle of the fourth century, when the masses were already flooding into the church.

All this took place within the local congregation. The baptisms with their preparatory forms which lasted for days were an annual climax in the worshiping life of the congregation. The act of baptism itself took place in the baptistery, but immediately after it the whole congregation celebrated the Eucharist with the newly baptized. Even when we take into account that some postponed their baptism a long time and that candidates could already be counted as Christians, it is still not saying too much to ascribe to every local congregation of the early church the character of a confessional congregation. In the persecutions they provided confessors in the highest sense of the word, the martyrs of Christ. They were confessors also in this that they admitted into full membership only those who had personally and clearly made a confession of the specific content of their faith. The *koinonia* of every congregation was a fellowship of faith, and, since the mouth must confess what the heart believes, it was a confessional fellowship.

Notes to Chapter 6

1. With the dative of the person and the genitive of the thing: Theodoret, Ep. 111: J. L. Schulze (1769—74), IV, 1182: καὶ τοὺς ἁγίους ἅπαντες κοινωνεῖν μοι τῶν εὐχῶν ἱκετεύω. Ep. 131 (p. 1,219): κεκοινωνήκατε τοίνυν ἡμῖν τῶν παθημάτων.

2. Justin, *Dial.*, 35, 5. Synod of Antioch, 341: Hahn, p. 187. *Ap. Const.*, VIII, 47, 30. Athanasius, *PG*, 25, 264c; 632c. Constantine in Athanasius, *PG*, 25, 273b. Cf. W. Schubart, *Justinian und Theodora*, 1941, p. 281.

3. Cf. the usage of the term in Ignatius, *Eph.*, 1, 2: *LCC*, I, 88; 20, 2 (93); *Philad.*, 1, 1 (108); 5, 2 (109); 11, 2 (111); *Smyrn.*, 7, 2 (114); 12, 2 (116); *Polyc.*, 4, 3 (119).

4. *Kirchenrecht*, I, 19 ff.

5. Acts 2:42. On *koinonia* here see H. Seesemann, *Der Begriff koinonia im Neuen Testament*, 1933, pp. 86 ff.

6. *Didache*, 4, 8: *LCC*, I, 173.

7. Karl Holl claims a use of the title "the saints" as synonymous with and limited to "the poor" in Jerusalem. But see W. G. Kuemmel, *Kirchenbegriff*, pp. 16 f. and O. Michel, *Das Zeugnis des Neuen Testaments von der Gemeinde*, p. 32.

8. Barnabas, 10, 11; 4, 10: *ACW*, VI, 52; 42.

9. Ibid., 19, 10: *ACW*, VI, 63; *Didache*, 4, 2: *LCC*, I, 173.

10. Hegesippus, in Eusebius, *H. E.*, II, 23, 4 ff.

11. *1 Clem.* 37, 2: *LCC*, I, 60.

12. *Sim.*, VIII, 9, 1 ff.; cf. *Mand.*, X, 1, 4.

13. In 1 Cor. 5:11 he mentions sinners against Commandments 1, 6, 7, 8, 9, and 10 (Reformed enumeration: 1, 7, 8, 9, 10).

14. ἐκκόπτειν, 2 Cor. 11:12. Later *terminus technicus* for excommunication. In *Ap. Const.* of a bishop for simony: ἐκκοπτέσθω παντάπασιν καὶ τῆς κοινωνίας.

15. Greenslade, pp. 108 ff.

16. Synod of Ancyra, 314, Canon 16: Stevenson, pp. 311 f. Basil, Canon 56: *PG*, 32, 797; Deferrari, III, 247 f.

17. Eusebius, *H. E.*, III, 32, 7.

18. *Haer.*, III, 3, 4: *LCC*, I, 374.

19. H. von Campenhausen, *Kirchliches Amt*, pp. 118 ff.

20. *Eph.* 15, 2: *LCC*, I, 92; *Magn.*, 13, 1 (97); *Magn.*, 8—11 (96); *Trall.*, 9 f. (100); *Philad.*, 6, 8 (104 f.); *Smyrn.*, 2; 6; 7 (95 ff.).

21. *Smyrn.*, 1, 2: ἐπὶ Ποντίου Πιλάτου καὶ Ἡρώδου τετράρχου καθηλομένον ὑπὲρ ἡμῶν ἐν σαρκί. *LCC*, I, 113. The otherwise unusual naming of Herod in this context is found also in the confession of Jerome, which probably derives from the circle of Antioch. See above, p. 8 and Excursus II.

22. *Apology*, I, 61: *LCC*, I, 282.

23. For Roman forms of interrogation at the beginning of the third century see Hahn, pp. 34 ff. Also Kelly, pp. 43 ff.

24. *Cat.*, 5: *LCC*, VI, 122 ff.

Bibliography for Chapter 6

Asting, R. *Die Heiligkeit im Urchristentum,* 1930.

———. *Die Verkuendigung des Wortes im Urchristentum,* 1939.

von Dobschuetz, E. *Christian Life in the Primitive Church,* trans. G. Bremner, ed. W. Morrison. London, 1904.

Holl, K. "Der Kirchenbegriff des Paulus in seinem Verhaeltnis zu dem der Urgemeinde," *Gesammelte Aufsaetze zur Kirchengeschichte,* II (1928), 44 ff.

Knopf, R. *Das nachapostolische Zeitalter,* 1905.

Kuemmel, W. G. *Kirchenbegriff und Geschichtsbewusztsein in der Urgemeinde und bei Jesus,* 1943.

Preisker, H. *Das Ethos des Urchristentums,* 1949.

Schlatter, A. *Die Gemeinde in der apostolischen Zeit im Missionsgebiet,* 1912.

Schlier, H. "Die Ordnung der Kirche nach den Pastoralbriefen," *Festschrift fuer F. Gogarten,* 1948.

Schubart, W. *Justinian und Theodora,* 1941.

Schweizer, E. *Das Leben des Herrn in der Gemeinde und ihren Diensten,* 1946.

Sohm, Rudolph. *Kirchenrecht,* I (1892).

Spoerri, Theophil. *Der Gemeindegedanke im ersten Petri Brief, Beitrag zur Struktur des urchristlichen Kirchenbegriffs,* 1925

7

CLOSED COMMUNION

It was quite impossible to isolate the Christian congregation from intercourse with its local social surroundings, no matter how desirable that might appear to a man like Hermas. At one point, however, the congregation was uncompromising. Firm boundaries were drawn around participation in the divine service. In the initial mission situation the apostolic message was given to all who would hear. However, as soon as there were "those within" and "those without",[1] that is, as soon as a congregation felt separated from its surroundings, it conducted a type of divine worship in which the distinction between within and without was made unmistakably clear. Admission was not for just anybody. Origen points out that the Christians are not like the philosophers whom anybody may attend and listen to. The Christians on the contrary test every man first and instruct him privately (κατ' ἰδίαν) until he gives demonstration of trustworthiness and an orderly life. Only then is he admitted to their assembly [2] as a "hearer." This goes only for the Service of the Word composed of hymns, lections, sermon, and prayers. Even this was obviously stoutly hedged about. Those outside were not denied the opportunity of hearing God's Word, but they must first prove their serious intention. Following the service of the Word came the celebration of the Eucharist. This was at least so from the middle of the second century (Justin). Before the Eucharist began, however, the "hearers" had to leave the assembly, and not only they but also the catechumens, even though they were already being solidly instructed toward reception. During the Eucharist the doors were guarded by deacons and subdeacons.[3] Tertullian severely rebukes the contrary way of doing things among the heretics, who did not maintain the distinction between catechumens and believers. "They assemble together, listen together, pray together; indeed when heathen come, they cast what is holy to the dogs, and the pearls, which to be sure are not in fact pearls, to the swine." [4]

The gathering for worship in the early church was not a public but a closed assembly, while the celebration of the Eucharist was reserved for the saints with the utmost strictness. Why? Some have explained this as part of the *disciplina arcani* in which the "initiated" were obliged to conceal the usages of worship from the "uninitiated." The heathen mysteries would in that case furnish the origin and pattern. In these such obligation was settled practice. We find the comparison with these actually already in Tertullian.[5] In the fourth century Baptism and the Eucharist are generally spoken of in the language of the heathen mysteries with the corresponding demand for secrecy. But the attempt to find in this the cause and basis of "closed Communion" in the early church is misguided. By "closed Communion" we mean the restricting of participation to full members of the congregation.

In the passage already mentioned, Tertullian is discounting the common slander about the criminal secret practices of Christians. If the slander were true, he says, then such facts would certainly be disclosed. But by whom? Certainly not the guilty [the Christians], for if in "all mysteries" [the Samothracian and Eleusinian mysteries are cited as examples] the promise of silence (*fides silentii*) is imposed, then it would be in force all the more if the Christians by their alleged evil practices would bring their fellow members into conflict with the law of the state. Outsiders (*extranei*) certainly could not disclose anything, for even in the *piae initiationes* (heathen rites for which the opponents of the Christians used this complimentary term) they would be excluded and thus not be in a position to bring in evidence against these practices. Tertullian is clearly striving, practiced lawyer that he is, to undermine the reliability of the witnesses for the prosecution on their own ground. The mysteries are simply introduced to help make this point. The Christians do indeed exclude those outside (*extranei*) from their mysteries, but there is no hint whatever that the reason for this is in any way the same as in the case of the heathen mysteries. When at the beginning of the chapter

Tertullian taunts his opponents with the question why no judicial investigation has been made of the closed assemblies of the Christians in which such crimes are supposedly practiced, he implicitly offers to give a full account of the "secret practices" of the Christians.[6]

In his customary rhetorical fervor Tertullian overlooked that besides the "initiated" and those outside (extranei) there was yet a third class, that of the lapsed. These were already fairly numerous when Pliny was governor of Bithynia. Their evidence concerning Christian worship was not only adequate but quite accurate. Besides, anyone who wished to learn about the Christian "mysteries" had only to read the Apology of Justin Martyr. Certainly no secret, this document was addressed "to Emperor Antoninus Pius . . . the sacred Senate, and the whole Roman people" a half century before Tertullian. Here we have an open and comprehensive account of the rites of Baptism and the Eucharist with all liturgical details that is still today the best source for its whole period. There is therefore in the second century still no disciplina arcani, and we really ought to have done with the notion that the "closed Communion" of the early church grew out of it.

The strict limitation of participation is clearly evidenced at the end of the apostolic age. It still remains to be shown that it was ever otherwise. The formative influence was not the keeping of secrecy but the keeping of unholy people from what is holy in accordance with the Old Testament understanding of holiness. In the Didache we read, "Let no one eat and drink of your Eucharist except those baptized in the name of the Lord; for here the word of the Lord applies 'Give not that which is holy to the dogs.' "[7] We have already heard the echo of this in the formula of the later liturgies: "The holy things for the holy ones" (τὰ ἅγια τοῖς ἁγίοις). Since only those baptized are admitted, they are obviously the holy ones for whom the holy things are reserved. This is in harmony with the early Christian understanding of Baptism.[8] Christ sanctifies and cleanses His church with the washing of water by the Word (Eph. 5:26). We have further the warning from Paul about the danger of "unworthy" eating and drinking, and he therefore enjoins rigorous self-examination upon every partaker (1 Cor. 11:27 ff.). For this reason alone not just any curious person could be admitted indiscriminately. The whole congregation is self-evidently together responsible for preventing anybody from ignorantly heaping guilt upon himself. Baptism is the basic requirement. A man baptized is one whose life has been proven and his trustworthiness demonstrated. Instruction has been given him. He has avowed his confession. Baptism itself is prerequisite inasmuch as that which is holy is to be received only by those who are holy.[9]

Baptism is the basic and crucial event which makes a new man out of the old, and so regarded it is the event of an individual. Its purpose, however, is not private or isolated. By Baptism we are drawn into the death and resurrection of Christ and so out of the domain of enemy powers, above all out of the domain of the Law into the freedom of that kingdom where Christ is Lord.[10] These thoughts are developed by Cyril of Jerusalem in his catechetical instruction of the newly baptized, and he finds in them the basis for the renunciation of the devil effected in Baptism as also for the *koinonia* of the baptized with the suffering and death of Christ.[11] Now Paul also describes the relationship with Christ which we enter through Baptism by saying that we are baptized in one Spirit into one body, and he derives from this the organic relationship of the members of the body of Christ also with one another (1 Cor. 12: 12 ff.). Through Baptism we become not only saints but also "holy brothers" (Heb. 3:1). All Christians share the same sonship, and Christ is "the firstborn among many brothers" (Rom. 8:29). Both the common bond of the ethos of an organized congregation, by which the church separates itself from its unholy surroundings, and specifically also its brotherhood rest on the fact that its *koinonia* is a baptismal fellowship.

The *koinonia* of Baptism is undeniably bound up with the *koinonia* of the Holy Communion. *Koinonia* as used by Paul in 1 Cor. 10:16 includes the fellowship of those who partake together (p. 27). As here the participants are bound to one another not by what they do with one another but by their common partaking of the body of Christ, so also the *koinonia* of Baptism rests in their being "baptized into the body of Christ." In both the baptismal and the Eucharistic *koinonia* the body of Christ comes first. In either case the body of Christ is not constituted by the action of men. Both are characterized by it and so demarcated by it. One cannot be a member of the body of Christ without Baptism and consequently also not a partaker of the Holy Communion. The Holy Communion of the early church is rightly "closed Communion" at least to this extent that no unbaptized person may partake of it. Church fellowship is as much Eucharistic fellowship as Baptismal fellowship and in both cases exclusive.

Nevertheless, both are not the same. Church fellowship based on Baptism became a problem for the early church when it faced the question of recognizing the Baptism of heretics or schismatics upon their entry into the Catholic Church. After heavy internal controversy the question was answered affirmatively. The Council of Arles (314) laid down, contrary to the previous practice of the African church, only that the entrant be asked if his Baptism was trinitarian. If this was the case, he was to be received only by the laying on of hands.[12] The Council of Nicaea did the same in 325 with the exception that Paulianists were to be rebaptized.[13] These followers of Paul of Samosata were regarded as denying the orthodox doctrine of the Trinity. Heretics who baptized in the name of the Trinity were thus implicitly conceded at least a connection with the church, although they were usually regarded as standing outside it. Otherwise nobody could be incorporated into the church of Christ by his baptism. Augustine later sought to resolve the contradiction by declaring heretical baptism valid but inoperative. The baptizing heretic, he maintained, could not impart the Holy Ghost because he did not have Him himself. This lack is proved for Augustine by the lack of love. If the heretic had love, it would lead him into the Catholic Church. On this basis the settled practice emerged of receiving people baptized by heretics or schismatics into the Catholic Church by the laying on of hands, which conferred the Holy Ghost.

Be that as it may, our interest is in the comparison with the Eucharistic practice over against these heretics and schismatics. Here the church also had to make decisions, but the problem was from the outset quite different. A valid Baptism is performed only once, whereas participation in the Holy Communion is repeated. The Baptism of the heretics had only to be pronounced valid or not. The same question could naturally be asked of their Eucharist. Augustine considered the question of their sacraments as such, and so the question of validity could be answered as in the case of their Baptism. In Eucharistic practice, however, the question was not about the validity of others' Eucharists but whether heretics or schismatics may be admitted to the Catholic Holy Communion. The question was the same for the others whose churches were regarded as heretical or schismatic by the Catholic side. Here the question is not of validity, which every church naturally claims for its sacraments, but of integrity.

This question was critical for the very reason that the early church still had a vital understanding of the Eucharist as *koinonia*. Is it in harmony with the *koinonia* of the body of Christ that Christians who are not at one should go to the Holy Communion together? By being partakers of the body of Christ in the Eucharist we become of one body (σύσσωμοι) with Christ, says Cyril of Jerusalem, and Cyril of Alexandria rightly concludes that we are then "in Christ" of one body (σύσσωμοι) with one another (p. 29). The partakers become "one body and one spirit." Therefore there may be nothing separating or dividing them, for that which divides would do injury to the *koinonia* and so to the unity of the body of Christ. Such divisions are a constant danger even among the baptized. Even though a man must first be baptized before he may partake of the Holy Communion, this does not mean that all the baptized may without distinction partake of the Eucharist together.

Divisions can be of various kinds. In the case of heresy it is a confessional division. The extending or refusing of Eucharistic fellowship is then always a confessional act of the whole congregation. In the case of personal divisions there would also be injury of the integrity of the *koinonia*. For this reason the formularies of the early church require that all such divisions be put right before partaking of the Lord's Supper. So already the *Didache*.[14] Here we come upon the passage from the Sermon on the Mount which calls for reconciliation before the bringing of an offering (Matt. 5:23 f.). It found a regular place in this context.

The gift that is brought is understood in the *Didascalia* as prayer and the Eucharist.[15] It directs that before the congregational prayer the deacon ask with a loud voice whether there is anyone who holds anything against his brother. If any division is disclosed, the bishop is to make peace between the contending parties.[16] The editor of the *Apostolic Constitutions* omits this last direction, probably because a reconciliation calling for the intervention of the bishop would too much interrupt the progress of the service. There could also be more than one case of dissension. The passage from the Sermon on the Mount is used by Cyril of Jerusalem as the basis of the kiss of peace. This is the sign which declares the souls united and all grudge-bearing set aside.[17] The kiss of peace [18] had its firm place in the liturgy either at the beginning of the Eucharistic section or later, but always after the catechumens were dismissed and before the Communion proper. According to the so-called Egyptian Church Order the catechumens were not permitted to exchange the kiss of peace "because their kiss was not yet clean." [19] The kiss of peace is that of Christian brothers, that is of "holy brothers," and they first become such through Baptism.

The obligation to be first reconciled and the kiss of peace coming before the partaking *(metalepsis)* of the Sacrament are there to prevent human divisions from breaking the unity of the body of Christ. If reconciliation is not achieved, then there is to be no partaking of Holy Communion. Clearly the appeal is to the consciences of all participating, for hatred and ill will in the heart cannot be discerned by others. If any man acts against his conscience, then the word of the apostle about "unworthy" eating and drinking is fulfilled.[20] For this reason alone we may not slight this call to fulfill a brother's obligation which according to the ancient liturgies rang out in every celebration of the Holy Communion. The liturgical kiss of peace was not like Schiller's "kiss for the whole world," but rather a demonstration of the Christian brotherhood. This is exactly what the local congregation declared itself to be by this concrete action of exchanging the kiss of peace. That it takes place at the Holy Communion reminds us that here the brotherhood aspect of church fellowship finds its purest expression.

Notes to Chapter 7

1. οἱ ἔξω and οἱ ἔσω, 1 Cor. 5:12 f. Cf. Col. 4:5; 1 Thess. 4:12; 1 Tim.3:7; Rev. 22:15.

2. εἰς τὸ κοινὸν, *Contra Celsum,* III, 51: Henry Chadwick, *Origen: Contra Celsum* (Cambridge, 1953), p. 163.

3. *Ap. Const.,* VIII, 11, 11.

4. *De praescr.* 41, 1 f.: *LCC,* V, 61.

5. *Apology,* 7, 6 f.

6. In *Ad uxorem,* II, 5, he betrays the desire that it would be good if strangers got no glimpse of the Christian usages, but at the same time he has to admit that they actually know of them anyway. *ACW,* XIII, 30.

7. *Didache,* 9, 5; cf. 10, 6: *LCC,* I, 175 f.

8. Cf. Bultmann, *Theology of the New Testament,* pp. 136, 338.

9. When Guenther Bornkamm asserts, "The Pauline epistles in no way give us the right to regard Baptism as being from the beginning the *conditio sine qua non* of participation in the celebration of the Lord's Supper" (*Das Ende des Gesetzes,* 1952, p. 126), we may add that they give us just as little right to suppose the contrary. His comment that *Didache* 9, 5 ("only the baptized are admitted": *LCC,* I, 175) "clearly presupposes that this regulation was not self-evident" is quite plausible, but this does not necessarily say that a new order is being instituted. It could just as well imply a defense against an encroaching abuse. If we look at the accounts in Acts in their actual context, we find repentance *(metanoia)* required before baptism, but thereupon baptism follows immediately even without catechumenate, and this in the early days. Both belong inseparably together. For some interim between repentance and baptism, during which participation in the Lord's Supper was already granted, there appears to be no ground even in the mission situation of the Pauline congregations.

10. Rom. 6:3 ff.; Gal. 3:27; Col. 2:9-15; 1 Peter 3:21 f.

11. *Cat. myst.,* I, 4; II, 2—7: Cross, pp. 13 f., 54 f.; 18 ff., 59 ff. Cf. Serapion, *Euchologion,* 20, 2: Funk, II, 182, 17; Brightman, p. 263, 31.

12. Canon 8: *CCL,* 148, 10 f.; Stevenson, p. 323. Cf. Frend, p. 152.

13. Canon 19: Stevenson, pp. 363 f.; Bright, pp. xv, 74 ff.

14. *Didache,* 14, 2: *LCC,* I, 178.

15. II, 53, 4: Funk, p. 152, 4; R. H. Connolly, *Didascalia Apostolorum* (Oxford, 1929), p. 116, 15.

16. II, 54, 1: Funk, p. 154, 2; Connolly, p. 117, 15.

17. *Cat. myst.,* V, 3: Cross, pp. 31, 72.

18. The "holy kiss," Rom. 16:16; 1 Cor. 16:20; 2 Cor. 13:12; 1 Thess. 5:26. The "kiss of agape," 1 Peter 5:14; later often simply called *pax*.

19. Cf. T. Schermann, *Die allgemeine Kirchenordnung*, 1914, p. 62 (II, 43); Funk, *Constitutiones Ecclesiae Aegyptiae*, II, 108, 5. Also see Justin, *Apology*, I, 65: *LCC*, I, 286; Tertullian, *De orat.* 18: Evans, p. 22; *Ap. Const.*, II, 57, 17; VIII, 11, 9, and other liturgies. On abuses of the kiss in the church, see Clement of Alexandria, *Paed.*, III, 81, 2.

20. Johannes Mandakuni, *Bibliothek der Kirchenvaeter*, 2d ed., *Ausgewaehlte Schriften der armenischen Kirchenvaeter*, trans. Simon Weber, II, 155: "Whoever approaches the body of the Lord while at odds with his neighbor receives not the life-giving body but a consuming fire, for he eats and drinks to himself damnation." There is further a censure on those who keep away from the Sacrament for many days merely to avoid having to be reconciled with their brother. Cf. Cyprian, *De orat.*, 23: T. H. Bindley, *St. Cyprian on the Lord's Prayer* (London, 1904), pp. 53 f.

Bibliography for Chapter 7

Andersen, Wilhelm. "Haben Taufe und Abendmahl einen verschiedenen Heils-bezug?" ELKZ, 1950, pp. 387 ff.

Bindley, T. H. *St. Cyprian on the Lord's Prayer*. London, 1904.

Bornkamm, Guenther. *Das Ende des Gesetzes*, 1952. See especially "Die Erbauung der Gemeinde als Leib Christi," pp. 113 ff., and "Das Anathema in der urchristlichen Abendmahlsliturgie," pp. 123 ff.

———. μυστήριον in *ThWb*, IV, 809 ff.

Casel, Odo. "Altchristliche Liturgie bis Konstantin der Grosse," *Archiv fuer Liturgiewissenschaft*, 1950, pp. 256 ff.

Chadwick, Henry. *Origen: Contra Celsum*. Cambridge, 1953.

Connolly, R. H. *Didascalia Apostolorum*. Oxford, 1929.

Cullmann, Oskar. *Early Christian Worship*, trans. A. Todd and J. Torrance. London, 1953.

Hahn, Wilhelm. *Gottesdienst und Opfer Christi*, 1951.

Hofmann, Karl-Martin. *Philema Hagion*, 1938.

Maurer, Wilhelm. *Bekenntnis und Sakrament*, I, 1939, pp. 11 ff.

Sasse, Hermann. *Kirche und Herrenmahl*, 1938, pp. 13 ff.

Schermann, T. *Die allgemeine Kirchenordnung*, 1914.

Sjoeberg, Erik. "The Church and the Cultus in the New Testament," *This Is the Church*, pp. 75 ff.

Staehlin, Rudolf. "Die Geschichte des christlichen Gottesdienstes," *Leiturgia*, I (1952), pp. 1 ff.

Voelker, K. *Mysterium und Agape*, 1927.

8

CHURCH DISCIPLINE
AND THE LORD'S SUPPER

The brotherhood of the local congregation was threatened from within already in the apostolic age. We have already noted Paul's instructions (p. 68). He is not very much upset by a quarrel between two women in the congregation. He simply admonishes them to compose their differences (Phil. 4:2). However, when "one who is called a brother" is seen to be guilty of immorality or greed, or is an idolater, reviler, drunkard, or robber, the others are not to eat with him (1 Cor. 5:11). This cannot be taken as a listing of offences according to which guilt and punishment can be determined from case to case in the manner of a penal judge. It deals not with deeds but with persons. Nonetheless a person shows what he is by his behavior. For the sake of simplicity we shall refer to these sins as gross sins and those guilty of them as gross sinners.

The deferred question of what is meant by "not eating with such a one" now calls for an answer. In another context the Christians are warned to withdraw "from every brother that walks disorderly" (ἀτάκτως, 2 Thess. 3:6). "Disorderly" means contrary to the instruction (παράδοσις) given by the apostle. In 1 Cor. 5:11, on the other hand, Paul is not only dealing with disorderly conduct but with men who so obviously live contrary to the commandments of God that they cannot inherit the kingdom of God (6:9 f.). In view of this we may expect that the congregation's ensuing response would be a striking break with the gross sinner. "Not eating together" could scarcely refer to ordinary meals. The reference may much rather be to the Lord's Supper, which is discussed in the same letter. Even if this is not specifically meant, it could certainly not be an exception. The completeness of the break is indicated by the apostles' categorial command: "Drive out the wicked person from among you!" (5:13). Obedience to this injunction would mean that the congregation would no more eat at all together with those previously characterized as gross sinners. Therefore they would also no more eat the Lord's Supper together with them. They are excluded from it.

Paul makes it expressly clear that he is not speaking of those "of this world" (5:10) but of those who bear the name of brother. Is he perhaps thinking of those who are already called Christians though not yet baptized? From the following chapter we see plainly that he is writing to people already baptized (6:11) and that he is mindful of the danger of their also falling into similar temptations (6:15 ff.). Those who bear the name of brother are in this instance the same as the baptized. The name of brother, which is the outward badge of belonging to the brotherhood, does not give the unconditional right to partake of the Lord's Supper, for notorious gross sinners are excluded from it even though they have the name of brother. If those of the fellowship of Baptism are identical with the brotherhood, then what goes for one goes for the others. If a man after Baptism shows himself to be a gross sinner of the sort described, he is to be excluded (ἐξάρατε, 5:13) from the congregation. The Eucharist is a "closed Communion" because participation is denied not only to the unbaptized but in certain circumstances also to the baptized.

For Paul this was an *ad hoc* injunction, a single instance in cleansing the congregation. The returning Lord should find that present congregation in a condition of virginal purity (p. 69). Paul did not live to see the Parousia, nor did his contemporaries. One generation followed another. A continuing congregation emerged from the assembly of saints of the last days, a congregation involved in history. That the church lived through the Parousia's delay without wavering in its faith in Christ is a miracle. As a consequence of that delay, however, new tasks were set before it. Of these the enthusiasm of the beginning neither as yet had nor could have had an inkling. The church would surely have given up as lost had it not known itself to be the body of Christ. It could consequently not ignore the implications which Paul drew from that fact.

The cleansing of the congregation which Paul did in a single instance naturally became for it a continuing responsibility. The way in which it discharged this responsibility experienced profound changes. These were accompanied by intense internal controversy. At first at least direction was given by the apostle's declaration that the "unrighteous," that is, gross sinners as defined by him, do not inherit the kingdom of God and therefore cannot be members of the body of Christ. Clearly and unanimously they also held that heresy, and of course complete defection, excluded a man from the fellowship of the church. When this cleansing meant complete and final exclusion from the congregation, there were no further problems regarding Communion practice. Whoever was no longer in the church self-evidently could no longer partake of the Sacrament.

Complete and final exclusion, however, did not remain the only way of cleansing. It came to be reserved for special cases. The hope of repentance prompted a looking toward the possibility of absolution and ultimately of full reconciliation with the church *(reconciliatio, pax)*. The principle remained that the unrighteous, that is, gross sinners, could not be in the church, but its application was guided by the possibility of repentance and consequent absolution. If the sinner has repented and is absolved, then he can be received again into the fellowship of the church. After some uncertainty and against the protest of rigorist minorities, the church at large granted full reinstatement to all gross sinners who changed their ways and showed their repentance in the required manner. This was true also finally of those who had fully defected *(lapsi)*. There is division of opinion about the historical beginnings and theological foundation of penitential discipline, which in its later development became an essential part of the Roman Catholic Church (Confession, Penance). We are concerned here only with its part in the Communion practice of the early church.

Protestant accounts tend at this point to sympathize with the rigorist critics of the majority church and to see in them the true heirs of original Christendom. In some respects this is understandable. The way in which repentance and absolution is ordered in the Roman Catholic Church coheres with an office of priest and judge which is quite alien at least from the pentecostal, spiritual, and charismatic beginnings of the church. It can also not be denied that in the controversies of the third century about repentance (Cyprian) the church came to be understood as an institution dispensing salvation. The consequence of this, if something of an overstatement be permissible, was the replacement of Christ by the priest in His role as mediator between God and man. On the other hand, attacks on the institutional understanding of the church appear dubious when they set in opposition to this a supposed associational understanding as original. This antithesis is elucidated by reference to the criterion of holiness. This the original church claimed because it wanted to be the "congregation of the saints," while the emergent Catholic Church claimed it as an institution dispensing salvation which controlled the means of grace, in particular the power of absolution.

Paul's understanding of the church as the body of Christ excludes, as we have seen, the associational understanding of the "congregation of the saints" as original. The above antithesis claims further support in the assertion that originally membership in the "congregation of the saints" was maintained only by the holiness of members, and this as a mandatory condition requiring a sinless walk of life after baptism. Proof is derived from the controversies about "second repentance" in the second century and the practice of absolution in the third. In these the rigorist critics of the developments in the majority church (Montanism, Hippolytus, Novatian; cf. Heb. 6:4-6) are said to preserve the original Christian rigor, albeit in gradually softened measure. But if we examine this antithesis, we find the majority church and its critics united in one significant point: their moralistic and legalistic understanding of salvation (p. 68). It was this understanding of salvation which made the emergent Catholic Church into a disciplinary institution, something that the original church for more than one reason neither was nor could be. In this respect there is only a difference of degree between the majority church and Tertullian, Novatian, and ultimately also the Donatists.

Roman Catholic research has long been engaged, and in part still is today, in the endeavor to demonstrate the existence in the apostolic age of the Sacrament of Penance as set down in later canon law. To this end a web of categories of later canon law has been drawn over the early Christian source material. Thus the sources were prejudiced for practical exegesis in a way that fails to convince. At any rate, the Catholic Church has since the third century claimed very wide, perhaps indeed in practice unlimited, power of absolution. The charge of innovation was made already at that time by Tertullian and Hippolytus. If the endeavor was and is to make a defense of such power, or to achieve the much heavier task of proving its existence in the beginnings of the church, the facts remain contrary. Absolution means forgiveness, which is not patient of being constricted by some sort of sacramentalizing. To say the least, we are here in the realm of the Gospel and not of the Law. If we examine the above antithesis from this viewpoint, that of readiness to forgive, it has a completely different complexion. Absolution can of course be regarded as a sign of weakness or laxity. Tertullian has basically no other criterion. The majority church saw in absolution a fulfilling of the responsibility placed upon it by Christ. Quite apart from all the possibilities of abuse, the question must be answered whether it was right in this. This is decisive for the claim whether at least at this point it was true to what was original and Christian.

In the early church, discipline regarding penitents developed from the Office of the Keys (Matt. 16:19). Here was found the right to bind and loose (16:19; 18:18), or according to John 20:22 f. the power to retain and remit sins. The power of the church based on this foundation may appear questionable, since critical scholars regard the words addressed to Peter about the keys as a later tendential interpolation. Others would derive the pericope Matt. 18:15-18 from a church tradition. According to this view the church regulations which gradually became necessary were put back into the mouth of Jesus Himself. The question of the genuineness of our Lord's words in 16:19 has received greater importance because of their connection with 16:18 ("on this rock I will build My church"). This is an importance they would scarcely have received if it were not for the claims of primacy and succession made by the Roman Church. These claims need not detain us here. The discipline regarding penitents developed in the early church before the claims gained significance for the church at large, particularly in the East.[1]

If we confine ourselves to the question of the church's right to bind and to loose, or more specifically the power of absolution, we find that the substance of what our Lord said to Peter is by no means isolated in this statement. This was certainly the view of the early church as shown by John 20:23 and the pericope Matt. 18:15-18. We cannot say more. It really makes no difference whether the early Christian church believed that this power was given by Christ before or after His resurrection; whether it was given first to Peter and then also to the *ecclesia* as a whole (without designation of any office or persons, Matt. 18:15-18) or the reverse; or whether, if the words to Peter should really be a later interpolation, the power of absolution was entrusted to the congregation alone. The pericope that tells of this is followed by our Lord's words about forgiving seventy times seven times, and then comes the story of the unmerciful servant. We see how the power of absolution is set in the wider context of the readiness to forgive, which is an altogether essential part of the preaching of Jesus.[2] Later exegesis has indeed discovered that the readiness to forgive generally enjoined by Jesus refers to "sins against men" and not to those against God, a distinction not made by the words authorizing absolution. This is not to be denied. The remarkable thing about these words authorizing the power of absolution is that the binding and loosing by those authorized are valid in heaven also. This is a development of what our Lord said of God's forgiveness coinciding with man's (Mark 11:25 f.; Matt. 6:12, 14 f.). Then, too, the authorizing words speak not only of loosing but also of binding. This does not say that loosing, binding, and loosing again are to be repeated in the manner of the "seventy times seven" when the brother sins against *me* (Matt. 18:21), or that loosing must always be the last word. In assessing the exercise of the power vouchsafed we must always set beside Paul's desire to cleanse Christ's congregation by the exclusion of gross sinners the balancing readiness to forgive. It was to this that the majority church appealed in Tertullian's time when it pointed its discipline of penitents toward reconciliation, and who would find fault with this?

In Revelation whole congregations are pointed to the possibility of repenting and so of escaping final rejection. There is no slackening of intense expectation of the Parousia here (2:5, 16, 22; 3:3, 19); nor could these congregations, against some of which such heavy reproaches are leveled, be composed only of the unbaptized. Tertullian is a little too facile in his use of these passages in his censures.[3] He may indeed be right in maintaining that what Paul says of pardoning the man punished by the Corinthians (2 Cor. 2:5-11) does not apply to the excluded fornicator (1 Cor. 5:1-5).[4] It cannot be denied, however, that Paul here appeals also for love and identifies himself with the pardon given by the congregation. And finally, never in the whole church was it ever completely forgotten that *all* Christians need forgiveness. Tertullian himself points out that the petition for forgiveness in the Lord's Prayer contains a confession of guilt.[5] As a rigorous Montanist he still concedes that all Christians are daily guilty of offenses for which they need forgiveness.[6] Other rigorists say the same. Church recognition of this fact is shown by the very early inclusion in the liturgy of a general confession of sin *(exhomologesis)* from which no one is excepted[7] and by the preaching of repentance to the whole congregation. Of this there are a host of examples from 2 *Clement,* a homily of the second century, to the great preachers of the fourth century. The same purpose was also originally to be served by the great fasts before Easter.[8]

To take sides in the controversy regarding penitential discipline in the second and third centuries is not simply a matter of saying that the original Christian line was followed by the rigorists and opposed by the majority church. That may be the case in the understanding of office, at least with Tertullian. With Hippolytus it is not so clear since for him a bishop is as hierarchical and priestly as with his opponents in the majority church.

The intention of penitential discipline is to apply the power of the keys given by Christ to the church. How then does rigor come to be the criterion of their use? A student of the history of law asks first *who* is responsible for their use. When the bishop is seen to be the answer to this question in the early Catholic Church, then, as we shall see, another question follows. *Upon whom* is the power to loose and bind to be exercised? This is the question which divides the parties in the third century. Even after the Catholic Church fixed its stand, the question still regularly appears on the synodical agendas of the following centuries.

A theological investigation must also ask the question in what spirit the power of the keys is exercised. The observation that from Matt. 18: 15-18 to the Pauline anathema Jewish patterns are followed does not help very much, however full of interest it may be. The *ecclesia* of the risen Christ is different from the Jewish one, and here the operative spirit can only be the spirit of Christ. When the question is put this way, we cannot automatically answer that the more rigorous penitential discipline is the more in harmony with the spirit of Christ. For this reason a theological investigation cannot simply decide in favor of Tertullian. The real problem in the power of the keys, from the viewpoint both of the Pauline kerygma and the Christ of the gospels, is not the loosing but the binding, not the forgiving but the retaining of sins. This is not the place to propose our own solution, but rather to inquire about the answer which the early church gave to this problem.

The first impression is that it got no further than a schematic solution. A welcome directive was found in the Johannine distinction between "sins unto death" and "sins not unto death." For the former case there is to be no prayer, while prayer for the latter will be granted (1 John 5: 16 f.). It sounds like an answer to the question who is to be loosed and who to be bound. All that remains to be determined is what sin unto death is. It was decided that mortal sins (in the Middle Ages also "capital sins") are idolatry, fornication (sins of the flesh), and murder. Against the background of this definition we can understand how Tertullian could be outraged by the actual absolution of sins of the flesh by the Catholic party. However, this classification was not final. What of other sins? Are all the others taken care of by the confession *(exhomologesis)* in the liturgy? Is there not a class in between? In the course of time the classification once begun almost compelled its further extension. The next step in the effort to maintain the classification was the inclusion of other sins under the three mortal sins: under idolatry, witchcraft; under murder, abortion; under fornication, the marrying of a girl without parental consent.[9]

This is the beginning of a casuistry which in its medieval completion patterned the structure of the whole practice of penance and absolution. The Synod of Neocaesarea (314) declared that a man who had the intention to lie with a woman but did not carry out his intention was obviously kept from it by grace.[10] This sounds quite harmless. Since, however, nothing more is said, we must take it as the view of that synod that the intention is only half as bad as its execution, a view that naturally has consequences for the penitential practice. That a man and his thoughts are all of one piece seems here to be quite forgotten (Matt. 5:28). The inherent danger of such casuistry is the externalizing of sin, for which a man may then compensate with equally external "works." It is not so in the Pauline procedure (1 Cor. 5:3-5) and that of the church which follows this. Here we have the opposite. An offense against one point of the Law means not partial but total guilt (James 2:10). Sin corrupts the whole man and so brings the whole person into the same condition. Only in the case of notorious sinners, when the offenders were recognized by the whole congregation, could there be church discipline. This does not, however, mean that the sins of thought and those sinful deeds which remained concealed weigh any less heavily before God.

The comparison with Paul's procedure yields yet another difference. His exclusion of the gross sinner took place in the expectation of the immanent Parousia. The present congregation must not be unclean when the Lord comes. The delay of the Parousia and the church's transition to historical permanence opened up a possibility apprehended by none at the beginning. This was the possibility of an extended educational program in dealing with such people. The time at the congregation's disposal now extended until the Last Judgment, and therefore it recognized this possibility as its responsible task. Only in the light of this realization can we understand the way it dealt with gross sinners, heretics, and the lapsed. No longer could it merely be a matter of their complete and final exclusion. In comparison with the procedure of Paul's day this is a quite new factor, but it need not necessarily for that reason mean a departure from him.

The original impulse to win many, Jews and Gentiles, the strong and the weak (1 Cor. 9:19 ff.), continued to be the essential mission motive for a long time. Should those, however, be passed by who were once in the church but had been excluded as gross sinners, or perhaps even those who had more than once quite fallen away? Such questions did not arise so long as the Parousia was daily and hourly expected with serious enthusiasm. Quite apart from Paul's conviction that he addressed a congregation about to experience the Parousia, we can see how the sinner who was excluded one day could not be absolved already the next without casting suspicion on either the sinner or the church, or both. However, after the passing of years or even decades things would appear different. From such a later point in time the church, it would seem, did the right thing in following up also the sheep lost from her midst and seeking "to win" them anew. It can scarcely be said that this program and the simultaneous use of the power of the keys were contrary to the spirit of Christ.

The congregations of Pontus were bidden by Bishop Dionysius of Corinth (c. 170) to receive those who turned again from any lapse or error or even false heretical ways.[11] This has the ring of a magnanimous summary. But since in another letter to the church of Cnossus he admonishes them to have regard for the weakness of most men, we may perhaps even sense motives which Hippolytus points out when speaking of his Roman opponent. He says that "he used the severity of other communions to draw the mass of Roman Christians to himself."[12] This note can be detected even in a man like Cyprian.[13] However, the entire practice of granting absolution to the gross sinner upon his evident repentance and of opening the possibility of readmission to those excluded cannot be made to bear the blame for this nor thereby be shown to be wrong. The task of teaching and leading such people is here in fact assumed by the penitential practice. Repentant sinners were first admitted as penitents who had to fulfill the test of longer or shorter penitential periods. Some of these were astonishingly long, even up to 27 years. For certain offenses the rule was given "never again to communicate" (*nec in finem communicare*). Such offenders remained lifelong penitents and had only the hope that on their deathbed they might receive the last Communion (*viaticum*, ἐφόδιον). For other offenders reconciliation took place with the laying on of hands after the fulfillment of their penitential periods. This was followed by their participation again in the Communion, the receiving *(metalepsis)* of the Sacrament.

How did this penitential procedure relate to Communion practice? Beyond doubt excommunication meant in practice exclusion from the Lord's Supper, and reconciliation readmission. The question must be asked whether this connection is merely external or fundamental. Excommunication (ἀφορίζειν) has a variety of meanings. To be sure the early church did not know the medieval terminology which distinguishes between the Greater and Lesser Ban *(excommunicatio major* and *minor)*. The excommunication formulas are so varied that one cannot always be sure of their practical implications.[14] The distinction is, however, in fact already there. The anathema formula which follows the Jewish pattern can only mean complete exclusion when directed against a person. It is used especially against heretics. It was so used at Nicaea (ἀνα-θεματίζειν) and was based on the heretics' departure from the doctrinal unity of the church.[15] The Fifth Ecumenical Council applied it even to dead Antiochenes who had died at peace with the church.[16] Similarly the formulas "to cast out of the church," [17] "to cut off completely from the *koinonia*," [18] "to be utterly cast out from the church," [19] and so on, leave no doubt of the completeness of the ejection from the church. In the local congregation this meant exclusion from all participation in the divine service and self-evidently also from the Holy Communion.[20] The believers should neither converse with the excommunicated nor pray together with him.[21] Whoever prays together with a man outside the communion of the church (ἀκοινώνητος) even at home, is himself to be excluded.[22] The communion *(communio, koinonia)* from which a man is here excommunicated is the church itself.

In other definitions of excommunication the communion is plainly only that of the Holy Communion. At times there is doubt at first sight whether it is the one or the other. We read, for example, that those who light candles by day in the cemeteries are to be barred *(arceantur)* from the communion of the church.[23] Chariot drivers and actors are to be excluded (separari) from the communion as long as they ply their trade.[24] It is possible that this may mean complete exclusion from the church, but that is most unlikely. The offense is not especially grievous. In the first case the reason given is that lighting candles would disquiet the souls of the saints. In the second case the exclusion applies only as long as they pursue the forbidden occupation. It is more natural to suppose that this being barred (arceri) and being excluded (separari) does not mean being cast out completely. Even if in the second case the exclusion is not only from the Holy Communion and we must assume that the believers were to have no dealings with people of the circus otherwise either, it is hard to imagine how, after complete exclusion from the church, they could be automatically readmitted upon giving up the doubtful occupation. In cases where from the outset communion is prohibited for a fixed time, we are forced to the conclusion that it cannot be a complete and final exclusion from the communion of the church but a temporary exclusion from the Holy Communion.[25]

In other cases, as already mentioned, it is immediately apparent that the prohibited communion is the Holy Communion. This is clear from the expressions of giving and receiving Communion (communionem dare or accipere). An adulterer may be "given the Communion" only after a penitential period of five years.[26] A believing wife who has left her husband because of his adultery and married another may not "receive Communion" until the first husband has died.[27] A believer who has fallen away and not been to church for a long time may "receive Communion" only after 10 years.[28] In Canon 78 we find the redundant formula "the Lord's Communion" (dominica communio), which surely leaves nothing in doubt.[29] The meaning is the same when we simply have communicare, which matches our "communicate."[30] Also the "last ἐφόδιον," which is not to be denied the dying,[31] refers to the Lord's Supper. Basil recommends that soldiers who have killed in war should keep themselves for three years from the Communion only.[32] For two or three years thrice-married people are to be allowed only "to stand together," that is, with the believers in the divine service, but without the "good of Communion." [33] In these two cases only the Holy Communion can be meant. The same is true when we read of the prohibition or granting again of "sacrifice" or "the holy things" (τὰ ἅγια) or "the Communion *(koinonia)* of the body of Christ," or of partaking of the consecrated elements.[34] In the light of these examples we may feel justified in supposing that in the formulas which at first seemed doubtful *(arceri, separari, abstineri a communione)* the exclusion only from the Holy Communion may at least be indicated in those cases in which the complete exclusion from the church is not established beyond doubt. Even if communion here should not be the Holy Communion but the communion of the church, exclusion from the latter would always mean from the former also.

In the East the penitential periods were divided into stages through which the penitent was to prove himself. This was certainly so in the fourth century and probably earlier. Basil says that a man who has killed intentionally must be excluded from the Sacrament for 20 years (ἀκοινώνητος τοῖς ἁγιάσμασιν). "With this man the 20 years are divided thus. Four years he must keep before the door of the house of prayer, and there confessing his offenses entreat the entering believers to pray for him. After these four years he is to be received among the hearers, and for five years he shall go out with them. Seven years he shall go out with those that kneel at prayer. Four years he shall only stand together with the believers but not have part in the sacrifice. Only after this shall he have part in the Sacrament." [35] The picture is quite clear. The penitential stages recall those of the catechumens.[36] The penitent must once more go the way that once he went to Baptism. He must leave the divine service before the Eucharist with the hearers. The stages vary in length as does the penitential period as a whole. What is prescribed in any case indicates the gravity of the offense. Since the procedure in every case excludes from the Holy Communion until it is completed, the extension of the penitential period into stages appears as a corresponding increase in severity.

The way the penitential stages correspond to those of the catechumenate reveals the intention to instruct and lead. Just as the catechumen is only step by step prepared for receiving Baptism and must discipline every impatience, so also the gross sinner is to be drawn up from the depth of his fall and gradually to be acclimatized again to the congregation gathered in the divine service before he may again receive Communion. The deeper the fall, the farther he has removed himself, the longer also the penitential period. The intention to instruct and lead is especially apparent when the rigid system is broken through or at least relaxed. The Synod of Ancyra (314) granted the bishops authority to shorten or to lengthen the penitential period. They were to do this in the light of their examination of the conduct of the penitent before and after his fall. The problem had to do with the lapsed who in the recent great persecution had taken part in heathen sacrifices under duress. The bishops were to be guided by brotherly love.[37]

The system, however, had another intention. Penitential discipline varied in specific cases according to their gravity. The whole arrangement operated also as a threat of punishment. The graver the offense, the heavier the penitential performance required. Karl Holl thought it possible to assign one intention to the East and another to the West. In the East, he thought, as far as the influence of the Alexandrians, Clement and Origen, reached, it was never forgotten that upon baptism a man was not yet complete and that therefore the church to the end of time had the task of teaching and leading *all* its members.[38] The basic intention of penitential practice was therefore to deepen the sinner's insight, to restore him to the right way, and so to heal him of his sickness. In the East the monks trained in the spirit of Basil therefore were able to spread his profound influence on the understanding and practice of penitence. In the West, on the other hand, penitential discipline developed one-sidedly into a penal procedure.

Holl's critics have rightly pointed out that the intention to punish is also not absent in the East, not even in Basil, while on the other hand the healing purpose was also pursued in the West. An indisputable proof of this is to be found in the concept of the "healing punishment" *(poena medicinalis)* which has retained its place in Roman canon law to this day. There is, however, no mistaking the different emphases of the East and the West. Gregory of Nyssa describes the whole procedure as a "therapeutic method," [39] while in the Western "healing punishment" the noun punishment is dominant. The emphases are about as different as those of moral improvement and corrective punishment. At least it was in the West that the bishop came to be known best as a judge who inflicted punishments in the secular manner. However, it is not our business here to play the East off against the West but rather to inquire how the two attitudes affected the Holy Communion.

The penitential stages of the East are not found in the West, and yet there are nonetheless gradations. "The smallest step in public penance was exclusion from the Eucharistic service or at least from the Communion. This remained at all times a part of penance." This is Rauschen's assessment.[40] The latter part of his statement is certainly correct, but with regard to the former we must ask what other steps of penance come into consideration. He answers, "Prayer, fasting, and various abstentions. In addition a man had to supplicate the priest, the poor, and the widows. Baths were also forbidden." Then he gives Tertullian's familiar description of penitents [41] which is along the same lines, and then the peculiarly Western prescriptions about changing clothes, shaving hair, the prohibition of worldly affairs, of conjugal rights, and also of marrying a second time even after the completion of the penance. Among these impositions exclusion from the Lord's Supper is said to be the smallest step.

This assessment by a modern Roman Catholic scholar rests on the assumption that penitential discipline is a punishment procedure.[42] The procedure begins with exclusion from the Holy Communion and ends with readmission to it. The exclusion is punishment because it deprives a person of rights which are regained only by the fulfillment of the imposed penances. Whether this exclusion was regarded in the early church as "the smallest step in public penance" is by no means certain. It is in any case only possible to regard it in this way when it is seen on the same level with the other impositions. If everything is punishment, then the punishment of exclusion from Holy Communion grows in severity with each added imposition of prayer or fasting. If no such impositions are added, this exclusion then remains "the smallest step." When the matter is understood in this way, no essential connection is discernible between the sin and the specific exclusion from the Sacrament.

In the therapeutic understanding of penitential practice things are different insofar as there is concern for inner healing *(Heilung)*. Gregory of Nyssa tried to divide sins according to the three Platonic functions of the soul. This affords differentiation of their gravity *(Can. Ep.,* 1) which then is to be reflected in the system of penitential stages. Worst are the sins of the intellect. Such sins are a denial of faith in Christ and apostasy to Judaism or Manichaeism. For these, even if a man turn again, penitence is lifelong. On the other hand, sins which spring from the lower impulses can in certain circumstances be ascribed to weakness. If we take into account Gregory's understanding of the Eucharist as that in which the faithful communicant is made partaker of the immortality of the body of Christ in both body and soul *(Or. Cat.,* 37), the inner logic of the exclusion from the Holy Communion becomes evident. The unrepentant sinner cannot have part in the body of Christ, for only that is immortal which is sanctified (ἁγιαζόμενον). The penitential procedure serves the goal of sanctifing a man. Without doubt there is forgiveness of sins in the Sacrament, but full repentance must precede forgiveness.

This must, of course, be true then for every sinner, even in the "small" offences. In fact, Basil points out that in the New Testament every sin is disobedience and it is not easy to find a distinction between small and big sins.[43] He applies the consequences of this to confession in the monastic communities. However, to go beyond the monks and compel the confession of all sins by all members of the congregations was neither possible nor desirable. How keenly impenitence was felt to contradict receiving the Sacrament is shown by the so-called *Testament of Our Lord Jesus Christ*.[44] Before the Eucharist the deacon calls: "Lift up your hearts to heaven. If anyone has enmity toward his neighbor, let him be reconciled. Is any conscious of unbelief, let him confess it. If any finds himself to be fallen, he may not keep it secret, for to conceal it is godless. If any is diseased in his soul, let him not come. The same is true of any unclean or wavering. Is any estranged from the commands of Jesus, let him depart. If any despises the prophets, let him step aside. Let him beware of the wrath of the Only-begotten — in order that we do not pour scorn on the cross." [45] This has the original ring. Every partaker is warned once more. If he is unrepentant, he should voluntarily keep himself from the Communion. Whoever partakes against his conscience does so at his own peril.[46] Those who have sinned unto death, whose sin is public and who have not yet fulfilled the penitential requirement of the church, are the only ones who can be restrained by the outward measures designed to preserve this order.

Here we find not merely an external but an essential connection between the penitential procedures and the exclusion from the Holy Communion. The reasons given by the Cappadocians may seem one-sidedly individualistic. This is even more striking in view of their forensic approach. Such individualizing, however, has as its practical aim the shaping of repentance to the need of the individual sinner. For his own sake the congregation cannot admit an unrepentant sinner to the Holy Communion when he is manifestly recognizable as such. Nor can the congregation do this for its own sake. It is not prompted by police-like narrow-mindedness when it protects itself from blemish and taint.[47] Behind the earnestness with which it watches over participation in the Holy Communion we see the Pauline understanding of the Sacrament including its communion character. The *koinonia* of Christians with one another is essentially the *koinonia* of the body of Christ (p. 17). Therefore the unity of the local congregation is most concretely expressed when its members celebrate the Holy Communion together. Each member gives personal testimony of this fact by his participation. The early church knew no private masses. The bishop "gathered his congregation." [48] In the prayers of the Eucharist the congregation united itself in praise and petition with the prophets, apostles and martyrs, and with the hosts and powers of heaven. That the congregation could not possibly admit the unrepentant sinner or heretic is utterly clear in the Post-Communion, where it turns to God and says: "Thou who hast separated us from the *koinonia* of the godless, unite us with those made holy to Thee." [49] It can pray *for* them but not *with* them.[50] And according to Paul, it can under no circumstances "eat together with them." There would otherwise be a simulated *koinonia* of the body of Christ which would be neither real nor true.

The early church made an exception of the deathbed. The Synod of Ancyra (314) declared that penitents about to die who had not fulfilled the imposed penitential period were to be "received" (δεχθῆναι). Here the lapsed were in question. Even murderers, who were excluded forever, should "at the end of their life be deemed fit for the Sacrament." [51] The Synod of Neocaesarea (314—25) made the same provision for a woman who had been excommunicated till death for marrying her deceased husband's brother.[52] The Council of Nicaea (325) declared that "always and in every case" the bishop should grant the Eucharist to a dying man who desired it after he had examined him (μετὰ δοκιμασίας).[53] If the sick man recovered unexpectedly, he was nonetheless to be put again with those who were permitted to participate only in prayer. According to the Second Council of Carthage (c. 387—90) the presbyter might accomplish the reconciliation in a case of necessity in the absence of the bishop.[54]

The ruling of the Council of Nicaea was based on "the old and canonical law" that "is also now to be observed." This does not sound like a reference to a synodical resolution passed a few years earlier. In fact we find the same principle already in Cyprian and in a letter of Bishop Dionysius of Alexandria (247—65). The only difference here from the Nicaean decision is that there is no mention of the bishop and that, should the sinner recover and not return again to his sin, the reconciliation should remain in force.[55] Dionysius gives the further basis that the dying men who have stood so close to their judgment and been steadfast in faith, and who have been absolved, have indeed received forgiveness of their sins, for God's mercy is true and reliable. We may conclude that all parts of church discipline, training, healing, and punishing are muted in the face of death. The church can do nothing else than let those who die in repentance and faith in forgiveness "depart as free." [56]

Notes to Chapter 8

1. The vast literature on this passage is mostly concerned with Matt. 16:18 and much less with v. 19. Against its genuineness: Kuemmel, *Kirchenbegriff*, pp. 20 ff., 50 ff.; H. von Campenhausen, *Kirchliches Amt*, pp. 140 ff.; T. W. Manson, *The Sayings of Jesus* (London, 1954), p. 203. In favor: A. Oepke,

"Der Herrnspruch ueber die Kirche Mt. 16, 17—19 in der neuesten For-schung," *Studia Theologica* (Lund), 2, 1948—50, pp. 110 ff.; F. V. Filson, *The Gospel According to St. Matthew* (London, 1960), p. 186. Cf. A. H. McNeile, *The Gospel According to St. Matthew* (London, 1961), p. 240. O. Cullmann, *Peter, Disciple, Apostle, Martyr*, trans. F. V. Filson, 2d ed. (London, 1962), pp. 184 ff. In deference to the synoptic parallels, Cullmann would transpose the passage from Matt. 18 into the situation of Luke 22:31 ff. E. Stauffer, "Zur Vor- und Fruehgeschichte des Primatus Petri," *Zeitschrift fuer Kirchengeschichte*, 1943—44, pp. 1 ff., regards the words as spoken by the risen Lord. Also G. D. Kilpatrick, *The Origins of the Gospel According to St. Matthew* (Oxford, 1950), p. 95. Cf. p. 43: "It must, however, be frankly recognized that, though suggestions of this kind may bear the speciousness of probability, they are patent conjectures, and in our ignorance point to no definite conclusions."

2. Matt. 18:21 ff.; 6:12, 14 f.; Mark 11:25 f.; Luke 11:4; 17:3 f. Cf. Matt. 5:25, 44; 7:1-5 (Mark 4:24).

3. *De pud.*, 19, 1—6: *ACW*, XXVIII, 109 ff.

4. *De pud.*, 13—16: *ACW*, XXVIII, 85 ff.

5. *De orat.*, 7: Evans, p. 12.

6. *De pud.*, 7, 14 ff.; 19, 23 f.: *ACW*, XXVIII, 71 f.; 114. Cf. R. C. Morti-mer, *The Origins of Private Penance* (Oxford, 1939), pp. 19 ff.

7. *Didache*, 4, 1; 14, 1: *LCC*, I, 178. Cf. 1 *Clem.*, 60, 1 f.: *LCC*, I, 71.

8. Holl, *Enthusiasmus und Buszgewalt*, p. 235 ff.

9. Elvira (306), Canon 6: Stevenson, p. 306; Basil, Canons 2 and 38: *PG*, 32, 672, 728. Catholic theory then sought another way — by raising the num-ber of mortal sins to eight or seven. Cf. already Tertullian, *De pud.*, 19, 24: *ACW*, XXVIII, 114; 274, n. 595; *Against Marcion*, 4, 9. On the other hand, concerning adultery, murder, and idolatry as a special class, see *De pud.*, 5: *ACW*, XXVIII, 62 ff., and (with reference to Acts 15:28 f.) 12:4 f.: Mortimer, pp. 12 f

10. Canon 4: Mansi, II, 539; Watkins, I, 270.

11. *H. E.*, IV, 23, 6. The meaning of δεξιοῦσθαι is in any case disputed. It seems rather doubtful that it should merely mean "to be concerned about."

12. Adolf Hamel, *Kirche bei Hippolyt von Rom*, p. 61.

13. *Ep.*, 55, 15.

14. F. Kober, *Der Kirchenbann nach den Grundsaetzen des kanonischen Rechts* (1863), p. 32, has collected 23 formulas from the Greek and Latin sources. This number could be enlarged.

15. Ancyra (358), Canon 1: Hahn, p. 202; Stevenson, pp. 310 f. Pseudo-Athanasius: Hahn, p. 139. In its Canon 3 the Council of Saragossa (380) imposed the perpetual anathema on those of whom it was proved that they had not eaten the grace of the Eucharist which they had received (into their hands) in church (eucharistiae gratiam acceptam in ecclesia non sumpsisse), as also upon those who between December 16th and January 6th (Epiphany) had gone about everywhere but not to church. This last instance shows clearly enough how wary we must be of leaning too heavily on the mere formula. It is impossible to suppose that such sinners should be more severely punished (in perpetuum) than the capital sinners who were granted reconciliation. Cf. P. B. Gams, Die Kirchengeschichte von Spanien (1864), II, 1, 370. "This is an ambiguous expression which was intentionally used and which may mean 'so long as he does not amend and show evidence of his conversion.' " (P. 28)

16. Hahn, pp. 171 f.; Bindley, p. 156.

17. Ap. Can., 51.

18. Ibid., 30.

19. Penitus ab ecclesia abjici, Elvira, Canon 49: Stevenson, p. 308.

20. Tertullian, Apology, 39, 4: "Let him be excluded from the fellowship of prayer, assembly, and every sacramental observance" (a communione orationis et conventus et omnis sancti commercii relegetur). Cf. J. E. B. Mayor, Tertullian's Apology (Cambridge, 1917), p. 388, note to p. 112, 3; Stevenson, p. 174.

21. Didascalia, VI, 14, 1: Funk, p. 340; Connolly, p. 210, 24. Antioch (341), Canon 2. Cf. Ignatius, Smyrn., 7, 2: LCC, I, 114.

22. Ap. Can., 11.

23. Elvira, Canon 34: Mortimer, p. 53.

24. Arles, Canons 4 and 5: CCL, 148, 10; Stevenson, pp. 322 f.

25. Elvira, Canons 40 and 54. Basil, Canons 34, 38, 58, 61, 81, 83: PG, 32, 727 ff.

26. Elvira, Canon 69.

27. Elvira, Canon 9: Stevenson, p. 306.

28. Elvira, Canon 46: Watkins, I, 264. Cf. Canons 1—3, 5—10, 12—14, 17, 18, 22, 31, 46, 55, 63—67, 71—73. Arles, Canon 22: CCL, 148, 13; Stevenson, p. 325. Gregory of Nyssa, c. 5: Pitra, I, 626, 6: κοινωνίαν διδόναι. Roman Catholic interpreters of the Canons of Elvira maintain that communio everywhere means church fellowship or the "sacramental absolution" (through the Sacrament of Penance). Hefele, however, is against this

(I, 157). Cf. Mortimer, pp. 45 ff. The presentation above also takes issue with the view notably propounded by Hinschius (*Kirchenrecht*, IV, 705 ff.) and adopted by others that "exclusion from altar fellowship only is virtually absent in the Councils up to the sixth century" (p. 709). Rather "the very earliest possible would be after the end of the fourth century, the positive earliest in the fifth century, and even then very rarely and as an arbitrarily constructed punishment imposed by the church officials" (p. 712). Gustav Krueger (*Handbuch der Kirchengeschichte*, 2d ed. [1923], I, 190) is also of the opinion that exclusion only from altar fellowship appears "apparently first in Basil." Cf. Mortimer, pp. 45 ff.

29. Cf. Turin (401), Canon 5.

30. Arles (314), Canon 14: *CCL*, 148, 12; Stevenson, p. 324. Carthage III (397), Canon 7. Toledo I (400), Canons 13, 17, 18.

31. Nicaea, Canon 13: Bright, pp. xiii, 50 ff.; Stevenson, p. 362.

32. Canon 13: *PG*, 32, 681; Deferrari, III, 43 f.

33. Canon 4: *PG*, 32, 673; Deferrari, III, 27. Cf. Canons 22 and 75. With his translation "bystanders," Watkins indicates that they were then put in a class — that above the "mourners, hearers, and kneelers" and below the "communicants" (I, 322 ff.). He also recognizes the Eucharist here.

34. Canon 82: μέθεξις τῶν ἁγιασμάτων. Canon 57: καὶ τῷ ἑξῆς εἰς τὰ ἅγια δεχθήσεται. Canon 58: ἀκοινώνητα τῶν ἁγιασμάτων. Cf. 56, 61, 70. Canons 22, 24, 55, 73, 75, 81: κοινωνία τοῦ ἀγαθοῦ. Canon 77: προσφορά. The same usage in Gregory of Nyssa, Canons 2, 4, 5: Pitra, I, 622, 4; 624, 18; 626, 5. The Synod of Ancyra (314) repeatedly uses the formula κοινωνεῖν χωρὶς προσφορᾶς (Canons 5, 6, 8, 9: Stevenson, p. 311). Cf. Nicaea, Canon 11. Hefele remarks on this formula that *prosphora* means primarily only the bringing of the gifts offered in the Eucharist, and that therefore the formula means no more than that the penitents were not permitted to bring their offerings with the others (I, 226 f., ET, I, 206 f.). He nevertheless concedes that this would involve their exclusion from receiving the Sacrament and that the whole act of the Eucharist can be called *prosphora*.

35. Basil, Canon 56: *PG*, 32, 797; Deferrari, III, 247 f. Similarly in Gregory of Nyssa, c. 5; here, however, the total is 27 years. Cf. Watkins, I, 326 ff.

36. See above, p. 75. Exact analysis of the parallels is given in Eduard Schwartz, "Buszstufen und Katechumenatsklassen" (1911), pp. 44 ff. In the following century we find the same thing without concession in Theodore's letter to Bishop Eulalius of Persian Armenia (*Ep.*, 77: Schulze, IV, 1130; *PG*, 83, 1245 ff.). The fallen (ὀλισθαίνοντες, lapsed?) are not to be hindered

from participation in the prayer of the catechumens, the hearing of the lections and the admonition of the teachers. They are, however, to be kept from "receiving the holy mysteries (μετάληψις τῶν ἱερῶν μυστηρίων), not until death but for a fixed time, until they acknowledge their sickness."

37. Canon 5: Mansi, II, 516; Watkins, I, 268. Philanthropy in the case of other offenses is found in Gregory of Nyssa, *Can. Ep.*, 2 and 5: Pitra, I, 622, 8; 626, 3.

38. That the desire to educate was the dominant intention of the Platonist Origen has been demonstrated by Hal Koch, *Pronoia und Paideusis*, 1932.

39. Θεραπευτικὴ μέθοδος, *Can. Ep.*, 1: Pitra, I, 619, 15; cf. 619, 2; 627, 31.

40. *Eucharist and Penance*, p. 137. Proof is adduced from Augustine, Serm. 351, 4, 7; 352, 3, 8. So also J. F. Bethune-Baker, *An Introduction to the Early History of Christian Doctrine* (London, 1903), p. 372: "the lightest form."

41. *De Paen.*, 9: *ACW*, XXVIII, 31 f.

42. E. Loening (*Geschichte des deutschen Kirchenrechts*, I, 268 [on the ancient church]) holds the view that only the exclusions from church and altar fellowship are punishment, not penance as such. Similarly Hinschius (*Kirchenrecht*, IV, 695) maintains that penance is not a duty legally required but a kindness. It therefore does not rank as the church's leading means of punishment or censure.

43. *Regulae brevius tractatae*, Question 293: *PG*, 31, 1288c.

44. Probably Monophysite of the fifth century. Cf. J. Quasten, *Monumenta Eucharistica*, V (*Florilegium Patristicum*, VII), 1936, p. 236.

45. Quasten, p. 260.

46. Chrysostom, *De David et Saule hom.*, III, 1: *PG*, 54, 695.

47. *Didascalia*, VI, 14, 10: Funk, p. 344, 10; Connolly, p. 214, 14.

48. *Ap. Const.*, II, 57, 2.

49. Ibid., VIII, 15, 3.

50. Ibid., VII, 12, 47. Gregory of Nyssa, c. 1: Pitra, I, 622.

51. Canons 6 and 22: Mansi, II, 515, 519; Watkins, I, 268 f.; Rackham, pp. 147, 201.

52. Canon 2: Mansi, II, 539; Watkins, I, 270.

53. Canon 13. See n. 36 above. Cf. Canon 76 of the so-called Fourth Council of Carthage, whose statutes are probably of Gallic origin.

54. Canon 4. Cf. Carthage III (397), Canon 32.

55. Pitra, I, 546. C. L. Feltoe, *The Letters of Dionysius of Alexandria* (Cambridge, 1904), pp. 60 ff. Cf. Watkins, I, 219. Perhaps the letter of Dionysius

quoted by Eusebius (*H. E.*, VI, 44, 4) has this document in mind. Dionysius there writes to Fabian of Antioch that he has issued a general instruction regarding the matter and he gives a drastic example of its application. Cyprian, *Ep.* 18, 1; 19, 2; 20, 3; 27. Lacey, pp. 16 f.

56. Pitra, I, 546, 32.

Bibliography for Chapter 8

Bartlett, J. Vernon. *Church Life and Church Order During the First Four Centuries.* Oxford, 1943.

Bethune-Baker, J. F. *An Introduction to the Early History of Christian Doctrine.* London, 1903.

Campenhausen, H. von. *Kirchliches Amt und geistliche Vollmacht in den ersten drei Jahrhunderten,* 1953, pp. 135 ff., 234 ff.

Cullmann, O. *Peter: Disciple, Apostle, Martyr.* Trans. F. V. Filson. 2d ed., London, 1962.

Deferrari, R. J. *St. Basil, The Letters.* Loeb Library, 4 vols. London and New York, 1926—34.

Feltoe, C. L. *The Letters of Dionysius of Alexandria.* Cambridge, 1904.

Filson, F. V. *The Gospel According to St. Matthew.* London, 1960.

Funk, F. X. *Kirchengeschichtliche Abhandlungen,* I, 1897. Especially on early penitential discipline, pp. 155 ff., and penitential stages, pp. 182 ff.

Galtier, T. *L'Église et la remission des péchés aux premiers siècles,* 1932.

Gams, P. B. *Die Kirchengeschichte von Spanien,* 1864.

Hamel, A. *Kirche bei Hippolyt von Rom,* 1951, pp. 59 ff.

Hinschius, Paul. *Kirchenrecht,* IV.

Hoh, J. "Die kirchliche Busze im zweiten Jahrhundert," *Breslauer Studien zur historischen Theologie,* No. 22 (1932).

Holl, Karl. *Enthusiasmus und Buszgewalt im griechischen Moenchtum,* 1898.

Kilpatrick, G. D. *The Origins of the Gospel According to St. Matthew.* Oxford, 1950.

Kober F. *Der Kirchenbann nach den Grundsaetzen des kanonischen Rechts.* 2d ed., 1863.

Koch, Hal. *Pronoia und Paideusis,* 1932.

Krueger, Gustav. *Handbuch der Kirchengeschichte,* 2d ed., 1923.

Laun, F. "Buszwesen," II in *RGG,* 2d ed., I, 1393 ff.

Loening, E. *Geschichte des deutschen Kirchenrechts.*

McNeile, A. H. *The Gospel According to St. Matthew*. London, 1961.

Manson, T. W. *The Sayings of Jesus*. London, 1954.

Mayor, J. E. B. *Tertullian's Apology*. Cambridge, 1917.

Meinhold, P. "Buszwesen," II in *RGG*, 3d ed., I, 1544 ff.

Mortimer, R. C. *The Origins of Private Penance*. Oxford, 1939.

Oepke, A. "Der Herrnspruch ueber die Kirche Mt. 16, 17—19 in der neuesten Forschung," *Studia Theologica* (Lund), 1948—50.

Poschmann, B. *Paenitentia secunda. Die kirchliche Busze im aeltesten Christentum bis Cyprian und Origines*, 1940.

Quasten, J. *Monumenta Eucharistica*.

Rackham, R. B. "The Test of the Canons of Ancyra," *Studia Biblica et Ecclesiastica*. Oxford, 1891, III, 143 ff.

Rahner, K. "Zur Theologie der Busze bei Tertullian," *Abhandlungen ueber Theologie und Kirche, Festschrift fuer K. Adam*, 1952, pp. 139 ff.

Rauschen, Gerhard. *Eucharist and Penance in the First Six Centuries of the Church*. St. Louis, 1913.

Schwartz, Eduard. "Buszstufen und Katechumenatsklassen," *Schriften der wissenschaftlichen Gesellschaft in Strassburg*, No. 7 (1911).

Stauffer, E. "Zur Vor- und Fruehgeschichte des Primatus Petri," *Zeitschrift fuer Kirchengeschichte*, 1943—44.

Watkins, O. D. *A History of Penance*. 2 vols. London, 1920.

Windisch, H. *Taufe und Suende im aeltesten Christentum bis auf Origines*, 1908.

9

THE LOCAL CONGREGATION

AND THE HERETICS

Heretics were treated in a way formally parallel to that shown to gross sinners, both in their exclusion and their readmission upon repentance. Their wrong was simply their desertion of the orthodox fellowship. Some of course were born and reared in a heretical communion. Heretics fell automatically into the category of capital sinners. No distinction was made here regarding heresy in the civil laws from Theodosius I onwards. Heresy was prosecuted and punished as such. The church for its part always regarded heresy as sin, although it conceded that the heretic who had never been orthodox sinned in ignorance. He was therefore received on easier conditions than the repentant apostate.

Heresy or schism is an old ecclesiastical distinction. Heresy is false doctrine, heterodoxy, contradiction of the orthodox church doctrine. Schism is division for some other reason such as divergence in order or disputed jurisdiction, but not division for doctrine's sake.[1] Basil claims ancient usage for adding a third class of division.[2] This is the parasynagog, the arbitrary formation of a separate local congregation. In this distinction heresy at any rate is seen as opposed to orthodoxy. This involves an understanding of the church according to which orthodox doctrine is an essential criterion of the church. Heretical doctrine is apostasy and the worst of all sins.

This juxtaposition of heresy and orthodoxy has prompted some critics to see in the insistence on orthodoxy a degeneration of the church and so has also prompted their sympathy for the heretics. They unconsciously assume that the opponents of orthodox doctrine also oppose the insistence on orthodoxy. This is the reverse of the facts. The great heretics of the ancient church claimed equally, though invertedly, that they were orthodox, and so they, too, must be numbered with those who give evidence of that degeneracy which insists on orthodoxy. These same critics naturally also regard the limitation of those permitted to receive the Sacrament as a cancer growing from this insistence on orthodoxy or, in other words, the confessionalistic degeneration of the church. The early church was never in doubt that unity in doctrine is a prerequisite of altar fellowship. No one who taught false doctrine might receive Holy Communion in an orthodox congregation.

Whether the ancient church was degenerate in this, that is, betrayed her original self, cannot be decided by mere terms. "Heresy" (αἵρεσις) is of profane origin. It can be used of a philosophical school or of any particular group without any implied judgment of what is peculiar to that group, or of the fact of its separation. The word is used this way in Acts, although in a few cases the connotation of blame is already perceptible.[3] There is clear condemnation in what Paul says when he lists heresies among the works of the flesh (Gal. 5:20) or when he regards heresies as inevitable "in order that those who are genuine may be recognized" (1 Cor. 11:19). There is, however, no clear reference to doctrine. Many exegetes doubt this reference also in Titus 3:10 and 2 Peter 2:1, even as they do in Ignatius. At the Synod of Elvira (306) we find the shortening of the 50 days between Easter and Pentecost to 40 called a "new heresy." According to our understanding of the terms this would hardly constitute false doctrine. Writing to Bishop Chrestos of Syracuse, Justinian can even speak of the "Catholic heresy." This is obviously intended in praise of the Catholic Church.[4]

Things are different with the men of the majority church who wrote against Gnosticism. Here heresy is the settled term for Gnosticism. It always implies false doctrine. In Irenaeus and Tertullian we find it differentiated from schism.[5] For the anti-Gnostic churchmen pure doctrine was quite unmistakably an indispensable and elemental factor for the life of the church. Here already we find men who are superorthodox indeed, and it might easily be thought that they slipped into this through their opposition to Gnosticism, which was eminently doctrinal. The "problem of heresy" is for Martin Werner, like everything else that can be related of the ancient church, a result of the crisis which the church faced because of the Parousia's delay. The breakdown of the "consistently eschatological" teaching of the apostles and Paul created a vacuum which Gnosticism and the doctrinal formulations of the church of the majority sought to fill, each in its own way. This is the real cause of the now progressive Hellenization.[6] Here Werner's thought flows into the same channel as that of the older historians of dogma, particularly Harnack, who derive both the dogma of the majority church and Gnosticism from the Hellenization of Christianity.

What can be said against this other than to point out that it overlooks or underestimates the continuity of the early catholic church, back through Werner's vacuum, with the original Christian beginnings? We cannot hope to make any impression with the Pastoral Epistles, which say enough about teachers and false teachers, confessions, sound and strange doctrine. In them Hellenization is already in full swing, and for Werner they are already a long way this side of the vacuum. Still, this intelligence is to be preferred to that of those who would wash the poodle without getting him wet. They allow these epistles to be of the apostolic age but try to assure us that sound doctrine does not mean anything like orthodox church doctrine. What is said of deceit ($\pi\lambda\acute{\alpha}\nu\eta$) and lies ($\psi\epsilon\tilde{\upsilon}\delta\circ\varsigma$) does not deal with "an intellectual difference in theological persuasions."[7] Obviously, how could the writer of the Pastoral Epistles ever come to think that there was a difference of theological persuasion between him and the false teachers, and an intellectual one to boot! Intellect indeed; that would mean superorthodoxy and confessionalism already in the New Testament. This attempt to whitewash the Moor of the Pastoral Epistles is only understandable against the background of the view taken of ecclesiastical orthodoxy. The historians of dogma have promoted this view. They have one-sidedly presented church dogma as a matter negotiated by recondite theologians, so that finally we find the dogmatics of John of Damascus put on the same level with dogma itself.

In actual fact it was out of the life of the early church that there grew not only the historical phenomenon of orthodoxy but also dogma as theological declaration. We must note well what was meant by dogma. Justin's teaching about the Logos is indeed a remarkable symptom of Hellenization, but it was never received as dogma. Only that is dogma in the early church which is worthy of the liturgy. "Mother of God" and the theopaschite formula were taken into the liturgy, but not the controversial writings which went back and forth about them. As Loofs rightly emphasizes, the Nicene Creed, like the Chalcedonian dogma, builds on the Rule of Faith of the second century. Everything that follows these dogmas is little more than supplementary and only serves to make them more explicit and precise. Their matter is salvation. This indicates their relation to life. The primary cause of their emergence is not the task of teaching and learning or some subsequent dogmatic document produced by revolution of a council, but lies rather in the "We believe" or "We confess." They relate to Christ. Jesus Christ is not "the Lord," but "our Lord" (Apostles' Creed and other baptismal formulas), "our *Kyrios,* God, Redeemer, King," incarnate "for our salvation" (Irenaeus), "crucified for us" (Nicene Creed), and "by His resurrection He set up a standard for all ages for His saints and believers" (Ignatius), and so on.[8]

Baptismal confession, Rule of Faith, and dogma are also life-related because they are witness (p. 57). Every baptized member of the church personally vouches for his baptismal confession. Similarly every heretic vouches for his heresy. The same confessional nature is indicated when Irenaeus calls "the faith received from the apostles" *kerygma,* as Athanasius also does of the Nicene dogma. *Kerygma* here certainly does not mean merely the missionary proclamation to men hearing it for the first time. It has continuing significance among Christians (Rom. 16:25). The proclamation of the death and resurrection of Christ[9] can never cease in the church, not because Christians must always be informed again about them, but rather because their confession is of the very stuff of the life of the church. "He who confesses the Son has the Father also" (1 John 2:23). Orthodox confession is divine worship. Such is its nature. It did not merely become so by the formal inclusion of the Creed in the liturgy.[10] The confession that Jesus Christ is the Lord joins together all who bow the knee at the name of Jesus (Phil. 2:10 f.). Bowing the knee is a liturgical act.

This Pauline confession links the first of the confessions to Jesus as the Christ (Mark 8:29) with all later confessions. It is a long way on from the first Messianic confession. The crucifixion and the resurrection lie between. But there is no break. As to the heart of the matter, it is a small step to the later baptismal confessions, rules of faith, and dogmas. The heart of them all is the Christological part, and this remained the center of their gradual amplification. In all Christ is named the Lord. This Pauline confession forms the essential continuity between the "consistently eschatological" beginnings, right through Werner's vacuum, and the following confessional formulations. Philippians 2 does not merely say that Christ is the Lord, but also why He is. This basis is thematic for the entire Christological dogma of the early church. There was no party in the controversies which did not appeal to it. The Nicene "of one substance with the Father" would explicate the "equal with God" of Phil. 2:6; the Chalcedonian "of one substance with us as touching the manhood" the "being found in human form" of Phil. 2:7. Leo the Great's *Tome*, which played a decisive role at Chalcedon, builds on Philippians 2. The same basis underlies the writing of Pope Agatho which influenced the decision of the Sixth Ecumenical Council regarding the two wills. This does not mean that the early church was united or came to be united in expounding Philippians 2. The understanding of *kenosis* (Phil. 2:7) caused the Christological rift between Alexandria and Antioch. The question of the relationship of the two "forms" (Phil. 2:6) caused the passionate Monophysite opposition to Chalcedon. Whether there was controversy or peace, however, no one will ever understand the Christological arguments if he sees in them merely the play of "intellectual theological persuasions."

The dogma of the early church is confession. It bears witness to the very heart of the confessions of the early church. Confession is divine worship. The reverse is also true: all divine worship is confession. In the

New Testament there are many forms of prayer, blessing, acclamation, and doxology which probably were very early in liturgical use.[11] In this confession or "proclamation" we see something essential to the existence and life of the church. It continues on from the missionary task. These statements of the New Testament are the beginning of all later confessional formulation. Their kerygmatic character Paul sees also in the Holy Communion.

In the light of all this we can see how the congregation's attitude is in its nature different toward heretics than toward gross sinners. According to synodical usage [12] we understand heretics to be false teachers, and congregations to mean first of all the local congregation. Gross sinners can be excluded, perhaps must be. Here complex and various factors are operative. Heretics on the other hand have plainly contradicted the confession of the congregation. They make division in the liturgical kerygma. No special procedure is actually needed to put them out of the congregation. The extreme case is presented by Paul where a man says "Jesus be anathema." No one can say such a thing "by the Spirit." "By the Holy Spirit" a man can only say "Jesus is the Lord" (1 Cor. 12:3). In such an extreme case the consequences follow automatically. According to the criterion of 1 John that spirit is of God "which confesses that Jesus Christ has come in the flesh." The spirit which does not confess this is "the spirit of the Antichrist." [13] The Antichrists "went out from us, but they were not of us; for if they had been of us, they would have continued with us" (2:19). They have excluded themselves. The heretic who speaks contrary to the confession of the congregation by that very fact excludes himself. The third synod summoned against Paul of Samosata, Bishop of Antioch, declared that "there is no need for any judgment first upon his deeds, since *he is outside*. He has departed from the canon (Rule of Faith) and gone over to false and illegitimate doctrines." [14]

Heterodoxy breaks church fellowship and therefore self-evidently and primarily also altar fellowship. Guenther Bornkamm points to the fact that the warning against false teachers frequently occurs in connection with references to the Eucharist.[15] The anathema, he maintains, "pronounces upon the particular case the decision given by God and gives the offender over to the sentence of God. The responsibility rests entirely with the man thus addressed. The anathema summons him to self-examination." [16] This is in harmony with 1 Cor. 16:22. There are certainly here, he continues, "no disciplinary directives for some human court [made up of either the congregation or a set of judges] to apply the power of the keys against this or that unworthy person, or to exclude this or that man." We must ask, however, whether this condemning anathema formula has *only* admonitory significance, whether it does not rather also call for the practical consequences. It is quite inconceivable that Paul could have celebrated the Sacrament together with those who preached "another Jesus than the one we preached, [through whom] you received a different spirit from the one you received [through us] or accept a different Gospel from the one you accepted." He calls them "false prophets, deceitful workmen disguising themselves as apostles of Christ" (2 Cor. 11:4, 13-15). The separation from false teachers which we find in the epistles (already Rom. 16:17), in Revelation, and often urged in Ignatius obviously applies in the first place to the divine service which includes the Eucharist. We are not informed how this separation was effected in the apostolic age. When we hear again and again the warning to avoid and flee heresies, heretics, and seducers, when we hear Ignatius warn against the heretical "fodder" and call for the enjoyment only of "Christian food," an obvious reference to Holy Communion,[17] we perceive heresy's strong attraction and power, particularly where it had the upper hand. This is certainly the case in widespread areas where there were Gnostic congregations and organizations. Here the problem of separation was reversed for the orthodox congregations. Here separation meant keeping its own members from participation in the heretical services.[18]

This situation changed to the extent that the orthodox gained the upper hand. This change was quicker in some areas, slower in others, and not uniform everywhere.[19] We continue to hear that heretics are excluded from divine worship and the Eucharist, but not of the means by which this was done. Justin says of the Eucharist: "This food is called the Eucharist among us. Only those are permitted to partake of it who believe the truth of our doctrine, who have been washed in the laver of the forgiveness of sins and regeneration, and who live accordingly, even as Christ has bidden us." [20] Here in addition to Baptism and a fitting walk of life we find "faith in the truth of our doctrine" as a condition of Eucharistic fellowship. This expression, more precisely translated "who believes that our doctrine is true," reflects the apologist's esteem for Christianity as a philosophical truth. However, the congregational order which Justin here reports certainly did not come into existence the day before. We see beyond all doubt that the heretics were in fact excluded from the Eucharist.

In the case of Marcion, in the middle of the second century in Rome, we find a formal procedure of excommunication. The consequences are the same as in the case of gross sinners. Altar fellowship is denied. The *Didascalia* accordingly enjoins upon the deacon the task of questioning every stranger whether he belongs to the church or to a sect *(haeresis)*.[21] The *Apostolic Constitutions* enlarge this with the direction that the deacon examine each one's church credentials *(systasis;* cf. below, p. 130). In the so-called Clementine Liturgy the deacon announces before the beginning of the Eucharist "that none of the hearers, none of the unbelievers, none of the heterodox [partake]." [22] The synods of the fourth century give further directions for carrying this out. As long as heretics remain in their heresy, that is, as long as they have not asked for admission or readmission, they may not enter God's house of the church. On the other hand believers may not pray or worship in the buildings in which the Jews or heretics have their services. Clergy who do this are dismissed, laymen excommunicated.[23] There is to be no intercourse with heretics and schismatics, in particular no praying together. A bishop or cleric who nevertheless does this is excommunicated.[24] Believers are not to let their children marry heretics. The festivals of Jews and heretics are not to be celebrated with them, nor are their festival gifts to be received.[25]

The development of penitential practice into a penal procedure (above, pp. 97 ff.) gave a vindictive character also to the procedure against heretics. At first, however, this was not so. The orthodox congregation separated itself from them, avoided them, and could not have Holy Communion with them, but "punishment" was God's business (2 Peter 2). The heretic condemned himself. (αὐτοκατάκριτος, Titus 3:10)

The particular way of dealing with heresy is shown in the procedure of admission or readmission. The man who went over from the Catholic Church to heresy and then returned had to endure 10 penitential years before he was granted Holy Communion. Thus the Synod of Elvira decreed.[26] Such penance is for committed apostasy. It was not required of those incoming heretics who had never belonged to the Catholic Church and who were not otherwise guilty, though heresy was always regarded as sin. The heretic as such had not to confess an offense, but rather to acknowledge his error and subscribe to the truth of the orthodox confession. According to the Synod of Laodicea those who turned from the Novatian, Photinian, or Quartodeciman heresy were to be received upon their saying anathema to every heresy and particularly their own former heresy. Those who were counted believers in their former congregations (those already baptized there) were to learn the orthodox confessions by heart and, after their anointing, were permitted to partake of the Sacrament.[27] The so-called Canon 7 of the Council of Constantinople of 381 (in fact a product of the following century) distinguishes two classes of heretics. The one group were to be received with anointing after they had given a written declaration and said anathema to all heresies contrary to the Catholic Church. The others were first to be received as catechumens and then also be baptized once more.[28] The Quinisext Synod of 692 repeats this canon and adds some recent heresies to the first group. It concludes, "thus (οὕτω, that is, after the conditions have been fulfilled) they are to partake of the holy *koinonia*."[29] Participation in the Holy Communion in every case completes the reception into the church fellowship. No church fellowship, no altar fellowship. The only exception is the deathbed.[30]

The reception into church fellowship of heretics and schismatics is in certain respects made easier than for excommunicated gross sinners. These had to fulfill longer or shorter penitential periods. Anastasius Sinaita gives the explanation that those guilty of the gross immoralities

which he mentions commit them willfully, while heresy comes of ignorance. Therefore conversion should be made easy for heretics, while
on the other hand for the gross sinners their sins should be made heavy.[31]
This is plausible, even though making things easy for heretics could be
understood as fatal opportunism.[32] We need not pursue here those classi-
fications of heresies and attendant consequences for reception which are
heavy going even for a man so well versed in church regulations as Basil
the Great.[33] From another point of view admission was by no means
made easy for the heretics. Their changing sides was no mere leaving
one association to join another. The man who stepped out of his former
heretical or schismatic congregation was indeed under no legal obligation
to justify his action to them. At least they could not apply compulsion.
The church, however, into which he wished to be received required evidence of his motives. He had to say an explicit anathema to his former
congregation, or rather its doctrine (*haeresis* can mean both). He had
to show that he recognized the differences, and in keeping with Canon 7
of Laodicea he had to learn the orthodox confession of faith by heart.

This may appear self-evident and at first sight no oppressive requirement. In times when membership in the orthodox state church brought
only social advantages while membership in a heretical or schismatic congregation meant equally many disadvantages there may be doubt as
to whether the declared better insight was always the ultimate motive
for transfer. However, even in such a situation we must acknowledge
that the church was not content with a mere application for admission.
The applicant was made to realize that he was changing his confession.
His rejection of the one and his making the other his own must be done
earnestly in keeping with so crucial a matter. Basil insists that at the
very least he must first be instructed in the Nicene confession.[34] Former
Montanists, even those who were ordained in Montanist congregations
and were their leaders, were to be instructed "with all possible care"
(Laodicea, Canon 8). Transfer with the necessary anathema was not
so easy when we consider that such men were already Christians, even
if not Catholic. They were linked in a brotherly fellowship and even
after transfer they felt the bonds of piety and certainly often of blood

with their former congregations. For admission no difference was made between heretics and schismatics. The only exceptions were those heretics who were received as catechumens because their baptism was not recognized.

The conditions of admission show that the "sin" of heresy was not regarded as on the same level with other sins. The purpose of the exclusion of heretics from altar fellowship is not identical with that of gross sinners. The heretic is not excluded so that he may be made a better man through submission to a penitential period during which Communion is denied. The heretic's exclusion falls under the original command that in the unity of the Lord's Table there may be nothing that separates one from another. Any disunity does injury to the body of the Lord. If this is true of personal divisions (p. 80), then certainly also of heterodoxy, which breaks the confessional unity of the congregation, always a liturgical and kerygmatic unity. In the course of time this truth was obscured by the growing feeling that the heretics ought to be punished. However, the primary reason for exclusion never disappeared from the congregations, as we shall see. This is testified to by the practice of "closed Communion," the theological foundation of which was never questioned in the early church. We may indeed wonder whether and how this was managed when the masses poured into the congregations, particularly in the large cities. Before we come to this question, however, we shall first look at an incident which might give rise to some divergent conclusions.

In the East the institution of "penitential priests" was in existence for some time. According to Socrates this dated from the beginning of the Novatian schism, that is, since the middle of the third century. These priests were responsible for hearing the confessions of those who had fallen away after Baptism. They were abolished in Constantinople by the Patriarch Nectarius (381—397) because of a scandalous incident which evoked public anger and brought the church (that is, the clergy) into disrepute. Sozomen also reports the incident and declares that "the bishops almost everywhere followed" this lead (H. E., VIII, 16). If this is so, the appointment of these penitential priests must have been a general practice.[35] Socrates limits the abolition to the Homoousians, that is, the orthodox Nicene party. Both historians agree that the institution continued to their time with "the other heretics." The Novatians were an exception. They never had the custom.[36] Sozomen makes the comparison with Rome, where penitential practice was concentrated in the hands of the bishop, and so indicates that the penitential priests were appointed to relieve the bishop of some burden.

The scandalous incident which led to the abolition of the penitential priests is variously reported by these two historians.[37] Socrates' account is the older and deserves more attention because he alone presents the course of events intelligibly. A woman of standing was confessing her sins to the penitential priest. He enjoined fasting and prayer. She, however, continued her confession with another matter. A deacon had committed sin with her. On the basis of this statement (τοῦτο λεχθὲν, that is, by the woman) the deacon was dismissed. Was the woman's confession public or private? If private, then the dismissal of the deacon calls for explanation. Socrates goes on immediately to say that the crowd broke into uproar. There is no question of an indiscretion by the priest. Plainly the woman's confession must have been heard by others and so have been public. Only thus can we understand the conclusions of Bishop Nectarius. He abolished the whole institution of penitential priests. The priest in this incident was himself quite innocent. He behaved quite correctly in receiving the woman's confession. It is possible, indeed probable, that he also heard confessions privately. This incident can only have been the cause of abolishing the whole institution if it involved also public confession, which then gave rise to this scandal.

We need not have looked into this incident were it not for the statement which is added by both historians. According to Socrates a certain presbyter from Alexandria, Eudaimon by name, advised the patriarch "to leave the decision of participation in the Sacrament to each individual's conscience, for only thus would the church remain free of slander." [38] This mention of slander, as well as the actual abolition of the penitential priesthood, is understandable only if confession was previously public. The statement about participation in the Sacrament, if it was really accepted by Patriarch Nectarius, would have to mean the end of the entire previous penitential and Communion practice of the early church. As it reads, it proclaims the principle of open Communion with no restriction whatever. Because the treatment of gross sinners and heretics is linked together in the church regulations, participation in the Sacrament would, according to this principle, have to be open to all heretics also.

The evidence of the institution and abolition of the penitential priests is frequently and indeed most diversely evaluated. The scarcity of other reports of penitential practice in this period helps to explain this. It is nevertheless incredible to see the weight that has been given to the advice of the presbyter Eudaimon. His suggestion of unlimited open Communion stands so absolutely isolated in the whole early church that one may well doubt whether it was at all seriously intended, or indeed whether it was even given. Sozomen asserts that this advice was given Nectarius by "several," but since Sozomen depends on Socrates for the whole story, it is best to rely on the latter. Socrates claims to have heard of the matter from Eudaimon himself. This we need not doubt, but it may well have been that the Egyptian presbyter exaggerated his own importance a little in private conversation with the ardently curious historian. Socrates reports his reply to Eudaimon. "Whether, Presbyter, your advice advances the good of the church or not, God knows. I at any rate see in it the pretext for men no longer laying their sins before one another and so no longer following the word of the apostle 'Have no fellowship with the unfruitful works of darkness but rather reprove them.' " [39] Socrates plainly disapproved, but he disapproved only of the advice which he reports as given by Eudaimon. Both historians report the abolition of the penitential priest, but neither makes bold to assert that the patriarch followed the advice to introduce unlimited open Communion instead. Sozomen confines himself to the general complaint that in his day the rigorous church discipline of the early church had slackened, an observation that required no very powerful insight in the middle of the fifth century.

Even if we suppose that Eudaimon's advice actually had some influence, it would at most be in the treatment of secret sins the confession of which was to be left to the individual conscience, and this with the bishop now replacing the penitential priests. It is quite impossible that notorius mortal sinners could set aside the required penitential procedure and they with the heretics be freely admitted to participation in the Holy Communion. Compelling proof is given by the two historians themselves. They tell of the reception of the "tall brothers" by Nectarius' successor in Constantinople, the patriarch John Chrysostom. The "tall brothers," four Egyptian monks, were admitted by him to participation in prayer but not in the Eucharist.[40] We shall return to this story later. It would be absurd to suppose that all the canons which dealt with refusal of Communion and admission to it upon completion of the penitential requirements had no meaning from then on beyond the paper on which they were written. Gregory of Nyssa (d. 394), whose *Epistola canonica* was quoted earlier, was a contemporary of Nectarius; Bishop Amphilochius of Iconium (died c. 400), to whom the three Canonical Epitsles of Basil are addressed, was a contemporary of Chrysostom. These very letters contain so many directions for concrete cases that no one can believe that because of the abolition of the penitential priests in Constantinople Amphilochius would feel prompted to throw Basil's canons out of the window and instead for the future "leave the decision of participation in the Sacrament to each individual's conscience." We find further that the canons of the fourth century and earlier were partly confirmed by later synods and partly added to on the basis of the same principles. Many of these are still today received as valid in the Nomocanon of the Eastern Orthodox Church, just as many still form a fixed part of Roman Catholic canon law to this day. It would be a hypothesis without any proof that the advice reported of Presbyter Eudaimon in any way makes doubtful the early church's basic principle of closed Communion. Nor is it altered by occasional infractions that may have occurred.[41] The word of the dogmatician John of Damascus suffices for the present on the relationship to heterodoxy. "We must maintain with all strength that the Eucharist is to be neither received from nor given to heretics."[42] He says this following the definition of *koinonia* given above (p. 33), where in comparison with Isidore of Pelusium he emphasizes the Holy Communion as fellowship.

Notes to Chapter 9

1. Greenslade, pp. 17 ff.

2. *Ep.* 188, Canon 1: *PG,* 32, 665; Deferrari, III, 9 f. Cf. Antioch (341), Canon 5

3. For Sadducees, Pharisees, and Nazarenes, 5:17; 15:5; 24:5. On the other hand, see 24:14 and 28:22.

4. Ignatius, *Eph.,* 6, 2: *LCC,* I, 89; *Trall.,* 6, 1: *LCC,* I, 114. Elvira, Canon 43. Constantine in *H. E.,* X, 5, 21.

5. Irenaeus, *Haer.,* IV, 26, 2; 33, 7. Tertullian, *De praescr.,* 5: *LCC,* V, 34. Constantinople (381/382), Canon 6: Lauchert, pp. 85, 34 ff.; Bright, pp. xxiii, 117 f.; Greenslade, p. 20.

6. Martin Werner, *Die Entstehung des christlichen Dogmas* (1941), p. 131; ET, S. G. F. Brandon, *The Formation of Christian Dogma,* pp. 48—52.

7. O. Michel, *Das Zeugnis des Neuen Testaments von der Gemeinde,* p. 72.

8. Irenaeus in his summary of "the faith received from the apostles," *Haer.,* I, 10, 1: *LCC,* I, 360. Ignatius in the doxology, *Smyrn.,* 1, 2: *LCC,* I, 113.

9. παραγγέλειν, 1 Cor. 11:26; κηρύσσειν, 15:12 ff.

10. Cf. J. A. Jungmann, *The Mass of the Roman Rite* (New York, 1951), I, 462 (New York, 1959), p. 292 f.

11. O. Cullmann, *Les premières confessions de foi chrétienne,* 2d ed., 1948. W. Maurer (*Bekenntnis und Sakrament,* pp. 4 ff.) finds the origin of church confessions in the sacraments.

12. Elvira, Canon 43, excepted.

13. 1 John 4:3. The text deals only with the fact of a supposed confessional contradiction. The second half of the sentence is textually uncertain.

14. τοῦ ἔξω ὄντος, *H. E.,* VII, 30, 6.

15. *Das Ende des Gesetzes,* pp. 123 ff. With R. Seeberg, Lietzmann, and others, Bornkamm holds that Paul expected his letters to be read in the assembly of the congregation. His bidding them to the holy kiss as well as the formulas with which he ends his letters (anathema, maranatha etc.) are taken as belonging to the Eucharistic liturgy and so make a transition to the celebration of the Sacrament. The negative statement in the anathema ("whoever does not love the Lord," 1 Cor. 16:22) calls for the affirmation of its opposite. A similar explanation is possible for the warning against false teachers in Rom. 16:17 which immediately follows Paul's injunction of the holy kiss. Bornkamm gives convincing confirmation of this from the *Didache* and Revelation (here following Lohmeyer's liturgical interpretation), and from Hebrews and Ignatius.

16. Bornkamm, p. 125.

17. *Trall.*, 6, 1.

18. Cf. also for the middle of the third century Heraclas of Alexandria in *H. E.*, VII, 7, 4.

19. Walter Bauer, *Rechtglaeubigkeit und Ketzerei*. See chapter 5, notes 7 and 12.

20. *Apology*, I, 66, 1: *LCC*, I, 286.

21. *Didascalia*, II, 58, 1.

22. *Ap. Const.*, VIII, 12, 2.

23. Laodicea, Canons 6 and 9; *Ap. Can.*, 64 (63).

24. Laodicea, Canon 33; *Ap. Const.*, VI, 181; VII, 28; VIII, 34, 12; *Ap. Can.*, 45 (44).

25. Laodicea, Canon 10, and somewhat more lenient, Canon 31. Cf. Chalcedon, Canon 14: Bright, pp. xliii, 195; Stevenson, p. 362; Laodicea, Canon 37.

26. Canon 22: Stevenson, p. 307.

27. Canon 7. From Canon 33 we see that this synod had already distinguished between heretics and schismatics. The teaching of the Novatians and Quartodecimans is dogmatically correct, and so strictly speaking they are not heretics but schismatics. Therefore Canon 7 establishes that the reception procedure is to be the same for them both.

28. First group: Arians, Macedonians, Novatians, Apollinarians, and others. Second group: Eunomians, Montanists, Sabellians, and others. Bright, pp. xxiv, 119 ff.

29. The new heresies are Nestorianism, Eutychianism, and Severianism (Monophysitism). Timothy of Constantinople, *De Receptione Haereticorum* (probably toward the end of the sixth century) differentiates the three groups (enlarged with a number of smaller groups). The first are to be anointed at their reception, the second baptized, the third neither baptized nor anointed. Only the anathema upon their former heresy is required of the third group. *PG*, 86, 13 ff.

30. Cf. above, p. 99, n. 53. Canon 13 of Nicaea concludes, "always and in every place." Stevenson, p. 362

31. *Hodegos*, c. 85: *PG*, 89, 712b.

32. Similarly Basil, *Ep.* 188, Canon 1: *PG*, 32, 669b; Deferrari, III, 18.

33. *Ep.* 188, Canon 1: *PG*, 32, 664 ff.; Deferrari, III, 5 ff.

34. *Ep.* 125: *PG*, 32, 545; Deferrari, II, 258 f.

35. Socrates: *PG*, 67, 613: οἱ ἐπὶ τῆς μετανοίας πρεσβύτεροι τῶν ἐκκλησιῶν. Sozomen: *PG*, 67, 1457: ὁ ἐπὶ τῶν μετανοούτων τεταγμένος πρεσβύ-

τεϱος. H. E. Feine (*Kirchliche Rechtsgeschichte*, 1950, I, 107) speaks of "the penitential priests of the bishopric," as if they were a generally known institution. This probably makes too much of the information given by the two historians. In his annotations on Socrates, Valesius already asks where a canon was ever published about this, although he does not cast doubt on the correctness of the reports (614c). In commenting on Sozomen he affirms that the penitential priest is not so much as hinted at in any Western source (1460c). Watkins, I, 350 ff.

36. *PG*, 67, 616a; 1460b.

37. Tillemont's (d. 1698) contemporaries were particularly interested in it. *Mémoires pour servir a l'histoire ecclésiastique des six premiers siècles*, X, 1 (1730), 391 ff.

38. συγχωϱῆσαι δὲ ἕκαστον τῷ ἰδίῳ συνειδότι τῶν μυστηρίων μετέχειν· οὕτω γὰϱ μόνως ἔχειν τὴν ἐκκλησίαν τὸ ἀβλασφήμητον, *PG*, 67, 617a; almost the same in Sozomen, 1461b.

39. Eph. 5:11; *PG*, 67, 620c.

40. Socrates, VI, 9: *PG*, 67, 693a. Sozomen, VIII, 13: *PG*, 67, 1549.

41. See below, p. 170, on the Armenians in the Balkans in the 10th century.

42. *De fide orthodoxa*, IV, 13: *PG*, 94, 1153b, eighth century.

Bibliography for Chapter 9

Bauer, Walter. *Rechtglaeubigkeit und Ketzerei im aeltesten Christentum*, 1934.

Feine, H. E. *Kirchliche Rechtsgeschichte*, 1950.

Goppelt, L. "Kirche und Haeresie nach Paulus," *Koinonia*, pp. 42 ff., also *Gedenkschrift fuer Werner Elert*, ed. F. Huebner, 1955, pp. 9 ff.

Gront, G. "La Lutte contre l'hérésie en Orient jusqu'au 9. siècle," *Pères, Conciles, Empereurs*, 1933.

Jungmann, Joseph Andreas. *The Mass of the Roman Rite: Its Origins and Development*. Trans. F. A. Brunner. New York: Benziger, 1951, 1955, 1959.

Kamlah, W. *Christentum und Geschichtlichkeit. Untersuchungen zur Entstehung des Christentums und zu Augustins "Buergerschaft Gottes,"* 2d ed., 1951, pp. 101 ff.

Kaesemann, E. "Ketzer und Zeuge," *Zeitschrift fuer Theologie und Kirche*, 1951, pp. 292 ff.

Tillemont, Sebastian. *Mémoires pour servir a l'histoire ecclésiastique des six premiers siècles*. 16 vols., 1693—1712.

Werner, Martin. *Die Entstehung des christlichen Dogmas*, 1941. ET: S. G. F. Brandon, *The Formation of Christian Doctrine*. London, 1957.

10

TRANSFERS AND CERTIFICATION

We have so far considered church fellowship in the local congregation. This is not to suggest that the movements into and out of the local congregation have only local significance. Such a notion is altogether inconceivable in the early church. When assembled together, the local congregation knows itself to be the *ecclesia* of God in undivided wholeness (p. 64). Only distance separates one congregation from another, and the church itself is not captive to space. John's way of speaking about this is to say that wherever the Father is worshiped in spirit and truth, there are no more local shrines (John 4:21, 23). Peter speaks of the elect as scattered throughout the provinces of Asia (1 Peter 1:1-2). In time past they were not a people. Even now they do not seem so to an unbelieving eye, and yet they are a holy people (2:9 f.), a single flock awaiting the chief Shepherd (5:4). According to Paul, the body of Christ, into which we are baptized (1 Cor. 12:13), is not a local association, but it also includes the Christians in Rome, though Paul has not yet seen them (Rom. 12:5). Self-evidently therefore Baptism received in Corinth is valid also in Rome. The strong churches support the weak ones. The name of brother rings back and forth in the greetings of letters. The local congregations are fully open and welcoming toward one another. Whoever is a full baptized member of one congregation is the same also in another congregation when he moves to that place. The only thing between them is distance.

It would therefore seem superfluous to ask whether exclusion from one local congregation was valid only for that congregation. Hatch asserts that it was,[1] and he has found followers. Campenhausen, who also takes this view, quotes Marcion as proof. Polycarp of Smyrna calls

Marcion the "firstborn of Satan" and bluntly refuses him fellowship, and yet he receives a friendly reception in Rome shortly afterwards.[2] It would seem that a man can be welcomed into one congregation of saints (Paul so characterizes the local congregation, 1 Cor. 14:33) even after he has been cast out of another. If this is so in the second century, then it certainly shows how things have changed from the early days. It is impossible to take what Paul says of the Corinthian fornicator as implying that only in Corinth is fellowship to be refused him, and that should he appear in Athens no attention need be given to it. In one spirit with the assembled Corinthians Paul gives him over to Satan (1 Cor. 5:4 f.). To the early Christians the kingdom of Satan is no more locally circumscribed than the kingdom of Christ. From 1 Tim. 1:20 we see that at the end of the apostolic age exclusion was still regarded as having general validity. Paul's anathema against false teachers strikes them wherever they appear, even as the hatred of the writer of Revelation strikes the works and teaching of the Nicolaitans in Ephesus as much as in Pergamum. (Rev. 2:6, 15)

If a change has developed in the second century, there are only three possible grounds for it. First, the spread of Christianity which was accompanied by the entangling spread of Gnosticism. Oversight became impossible. Who should have fellowship with whom could only be decided from case to case (above p. 48). Consequently also one could not without hesitation assume the reliability of an exclusion made in some other place. Secondly, the settling of local boundaries between local congregations which demarcated their constituted government and hierarchy. There is already some evidence of this in First Clement. It is full blown in the bishop's church of Ignatius, where the bishop is almost everything for his *ecclesia,* and yet only for his.[3] Evidence is not so easily come by which would indicate that the boundary the bishop draws between his *ecclesia* and heresy is intended as a judgment upon the heresy only within the region of his control. This is certainly not the intention of Polycarp's judgment upon Marcion. Ignatius, too, expects that the boundary he himself draws for his *ecclesia* will be respected by the others to whom he writes. The only question is whether or how far his judgment has influence. The hindrance here would be the very division of the church into many episcopal domains. The third change from the early days would be the progressive formalization of the exclusion procedure, which finally became a fixed part of canonical penitential discipline. Only after exclusion had become statutory excommunication could it be "officially" transmitted to other congregations.

Campenhausen finds in Tertullian the first hint of one congregation's informing another of an exclusion. Following Tertullion again, he assumes this to have taken place also in the anti-Montanist decisions.[4] These decisions are, for all that, several decades prior to Tertullian. But the reference leads us further for another reason. The first synods of which we have records are those held against the Montanists. By these synods the followers of Montanus were "put out of the church and excluded from the *koinonia*." [5] This has all the marks of a formal excommunication. But in the first place it is enacted not by an individual bishop but by the synods in which "the believers of Asia assemble." These are not represented exclusively by bishops, though certainly there are some bishops present too. In the second place the exclusion is not from "an" *ecclesia*, but without limit or qualification from "the" *ecclesia*. Informing other congregations is here no great problem, for all the congregations of Asia represented at the synod would learn of the exclusion from their representatives. Beyond doubt the synods assume the right to exclude the heretics from the *whole* church.

Here the local congregation is finding a way out beyond the walls erected to establish boundaries between episcopal domains. We shall look at this more closely later. As far as excommunication is concerned, the road we have noted seems to reach its goal, at least for the time being, in Canon 5 of the Ecumenical Council of Nicaea.[6] Exclusion from one congregation is valid for all congregations. Because of possible abuses care is taken at the same time to have the exclusion enacted in one congregation checked by the provincial synod. This checking of each local excommunication by the now synodically organized and established church not only formally pronounces it binding on all but also insures against local arbitrariness. This general validity is no departure from the early days. On the contrary, if we are to suppose that a different view prevailed for a time, it marks a return to them. This does not answer the question whether the criteria of "unity" have not meanwhile considerably changed. To this question we shall also return later.

Canon 5 of Nicaea did not start anything new. From the time of Tertullian there is evidence enough of congregations advising one another of the excommunications that have taken place. Such communications naturally intend that the other churches will apply the practical consequences. Cyprian and Cornelius of Rome informed one another of the excommunications they had dealt with. Cyprian defended himself against the aspersion that he had omitted to do this in one case. The Synod of Antioch (268) which put Paul of Samosata out of the church sent word of this exclusion to the bishops of Rome and Alexandria as also to "all bishops who bear office with us in the whole world, to the presbyters and deacons and every Catholic *ecclesia* under heaven." In the same way Bishop Alexander of Alexandria sent a circular letter (κατὰ πόλιν) to all his fellow bishops informing them that he, together with other bishops, had put the anathema upon Arius and his followers.[7] This is also before Nicaea. Later Bishop Synesius of Cyrene sent a similar statement in the name of the church of Ptolemais to "all her sisters in the whole world." Here Andronicus and Theonas had been excluded together with their associates (*Ep.* 58). Self-evidently also the excommunications decided upon by general synods were made known through "the whole world."

This procedure could be more easily applied to notable heretics than to their many or few followers and sympathizers who were often scattered over whole provinces. The local congregation or bishop who knew them personally could indeed impose the regular consequences, but they could not prevent them from leaving that place and seeking admission in congregations elsewhere. Especially in large congregations the layman in particular would have no great difficulty in remaining undisclosed. In Alexandria it happened that a man heretically baptized, who never said a word about it, participated for years in the Eucharist of the orthodox congregation. Only after his conscience got the better of him did he denounce himself and so put Bishop Dionysius in confusion.[8]

Even after the ecclesiastical communication system was perfected in the established church, there was chance enough for the heretic to move elsewhere and so evade the excommunication which applied to him even though he was not expressly named in it. He was particularly tempted in this direction after he became liable also to police reprisals. The Council of Nimes (Nemausus, 396) had to deal with certain clergy who had come to Gaul after it was made clear that they were not welcome in the East. Their certification papers aroused suspicion because the signatures were unknown. They had most likely slipped out to the West under pressure of the heresy laws. Since their membership in a forbidden communion could not be clearly proved, they were, on the basis of their inadequate evidence of identity, excluded only from serving at the altar.[9] Others, excommunicated in Carthage, tried to sneak into church fellowship in Italy.[10] Theodoret called for the help of the imperial prefect against a cleric who did not seem to bother at all about the excommunication imposed on him. Empress Pulcheria herself did the same against a bishop for the same reason.[11] Still later Leontius of Byzantium knew of a Nestorian who under pressure from his brethren in the faith had himself numbered among the clergy of the majority church in order to fish in troubled waters.[12]

The anonymous heretics were not the only reason for the church's devising an ordered defense against deceivers. Already in the ardent early days the *Didache* is forced to give criteria for distinguishing between true and false itinerant prophets. If he stays longer then two days, he is a false prophet. "If one 'in the spirit' says, 'Give me money,' pay no attention to him" (cf. 1 Cor. 12:8-12; 2 John 10). An informative warning. It is not surprising that the vast social welfare work especially of the large congregations should also attract some less admirable characters. In the days of the great party strife this latter sort of attraction alternated with the party in power, that is, the party which at the moment enjoyed the favor of the civil government and its police force. From the fourth century there were congregations of differing confessions next to each other in the large towns and in many other places. Socrates tells of a man who had himself baptized several times in Constantinople and

"earned money by this technique." [13] He was first with the Arians, then
the Macedonians, and finally at his attempted entry among the Novatians
he was unmasked by Bishop Chrysanthos as a Jew. Because of such
attempts at deception, care had to be taken with every unknown applicant.
If it was possible to deceive in the same town by such switching back and
forth and sneaking in, then what of the traveler who turned up fresh
in quite another place?

As a defense against deceivers of one sort or another the church
developed its own methods of identification. In doubtful cases written
credentials were required before admission to the *koinonia*. The credentials vary in name and character. The oldest form are the *systatica*
(γράμματα συστατικὰ), Letters of Commendation, which are mentioned
already by Paul (2 Cor. 3:1). He himself furnished such a letter for the
deaconess Phoebe and gives notice of other similar letters. [14] The brethren
in Ephesus commend Apollos to the disciples in Greece, Ignatius his
countrymen who precede him to the congregation in Rome, and Polycarp
Crescens to the congregation in Philippi. [15] There has always been
the informal use of such commendations in the church. The first sort
of formal identifications are the Letters of Peace *(literae* or *libelli pacis)*.
They play a role in the controversy regarding the readmission of those
who lapsed in large numbers during the Decian persecution. We find
Cyprian occupied with them. These proceed from the idea that the
intercessions of the martyrs have power to wipe away the sins of the
lapsed. They were written up by the confessors who plead in them that
church fellowship be granted again to the lapsed. [16] These letters in themselves have nothing to do with intercourse between congregations or practically only insofar as the confessor and the lapsed for whom he vouches
might not have been of the same congregation.

The Council of Arles (314) directs that these letters from confessors
are to be taken from those who present them and be replaced by Letters
of Fellowship *(literae communicatoriae)*. [17] But why? These persons
obviously had been in need of the certificate issued by a confessor because there was something not in order with their membership in the
church fellowship. If this was given them, which is here presupposed —

otherwise they would have no credentials at all — then no further certification was necessary in their own congregation. The new certificate could only be designed as evidence of identity for a transfer to another congregation. This is demonstrated also by the Council of Elvira (306), which also uses the term Letters of Fellowship. Those who have these certificates are always to present themselves, particularly at the seat of the bishop, for the examination of their testimonials, to see if they are in order (Canon 58). Only travelers arriving from elsewhere are here obviously in mind. About local people everybody was informed. This synod is concerned to curtail the influence of confessors. It directs that only Letters of Fellowship should be issued. These do *not* contain the name of a confessor "because all simple folk are awed by the aura of this name" (Canon 25). This does not alter the fact that the certificate is intended for travelers who have to give proof of their identity in another place. The rule that women may not make bold to write to lay believers without their husbands' names or accept Letters of Peace *(literae pacificae)* in their own names (that is, without those of their husbands) is to be understood as referring to Letters of Commendation (Canon 31). The term used by this synod for the official certificates for travelers is Letters of Fellowship.

In the East we find the term Letter of Peace used for this. The Synod of Antioch (341) directs that "no stranger is to be received without a Letter of Peace" (Canon 7). Here the requirement of the certificate for every transfer is made a general rule.[18] These Letters of Peace (εἰρηνικαί) can no longer be serving the purpose of those *(libelli pacis)* issued during the persecutions. The last persecution already lay a full generation behind them. They have rather the same significance as the Letters of Fellowship mentioned in the councils of Spain and Gaul. They are the certificate universally required of Christians in a strange place as evidence toward their reception by a new congregation or its bishop. Special weight is laid on the reliability of the man who issues the certificate. Village priests are not allowed to issue any canonical communication but may only give informal information to their neighboring bishops. "Canonical" (κανονικὸς) here means testimonials which fulfill the requirements of the church canons.[19] On the other hand recognized "suffragan" bishops (rural bishops, found only in the East) may issue Letters of Peace. (Antioch, Canon 8)

A clear distinction between the terms seems not yet to have been made in the East at this time. The credentials *(systasis)* which according to the *Apostolic Constitutions* (c. 380) every stranger is to present to the deacon upon his entry into the congregation assembled for worship may well be the same certificate which is called Letter of Peace in Canon 7 of Antioch (above p. 131). In the following century the Council of Chalcedon distinguished quite sharply. It ruled that those without means of their own and those who needed help might travel only with "epistles or church Letters of Peace, not with *systasis* letters." The *systasis* letter, that is, the Letter of Commendation, should be reserved for those entitled to a special reception.[20] When we recall that the *systasis* letter was the customary certificate in the early days of Christianity, even though not formally called this, which was given even to a runaway slave to take along with him (Paul to Philemon), the change in the social structure of the church becomes only too clear. The Chalcedonian rule is remarkable not only for the preference shown to some people, but it also indicates the abuses that had to be contended with when the church became the church of the masses. This situation did not first arise after Chalcedon but was already there in the second half of the fourth century when those other synods took place. The regulating of the Letters of Fellowship or Letters of Peace was not prompted by the desire to solicit support for the bearers in other congregations. Such solicitation was of course not out of the question. For example, the letters of Bishop Basil of Caesarea are full of it, and the collected letters of Bishop Theodoret contain a whole series on behalf of one and the same Celestiacus (Epp. 32—36). But canonical testimonials, which every Christian was required to produce where he was a stranger, had a different purpose.

The conclusion that we drew from the prescription of the *Apostolic Constitutions* is confirmed by the Council of Carthage (345—48). It directs that no person, clerical or lay, may commune in another congregation "without a letter from his bishop" (Carthage I, Canon 7). Here the practical purpose is clearly expressed. Bishop Gratus gives the following basis for it. When a man is received by letter and the bishops are united, no one can slip unchecked *(latenter)* from the *communio* of one to that of another. Two things are apparent from this basis approved by the whole synod. The certificate issued by the home bishop contains first a declaration that there is no impediment to a man's being received forthwith. The applicant enjoys full church fellowship in his home congregation, is neither excommunicated nor in the class of the penitents. He can therefore be admitted to the Holy Communion without further ado. Secondly, by presenting his certificate he comes under the care of the bishop of the new congregation. He cannot then at will commune elsewhere.

This second operation of the certificate already becomes evident in a decision of the Council of Arles (314). Here they faced the question of how to deal with Christians who entered the service of the state. The Council of Elvira (306) still ruled that those who held the office of magistrate are "to keep away from the church" during their year of office, that is, they are not to attend the divine services (Canon 56). This was indeed self-evident since because of their office they could not avoid being implicated in the heathen state religion. Meanwhile, however, things had radically changed under Constantine. Arles directed that "presidents" *(praesides,* "governors") are to be given Letters of Fellowship. In contrast with the previous ruling, they may now participate in full church fellowship and so also the Holy Communion. Then the instruction is given that wherever they may be staying they are to receive the *cura* of the officiating bishop in that place.[21] *Cura* is ambiguous. It can mean care, that is, the bishop should give the governing official his counsel and aid. What follows, however, indicates that this is not what is intended. "If they begin to act contrary to the discipline (of the church), they are then finally to be excluded from the communion." The same is to be done with other state officials. This *cura* for leading state officials committed to the bishop evokes thoughts of the claims and conflicts we know of in the Middle Ages. Such thoughts would scarcely have been in the minds of the fathers at Arles in 314. No one can fault their applying the same standard to the highest persons in the state as were applied to other Christians, which meant also in some cases their excommunication. In any case this threat is only the reverse side of the Letters of Fellowship, which were furnished for them as for everyone else. Their certificates have the same significance as that established for all Christians by the Council of Carthage. They give the right to receive the Sacrament in another place and at the same time bind them to the bishop there.

The Letters of Fellowship or of Peace are evidence of the freedom of transfer in the church. The barrier of distance is overcome, and yet there are church boundaries. The assignment to the bishop of the new place indicates that no one can belong to "the church" without belonging to a specific parish. Here lies the guarantee that the boundaries of the orthodox confession will not be transgressed. Credentials are naturally only acknowledged by a bishop if they are issued by a man in church fellowship with him. The unorthodox churches next door do exactly the same.[22] The clerics already mentioned that occupied the attention of the Council of Nimes presented letters (epistolia) but with an "unknown signature." This was taken as evidence of "simulated religion."

Within the boundaries thus drawn there was an open welcome. By his enjoyment of church fellowship in the local congregation a Christian had part in the universal church fellowship of the whole church. The inclusion of the small circle in the great one found concrete expression in this that a Christian who transferred from one congregation to another might join in the Holy Communion there. Thus the altar fellowship of the local congregation was also embraced and upheld by the altar fellowship of the whole church.

The credentials of which we have spoken so far served as identification for laymen. For the clergy there were special arrangements, to which we shall come later.

Notes to Chapter 10

1. E. Hatch, *The Organization of the Early Christian Church* (London, 1888), pp. 171 f.
2. H. von Campenhausen, *Kirchliches Amt*, pp. 157 f.

3. Ibid., p. 156: "The bishop must content himself with holding his sheep together, and the judgment he can give on heretics has significance at most for his own but not for these themselves." The last part of this sentence is unintelligible to me. Does it mean that Bishop Ignatius indeed warns his own against the heretics but does not thereby pronounce a judgment upon the heretics themselves which has significance for his flock? There is no doubt about what Ignatius means when he declares that whoever denies that Christ is a "bearer of flesh" is himself a "bearer of death" (*Smyrn.*, 5, 2: *LCC*, I, 114), or further, "whoever sullies the faith of God with bad teaching" is " become unclean and will go into fire unquenchable." And then he adds, "so also whoever hearkens to him" (*Eph.*, 16, 1: *LCC*, I, 92). Or does Campenhausen mean that the heretics for their part did not acknowledge the judgment of the bishop? But where in all the world have heretics ever acknowledged the judgment of an "orthodox" bishop, especially when as in the case of Ignatius' congregations they are already "outside"? The moment they do that they are no longer heretics.

4. Ibid., p. 158, n. 3. Tertullian, *De pud.*, 7, 22: *ACW*, XXVIII, 72; *Against Praxeas*, 1: E. Evans, *Tertullian's Treatise Against Praxeas* (London, 1949), pp. 89 f., 130 f.

5. Thus the anonymous report in *H. E.*, V, 16, 10: Stevenson, p. 109.

6. Mansi, II, 672: Bright, pp. xf., 15 f.; Stevenson, pp. 359 f.

7. For Cyprian: *Ep.* 59, 1 and 9: Lacey, pp. 70 f.; for Antioch: *H. E.*, VII, 30, 2: Stevenson, pp. 354 ff.; for Alexander: Socrates, *H. E.*, I, 6: *PG*, 67, 44 ff.

8. *H. E.*, VII, 9, 2 ff.

9. Canon 1: *CCL*, 148, 50; Lauchert, pp. 183 f. Cf. Excursus II.

10. 11th Council of Carthage (407), Canon 11.

11. *Epp.* 42, 43; cf. 44 ff.: Schulze, IV, 1100 ff.

12. When he had qualms of conscience, the men who led him astray gave him the comfort that the bread consecrated by him as a type of the body of Christ carried at any rate more blessing than bread bought in the market or than that offered by the Philomarianites (Catholics) in the name of Mary. Leontius, *Adv. Incorr. et Nest.*, III, 6: *PG*, 86, 1364b.

13. διά ταύτης τῆς τέχνης χρήματα συνελέγετο, *H. E.*, VII, 17: *PG*, 67, 772c, d.

14. συστατικαὶ ἐπιστολαὶ, 2 Cor. 3:1; Rom. 16:1: συνίστημι; 1 Cor. 16:3.

15. Acts 18:27; Ignatius, *Rom.*, 10, 2: *LCC*, I, 106; Polycarp, *Phil.*, 14: *LCC*, I, 137.

16. The formal reconciliation, the readmission itself, was performed by the

bishop. Cf. Poschmann, *Paenitentia secunda,* pp. 2741, 374 ff., 399. Cyprian, *Epp.* 15, 22, 23: Lacey, pp. 9 ff.; Mortimer, p. 25.

17. Canon 9: *CCL,* 148, 11; Stevenson, p. 323

18. Zonaras, the medieval commentator, maintains indeed that the canon does not apply to all who remove to another place but only to the clergy (*PG,* 137, 1297). This is sheer eisegesis. The prescription of the preceding Canon 6 is expressly applied to laymen. Nobody is to be received who has been excommunicated by his own bishop, unless the synod as the court of appeal has decided in his favor. Canon 7 goes on immediately μηδένα ἄνευ εἰρηνικῶν δέχεσθαι τῶν ξένων. If the synod had intended to restrict this to the clergy, it would have been obliged to say so explicitly.

19. In the West *literae formatae,* 11th Council of Carthage (407), Canon 12; cf. *formata commendatio,* 3d Council of Carthage (397), Canon 28.

20. Canon 11: διὰ τὸ τὰς συστατικὰς ἐπιστολὰς προσήκειν τοῖς οὖσιν ἐν ὑπολήψει μόνοις παρέχεσθαι προσώποις. Zonaras and Balsamon take ἐν ὑπολήψει to mean of doubtful repute. The words permit this, but this would make no intelligible contrast with the first part of the canon which refers to πάντας τοὺς πένητας καὶ δεομένους ἐπικουρίας. The canon cannot mean that poor people of doubtful repute — a conceivable circumstance, to be sure — should be regarded as of doubtful repute because they are poor, and hence be denied Letters of Commendation. Zonaras would take the Letters of Peace of the first part about the poor to be ἐπιστολαὶ ἀπολυτικαὶ (*dimissoriae*) for the clergy. Balsamon follows him in this. *PG,* 137, 426a, 428b. This restriction to the clergy is simply read in here as also in Canon 7 of Antioch. Apparently these commentators (Zonaras, c. 1160; Balsamon, c. 1200) no longer have any notion that there was so much concern shown for laymen in the early church. In their day there was evidently no such thing any more as credentials for laymen. The contrast only makes sense when ἐν ὑπολήψει is understood of *personae honoratiores* or *clariores.* So it was taken by the old Latinists Dionysius Exiguus and Isidore, as Hefele points out, III, 398. He therefore also translates the ὑπόληψις of Canon 21 with "repute" (*Leumund,* ET p. 406: "testimony").

21. *Ab episcopo ejusdem loci cura illis agatur,* Canon 7: *CCL,* 148, 10; Stevenson, p. 323.

22. The Eunomians did not pray with anyone newly arrived, that is, they did not permit him to participate in their divine service unless he could prove that he was in doctrinal agreement with them (*homodox*). The written credentials they required had to show marks known only to them. Sozomen, *H. E.,* VII, 17: *PG,* 67, 1465a, b.

Bibliography for Chapter 10

Balsamon, Theodoros, Johannes Zonaras, and Alexios Aristenus. *In canones sanctorum apostolorum, conciliorum et in epistolas canonicas sanctorum patrum commentaria.* In W. Beveridge, *Synodicon* (Oxford, 1672), reprinted in *PG*, 137 and 138.

Evans, Ernest. *Tertullian's Treatise Against Praxeas.* London, 1949.

Harnack, A. "Literae formatae," *Realenzyklopaedie fuer protestantische Theologie und Kirche*, II, 536. Here also earlier literature.

Hatch, E. *The Organization of the Early Christian Church*, Bampton Lectures. 3d ed., London, 1888

Kober F. *Die Suspension nach den Grundsaetzen des kanonischen Rechts*, 1862.

―――. *Die Deposition und Degradation nach den Grundsaetzen des kanonischen Rechts*, 1867

Suicer, J. C. *Thesaurus Ecclesiasticus e Patribus Graecis*, 3d ed., 1764. Vols. 1 and 2. See ἀπολυτικὸς, εἰρηνικὸς, κανονικὸς, συστατικός.

11

FELLOWSHIP BETWEEN CHURCHES

For the individual Christian who removed to another place the problem of church fellowship was practically solved by the Letter of Peace. This certificate indicated to whom he should attach himself in the new place and guaranteed his reception into the fellowship of the local congregation there. The certificate did not only protect against deception, nor did it have only private significance. It also expressed the fellowship between the congregation which issued it and the congregation which acknowledged the document presented by the traveler. If now for "local congregation" we again say "church," we have here fellowship between churches. The term "local congregation" has been useful in the discussion where locality has been the major consideration (p. 64). Early Christian usage in fact uniformly employed *ecclesia* for both the local congregation and the whole church. Churches in the plural were long designated by the name of their town or province. However, as the individual episcopates emerged during the course of the second century, *ecclesia* came to mean the church under its bishop. There were exceptions. The bishop was not necessarily bound to a local *cathedra*.[1] For the fellowship of the whole church (κοινωνία τῆς καθολικῆς ἐκκλησίας, e. g., Chalcedon, Canon 4) these exceptions were incidental both to the theory and to what actually happened.

This fellowship, whether granted or refused, was determined by the corporately organized churches which after the second half of the second century were represented by their bishops. Eusebius records that the "catholic letters" of Bishop Dionysius of Corinth, by which he maintained fellowship beyond the borders of his own parish,[2] were directed to the individual churches. However, when he speaks of the Letter to the

Romans, he adds that it is addressed to the bishop there (Soter). In reply
to his letter to the Knossians, Dionysius received an answer from Pinytus,
the bishop there. Letters to the churches involved their bishops, and the
letters between bishops regarding their fellowship with one another involved also the churches they represented. The protagonists in the controversy about the date of Easter were all bishops. They assembled in
synods to deal with it and wrote letters expressing their position. Eusebius,
however, begins his report about all this with the information that the
controversy has divided "the parishes of Asia" and the "churches of all
the rest of the world." Bishop Polycrates of Ephesus "was the leader"
of the bishops of Asia. What he had written was approved by them when
they met together with him. Thereupon "the head of the church of the
Romans, Victor, attempted to exclude as heterodox all the *parishes* of
Asia en bloc together with the neighboring churches from the general unity and branded the brethren there as outside the fellowship
(ἀκοινωνήτους).[3] For better or for worse the churches were involved
in the lot of their bishops. They were received into fellowship with
them, and with them they were excluded.[4]

According to this it appears as if the bishops are solely responsible
for the fellowship. Church fellowship is, then, merely bishops' fellowship.
This would be in harmony with Cyprian's theory that the unity of the
church is guaranteed by the unity of the bishops. Even if this were so,
there are other things that must be settled first. Episcopal polity does
not by itself qualify for church fellowship. It is not the exclusive criterion
of orthodoxy.[5] Nor did the apostolic succession altogether achieve what
was expected of it (p. 53). In the second century the individual bishops'
churches lay next to one another independent in the management of their
affairs. Despite their similar polity they had their own peculiarities.
Each bishop had the obligation and power to examine his neighbors and
decide according to his own standards whether to practice fellowship with
them or not. As long as this was so, fellowship was rather fragilely constructed. It was in constant danger of being broken by divergent episcopal decisions. Far-reaching examples of this are the schisms between
Rome and the East on account of the date of Easter and heretical baptism.

The situation changed with the growth of synods and the development of metropolitan polity. From these emerged the possibility of bishops being unseated. Fellowship is then maintained between churches without the bishop and indeed in opposition to him. The Synod of Antioch (268), which was against Paul of Samosata, records a letter of Bishop Dionysius of Alexandria addressed "to the whole parish of Antioch" in which the bishop there "is neither honored with a greeting nor addressed in person" (*H. E.*, VII, 30, 3). We see from this that the connection between church and bishop is only conditional. It can be sacrificed for the unity of the church according to a higher criterion of unity. From this we may conclude that, in the case of a conflict, fellowship with the parish has precedence over that with its bishop. In this particular instance the Bishop of Alexandria dealt with the congregation of Antioch over the head of its bishop, and this before his dismissal. What here appears as a single instance was often repeated later.

To form larger working units, the bishops' churches joined together under the metropolitan and combined in synods. In the West this happened principally under the Bishop of Rome who there enjoyed precedence. One may speak in the plural of churches, for there were those of Africa, Spain, and Gaul, each united under its primate, and with the plural mean provincial churches. From among the metropolitans there emerged the chief metropolitans, who were later in the East called patriarchs. Thus the scope of action regarding fellowship grew ever wider. Common decisions for the whole church were made for the first time by the synod of "the 318 fathers" in Nicaea in 325. Whether it was in fact only a synod of the Roman Empire is not crucial here, for the same claims were made also by the following "ecumenical" councils.

Are we then to regard not only the unity of the church but also episcopal accord as the achievement of polity? What happened in the second and third centuries may then be regarded as the sicknesses of childhood. They simply lacked laws of ordered supervision. The cure was then in combining the bishops' churches together into a pyramid in which the middle ones, or in desperate cases the top one, could apply disciplinary measures to prevent or heal breaches in the fellowship. Our problem of church fellowship as fellowship between churches would then be no problem at all after Nicaea. At most it would remain merely a matter for disciplinary action.

In actual fact, however, the moment Nicaea had achieved the apparently maximum unity, the problem returned even more acutely. Now it became a thoroughly confessional problem. Each dissenting synod and party of the fourth century stood for some usually settled dogmatic formula of a particular confession. Episcopal polity appears wholly inadequate for holding things together. After Nicaea as before, the bishops were exponents not only of unity but also of disunity. The great anti-Nicene parties were lead by bishops. In this the following century shows not the slightest change. The great heresiarchs Nestorius, Dioscurus, and Severus were legitimate patriarchs of the established church. After Chalcedon the church in Armenia separated itself. In Persia it became Nestorian, in Syria and Egypt Monophysite. All had episcopal polity, and all were mindful to maintain the apostolic succession. There appears to be very little left of the unity of the episcopate which should, according to Cyprian, guarantee the unity of the church. In the great Councils we do not find anything like the ability to overcome an actual division by the dissidents being won over for the consensus by those who made up the majority at the time. The minority was outvoted or they walked out of the assembly before the decision was made. The consequence was the formation or fostering of separate churches.

There is no period in the early church when the question of the conditions and boundaries of church fellowship was not acute. It was already so in the time of Hegesippus, and quite intensely so after Nicaea. In the conflicts between provincial churches in the second and third centuries it is possible to indicate geographically the boundaries between the protagonists, and so also between one fellowship and another. After Nicaea the boundaries, at least in the East, cut right through the provinces and even through individual parishes.[6] Nicaeans, Semiarians, Eunomians, Macedonians, and Apollinarians confronted one another in the same locality. At the same time the pre-Nicene Novatians had their network of congregations through the same area, many parts of which still remained theirs for a long time. After Chalcedon the Monophysites must be added. They split further among themselves. All these often had their houses of worship next to one another, especially in the large towns. When the Emperor Anastasius I transferred (c. 500) the right of asylum from the "big church" in Constantinople to the churches of the heretics [7] the confessional scene in the capital may well have been as multicolored as in some cities of today.

There are grounds for the denial of fellowship which are acknowledged by only one party as divisive. When Victor of Rome broke fellowship with the churches of Asia Minor in the Easter controversy, Irenaeus' opposition to him was based on the principle that differences in customs do not give churches the right to deny one another fellowship.[8] He can quote the practice of Victor's predecessors, and Eusebius still acknowledges him to be in the right. The controversies about penitential practice, readmission of the lapsed, and heretical baptism went deeper. In the West particularly they divided and shook the church for a long time. They gave rise to the Novatians as a separate church. The orthodoxy of the Novatians was never called in question. They declared themselves for the dogma of Nicaea. Their separation was based on questions of discipline. Later in the East their record was so unblameworthy and they enjoyed such high respect that the only opposition to reunion came from their side.[9]

The schism of the Donatists was also based on differences in discipline. They could as little be charged with heretical dogmas as the Novatians. Nevertheless, their churches were seized with the help of the police, and participation in their divine service was made a capital offense. That their fate was different from that of the Novatians cannot merely be blamed on the civil heresy laws, which were the same in both East and West. Rather we must say that the way in which the relationship between churches was regulated in Africa would not have been what it was but for the theological basis provided for it by Augustine. The method of execution had indeed already been applied to Priscillian and other leaders of the movement in Spain named after him. In this instance we find Bishop Martin of Tours in brave but fruitless opposition. The way he

FELLOWSHIP BETWEEN CHURCHES

FELLOWSHIP BETWEEN CHURCHES

dealt with heretics shows that the whole catholic church of this period did not suffer the incubus of Augustine's almost frivolous arguments. Fellowship with orthodox but intriguing bishops seems to have caused the saintly Martin much distress.[10]

There is one ground for the denial of church fellowship about which there was never anywhere a difference of opinion in the early church, not even between East and West. Heterodoxy breaks the fellowship ipso facto. The basic foundation for this we have seen when considering the local congregation. What is true there is true also between churches. The divisive significance of dogma is only one side of the matter. Dogma is not only the binding doctrinal norm for those who teach in the church, but it is also the confession of all the members who are included in the "We confess" or "We believe." For this reason doctrine is the point at which the unity of the church is most grievously wounded and therefore the point at which also the wounds must again be healed. Where church fellowship is broken by heterodoxy, it can only be restored by the achievement of doctrinal unity. Doctrinal unity is part and parcel of orthodoxy. The truly sound faith leads "to fellowship and unity with those who believe the same." [11] Until the opposite is proven, what a man says is accepted as that which he really thinks (φρονεῖ). In the excommunications of the heresiarchs all who think "his thoughts" or "the same" are also included.[12] Similarly the heirs of the Nicene Fathers "who proclaimed the same *kerygma*" are at one in their "thoughts of the faith." Threatening divisions are to be avoided by a renewal of the Nicene faith so that thus those "who think the same would be led to unity." [13] What episcopal polity was to have done for the unity of the church was first achieved by dogma: doctrinal unity in orthodoxy. Doctrinal unity means accord in the "understanding of the faith" (φρόνημα τῆς πίστεως). This may not be subjectively misunderstood. Dogma is an expression of the faith, a confession of what is believed. It is not the personal act of believing that forms the unity but what is believed.

This is true for all Christians. It is true in a special way for bishops. Unless he is contradicted, a bishop may regard himself as united in the faith with his own congregation. Since he has the office of teacher, he represents what is taught both within and without. For this he does not have to be a professor. Dogma is the basic stuff of the whole divine service (p. 111). He is thus a constant defender against heresy. As soon as some alien doctrine arises, he is drawn into controversy by virtue of his office. Once, in the time of Hegesippus and Irenaeus, the bishops stood next to one another in isolated independence. The orthodoxy of another had to be determined from case to case. This was no longer so already in the third century and certainly not in the fourth. Then the bishops met one another at synods, which were soon regular practice. As theological questions arose, they became the common concern of the bishops. In their letters to one another the voice of each had its place in asking questions and offering answers. We see how doctrinal unity is always in question. It is not an assured possession but an unremitting task. Since doctrinal unity is always corporate, it can only be maintained jointly. Church fellowship which depends on doctrinal unity needs its special channels of communication.

Before we come to these, however, there is one notion that we must deal with first. This is the idea that only the bishops, or at most only the intellectual upper crust, had any interest in the dogmatic disparities. This notion was fostered in the church by Origen's distinction between the learned and the simple. Origen made theology a science, and every science is by nature aristocratic. A great deal of the literature of that whole period is plainly beyond the majority of laymen. The same could probably be said of many a bishop. This, however, does not prove that the many had neither understanding nor concern for the theological controversies. To be sure, the unrelenting prosecution of the dogmatic controversies was at no point halted out of consideration for the "immature." Nothing, however, was hidden from them. For Athanasius theology was no occult science, nor did it become so wherever his influence reached. Gregory of Nyssa records that a man became involved in discussions about the Christological controversies with the money changer, the baker, and at the baths.[14] He himself found this burdensome, and like Origen he distinguished between theological experts and greenhorns. The very thing that is tiresome to him is vivid evidence of the responsiveness of the bulk of church members. The great "theological addresses" of Gregory of Nazianzus were given publicly in the capital. They summarize the results of the whole theological controversy since Athanasius even to the fine dogmatic points. Tireless shorthand reporters, who as in our own day were the ears of an interested public, took them down and so preserved for us the doctrinal theology of many teachers of the church.

Lay participation was, one may almost say self-evidently, not less vigorous among the opposition parties, for contradiction of orthodox church doctrine has always enjoyed an appreciative public. Already in the first Christological controversies at the end or the second century and the beginning of the third the spokesmen were no "theologians." Two of them who happened to share the same name Theodotus were distinguished as the Cobbler and the Money Changer. There was hardly anything which irritated Bishop Basil of Caesarea quite so much as the close ties between the heretics and the people.[15] Church political agitation cannot alone explain the uproar among the masses concerning Mary's title of Mother of God. The battle about Chalcedon raged through all classes. In the "big church" at Constantinople there was a general brawl caused by Monophysite heckling during the liturgy.[16] The circus parties, the "Blues" and the "Greens" which divided internal Byzantine politics, aligned themselves on opposite sides in the conflict between orthodoxy and Monophysitism.[17] These none-too-pleasant accompaniments nevertheless destroy the notion that confessional differences had interest only for professional dogmatists and left the mass of church members unmoved. Monophysitism was altogether a movement of the masses. Theology first became a secret science when it became scholastic and a craft of interest only to the guild. This was far from the case at the time of the great doctrinal controversies and consequent divisions.

Notes to Chapter 11

1. Eusebius reports that "it is said" that the Evangelist Mark founded "churches" in Alexandria, that is, several in one and the same town (*H. E.*, II, 16). Obviously this means congregations and not church buildings. We also find Bishop Julian in 178 receiving "the episcopate over the churches

(plural!) in Alexandria" (*H. E.,* V, 9). At this time there was only one bishop in all Egypt. He is called Bishop of Alexandria according to his *cathedra,* and yet he exercised his episcopal office over the churches (i. e., congregations) throughout Egypt.

There still are other examples of local congregations which have the name *ecclesia* but not their own bishop (Karl Mueller, *"Beitraege,"* pp. 5 ff.). On the other hand, there are bishops unconnected with a local *cathedra.* The best-known examples of this are the "bishops of the Goths," and on the eastern boundary of the Roman Empire there were the bishops of the nomadic Arab tribes who were called "bishops of the Saracens" or something similar.

2. This is the usual term for a diocese in the ancient Eastern church (1 *Clem.,* 1, 1: *LCC,* I, 43; similarly the preface of the *Martyrdom of Polycarp* sent by Smyrna to Philomelium: *LCC,* I, 149). Diocese is the customary term in the West (*H. E.,* IV, 23, 1).

3. *H. E.,* V, 23 and 24: Stevenson, pp. 147 ff.

4. As a Montanist Tertullian repudiated the spiritual authority of the "church as the sum of the bishops" (*De pud.,* 21, 17: *LCC,* V, 77; *ACW,* XXVIII, 122). However, in his earlier polemic against the heretics he regarded the succession of bishops as a guarantee that "we have fellowship with the apostolic churches" (*De praescr.,* 21, 7: *LCC,* V, 44). In the controversy about heretical baptism Stephen of Rome declared that he would have no more fellowship "with Helenus, Firmilian, with all of Cilicia, Cappadocia, and Galatia, and so in turn with all neighboring peoples." This put an end to the fellowship of the *church* of Rome with all the *churches* of these provinces (*H. E.,* VII, 5, 4). Basil wrote to the congregation at Neocaesarea that the maintenance or final severance of the ties with it would depend on which shepherd (i. e., which new bishop) they would support. (*Ep.* 28, 3: *PG,* 32, 309; Deferrari, I, 168)

5. The Theodotians put up the Confessor Natalius as their own bishop in Rome — at a monthly salary of 150 denarii, adds the malicious report of Hippolytus (*H. E.,* V, 28, 10: Stevenson, p. 157). In Syria and Pontus bishops of the majority church attached themselves to the Montanists. They had village bishops and later indeed bishops in Constantinople (Hippolytus, *Comm. on Daniel,* IV, 18 f.; Sozomen, *H. E.,* VII, 19: *PG,* 67, 1476a; *Justinian Code,* I, 5, 20). In Adamantius even Marcion is called bishop by one of his followers (*Dial.,* I, 8: *GCS,* 16, 34). The polity of the Novatians was the same as that of the majority church. Augustine speaks of bishops among the Manichaeans (*De haer.,* 46).

6. Naturally, the parties could still be given some geographical boundaries. After the separation of East and West at the Council of Sardica (c. 343), the church boundary was a range of mountains between Illyria and Thrace. To Socrates, who points this out (*H. E.*, II, 22), such a drawing of a boundary seemed an especially sad sign of church confusion because a part of the church in the East was conformable with the West, although it had not at this time broken fellowship with the party whose dogma was opposed by the West

7. Theodore the Lector, II, 24.

8. *H. E.*, V, 24, 13 ff.: Stevenson, pp. 149 f. This statement of Irenaeus is referred to in the Augsburg Confession, XXVI, 44.

9. Basil later lumped them together as Cathari with the Encratites and Hydroparastatae (*Ep.* 188, Canon 1: *PG,* 32, 668; Deferrari, III, 15). That relentless foe of all heretics, the Emperor Theodosius I, granted the Novatians freedom to practice their religion beside the established church (Socrates, *H. E.*, V, 10 ff. Cf. N. Q. King, *The Emperor Theodosius and the Establishment of Christianity* [London, 1961], pp. 54 ff.). Socrates relates of the Novatian bishop in the capital (Paul, d. 439) that "at his funeral he in a way made all the different confessions (αἱρέσεις) into one church, for they all accompanied his body to the grave with the singing of psalms" (*H. E.*, VII, 16). Of what other bishop of the early church do we hear such a thing?

10. Sulpicius Severus, *Chronicle*, II, 50, 5; *Dialogue*, III, 11 ff.

11. ὁμοδόξοις, Basil, *Ep.* 28, 3; 82: *PG,* 32, 309c; 460b; Deferrari, I, 170; II, 98.

12. Flavian against Nestorius: πρὸς τὰ αυτοῦ φρονοῦντας ἢ λέγοντας, Hahn, p. 321. Union formula of 633, Canon 8: τοὺς τὰ ὅμοια αὐτῶν φρονήσαντας ἢ φρονοῦντας, Hahn, p. 339.

13. Basil, *Ep.* 52, 1; 92, 3: *PG,* 32, 392 c; 481 c; Deferrari, I, 128; II, 140.

14. *PG,* 46, 577b. Cf. D. L. Sayers, *The Emperor Constantine* (London, 1951), pp. 119 ff

15. *Ep.* 243, 4 *fin.; PG,* 32, 909; Deferrari, III, 447.

16. Theodore the Lector, II, 26

17. The literature about the Blues and Greens (Y. Janssens and H. Grégoire) discussed by F. Doelger (*Byzantinische Zeitschrift*, 1937, pp. 525 ff., 542 f.) was inaccessible for this study. Cf. W. Schubart, *Justinian und Theodora*, 1943, p. 85. For the same parties in Antioch, see V. Schultze, *Altchristliche Staedte und Landschaften*, III, *Antiocheia*, 1930, p. 363.

Bibliography for Chapter 11

Algermissen, K. *Konfessionskunde,* 6th ed., 1950.

Foerster, Erich. "Genossenschaft und Konfoederation in der alten Kirchenge-schichte," *Zeitschrift fuer Kirchengeschichte,* LXI (1942), 104 ff.

Harnack, A. *The Constitution and Law of the Church in the First Two Centuries,* trans. F. Pogson, ed. H. Major, London, 1910.

Heiler, F. *Urkirche und Ostkirche,* 1937.

Kattenbusch, Ferdinand. *Lehrbuch der vergleichenden Konfessionskunde,* I, 1892.

King, N. Q. *The Emperor Theodosius and the Establishment of Christianity.* London, 1961.

Koeninger, A. M. *Grundrisz einer Geschichte des katholischen Kirchenrechts,* 1919.

Milasch, N. *Das Kirchenrecht der morgenlaendischen Kirche,* trans. R. von Pressic, 1905.

Mueller, Karl. "Beitraege zur Geschichte der Verfassung in der alten Kirche," *Abhandlungen der preussischen Akademie der Wissenschaft, Phil.-hist. Kl.* (1922), No. 3.

Schultze, Victor. *Altchristliche Staedte und Landschaften, III, Antiocheia* (1930).

Sohm, R. "Das altkatholische Kirchenrecht und das Dekret Gratians," *Festschrift fuer Ad. Wach,* 1918.

12

FELLOWSHIP BY LETTER

Fellowship between churches was actually practiced for the most part by messengers, traveling clergy, and visiting bishops. The churches, however, did not only wish to have ties with one another but also wanted to participate in the *koinonia* of the whole church. Individual visits or messages were not enough. There was a need for the development of written communications. These could be copied many times and sent on from place to place and so reach even the remotest congregation called Christian.

Circular letters (Letters to Everywhere) were sent out by the episcopal synods convened in Palestine, Rome, Pontus, and Osroene to deal with the Easter controversy. In these letters they declared their position.[1] The Palestinians asked that every congregation receive a copy of their document. They reported that they themselves had forwarded letters to Alexandria and received them from there (*H. E.*, V, 25). In this statement they volunteered as postal transmitting station for their area. In the third century it was regular procedure in the West for noteworthy communications between churches, which now means practically between bishops, to be forwarded from the smaller to the larger and so on to the provincial seat and thence to Rome, from where they were forwarded in reverse sequence to the other provinces.[2] In the East there was no central clearing house, but presumably there, too, regular reports on official business — for example, the appointment of a new bishop — were passed along in a similar manner.[3] In addition, official letters were naturally exchanged directly between the bishops and especially the great metropolitans. The bishops of Rome, Carthage, Corinth, Alexandria, Antioch, and others wrote without any intermediary even to distant congregations not within their own pastoral care.

The Synod of Antioch (268) informs all the bishops and churches of the whole world that Paul of Samosata is deposed (p. 128). At the end of its encyclical it announces the appointment as bishop of Antioch of Domnus, a man adorned with all the qualities of a bishop, in the place of the excommunicated Paul. It then adds that people should write to him and receive from him "the Letter of Fellowship."[4] The definite article suggests that already then it was customary for bishops to exchange Letters of Fellowship upon entry into their office. The specific instruction given in this case had some particular point. The deposed Paul of Samosata refused to surrender the church building. His opponents appealed to Emperor Aurelian to take a hand. The emperor's decision was to give the building to those with whom the bishops of Italy and the city of Rome exchanged letters.[5] This action of the emperor came four years after Bishop Paul was deposed and shows that even then a considerable part of the congregation must still have held to him. The heathen emperor had no notion of the dogmatic issue himself. His criterion for deciding for one of the local parties was its fellowship with the bishops in Italy and in the imperial capital while the other party stood isolated. The more widely connected fellowship of the party approved seemed to him to be demonstrated by its exchange of letters. This explains why the synod was so insistent about the exchange of Letters of Fellowship between Bishop Domnus, whom it appointed, and the other churches. Aurelian was most likely prompted by political considerations. Christians indeed may have suggested to him that the exchange of letters produced and demonstrated a good piece of effective church government and also a piece which may have achieved some notoriety during those years because of the synod's pertinacity.

Nowadays the exchange of letters seems to us no more than a mechanical means of exchanging views and reports, at times indeed an unavoidable evil or a bother which might just as well be disposed of over the telephone. It meant rather more in the early church. The letters between Cyprian of Carthage and Cornelius of Rome and his successors disclose their eminently practical significance both in the time of persecution and for the government of the church as it faced threatening divisions. Such letters meant even more. They were part of what was essential for recognizing the *koinonia*. That the whole church is one body is the fact on which Alexander of Alexandria bases his circular letter in which he tells of the exclusion of Arius and his followers. Because the Holy Scripture bids us keep the bond of unity and peace, it follows (ἀκόλουθόν ἐστιν) that we are to write and to tell one another what is going on so that when one member suffers or rejoices, we also suffer and rejoice together with him. Theodoret makes the same request of Domnus of Apamea on the basis of the "law of brotherly love." Basil writes to Ambrose that the Lord has given us two ways of mutual recognition: personal meeting and correspondence. In writing to the congregation in Neocaesarea he enumerates 15 provinces in the East and West and proves his fellowship with their bishops by the fact that they all "write letters to us and receive them from us." He does not need to tell what the letters were about; the fact of their exchange is itself proof of church fellowship.[6]

When their matter was theological or ecclesiastical, they were not merely a means of doing business but had the character of a confession. In both an exchange of letters and a conversation there is a certain back and forth. In conversation there is no finality about each statement. Correction is possible without shame even if there are stenographers present. At the end there may be unity or disunity; from the beginning both are possible. The same can also be the case with an exchange of letters, and there are numerous examples of this in the collections of letters from the early church. However, the church letters cited above and those which the bishops regularly exchanged as Letters of Fellowship are not of this tentative, conversational sort. They do not strive toward unity but are its evidence and proof. Such letters document the man who writes them. He is identified with what leaves his hand "black on white." The man who receives the letter has in his hand not merely a letter but also the man who wrote it. This need not bother anybody, however, for unity is a presupposition not subject to doubt by either party. Such an exchange of church letters, whether between two or many, does not purport to carry on a conversation with the proviso of subsequent correction. This is meant to be solid documentary evidence of churchly harmony, accord, and doctrinal agreement.

We see from many Synodical Letters [7] that this state of affairs was not something to be taken for granted. Every such letter was indeed the product of a synodical resolution and therefore a document of fellowship, but for the time being this was true only of its own synodical compass. Synodical Letters could indeed be directed to another individual church and become an expression of mutual fellowship with it.[8] Or this might be more widely achieved as in the case of the letters mentioned earlier which were written by the synods engaged in the Easter controversy and which were directed "to all." In this case the fellowship thus expressed embraced considerable sections of East and West. Eusebius mentions further concurring letters from the congregations in Gaul under Bishop Irenaeus, and a similarly concurring personal letter from Bishop Bachyllus of Corinth (*H. E.*, V, 23). The fellowship, however, did not embrace the whole church, for those of Asia Minor dissented. Later the Synodical Letter developed into an important weapon in the dogmatic controversies. It often contained a comprehensive statement of church doctrine and thus had the character of a confession. An example of this is the Synod of Alexandria's Synodical Letter which was composed by Cyril of Alexandria and directed against Nestorius.[9] Synodical Letters also warned heretics or pronounced their excommunication, and blow followed blow. Theodoret tells of more than 50 Synodical Letters (and that means as many synods) which came out against Cyril's "Twelve Articles." [10]

The Letters to Everywhere (πανταχόσε or πανταχοῦ, encyclicals, circular letters) do not expect an answer. They appeal in their way to the unity of the church or presuppose it. They do not, however, always give evidence of that accord as may be seen in those of the Easter controversy.[11] They serve, for example, as the method of announcing excommunications to the "whole church" or "all the world" (p. 128). In the encyclical already mentioned Alexander of Alexandria complains that Bishop Eusebius of Nicomedia has also "dared to write everywhere." [12] And what he writes, Alexander feels, is evidence not of like-mindedness but of evil-mindedness, that is, sheer false doctrine. All this is still before Nicaea. That synod was to restore concord. Yet even after it the same Eusebius together with two other bishops sent out "the symbol of their heretical unbelief everywhere." [13] Similarly the followers of Eudoxius and Aetius spread their heretical tomes "everywhere." Each general encyclical laid claim to catholicity. Here there are two, and later three, claiming catholicity against each other. The general encyclical became a document of fractured unity. [14]

In this situation the Letters of Fellowship assume a new function. As before they are evidence of harmony and doctrinal concord, but their compass is now bounded by the presence of heterodoxy. Heretics can and must be combated. Spoken and written appeals can publicly be made to them to return, but no Letters of Fellowship can be exchanged with them. The last resort is to tell them that fellowship with them is at an end (ἀκοινωνησία). This is what the Egyptian monks did with Simeon Stylites because he lived on a pillar, such a thing as they had never heard of before. [15] The call to demonstrate an existing unity of faith was the more urgent when it was confronted by some outbreak of division. Firmilian of Caesarea gives thanks to God that Cyprian's letter regarding heretical baptism had, despite the distance between them, assured their fellowship as much as if they lived in the same house (Cyprian *Ep.* 75, 1). He then makes it clear that for this they are indebted to their common opposition to Stephen of Rome, who threatened to break off fellowship with the people of Asia Minor on account of this question. Basil complains of the growing pressure of the anti-Nicene majority in his domain. The pressure is not merely external. Already the congregations have grown used to heretic baptisms, funerals, visits to the sick, charitable works, and celebrations of the Eucharist. If this state of affairs continues any longer, the congregations will lose their appreciation of the truth. [16] In this situation he turns to the brethren and bishops in Italy, Gaul, and all the West, with whom he knows he is in doctrinal agreement, and calls to them with the repeated appeal: "Write us letters!" [17] They not only strengthen us, he says, but also give proof before the whole world of the great fellowship of the orthodox. He entreats Athanasius for a clear word against Marcellus of Ancyra, who is deposed in the East but has again found recognition in Rome. This he asks "so that it may not be like fighting in the night, when friend and foe are indistinguishable." [18] In the struggle with the Arians he asked Athanasius to write to those who are in doctrinal agreement and are ready for *koinonia* and unity, and to ask them to begin meeting with them.[19]

We find the same thing in the other parties. Especially where they are in a minority or under political pressure they feel a particular urgency to express their fellowship by demonstration of the doctrinal concord. This is true of the three Monophysite patriarchs, Theodosius of Alexandria, deposed Severus of Antioch, and Anthimus of Constantinople, who voluntarily withdrew from his office in the established church. In 536 they exchanged "letters of fellowship," "letters of the league of fellowship," "canonical letters of agreement and unanimity," and "letters of agreement and fellowship." By rejecting the teaching of the Council of Chalcedon in these letters, they confessed adherence to the Nicene Creed and the Henoticon, and on the basis of this doctrinal agreement they assured one another of fellowship. Here is a classic example of a multilateral exchange of Letters of Fellowship in the early church. Zacharias Rhetor gives a full account of these writings.[20] The fellowship existing among the three bishops was confirmed and put into proper and legitimate order by their exchange of letters.

It is impossible to idealize the polemical methods employed in the early church, the partisan strife, or the use of police repression. From Paul of Samosata to Luther we find, it seems almost inevitably, the ascription of loose morals to the dogmatically suspect. But such slander was usually mutual. To each of the heterodox from Arius to Severus orthodox usage regularly affixed the epithet "scandalous" (δυσσεβής). On the other side the Arian Philostorgius could not keep himself from spreading evil rumors about even such a man as Athanasius. There are indeed some modern historians who believe that the dogmatic position of Cyril of Alexandria finds its explanation in his bad character. There were indeed also those like Theodoret who knew how to leave a sinking ship in time and the next instant bob up among the victorious party.

Incomparably more numerous, however, were those in all parties who also suffered for the dogma they upheld. If we review it all, we may well agree here with the historian Evagrius, who already sees the Christological controversies from some distance. He observes that none of the participants, not even the heretics, "deliberately wished to revile." Rather, while all stand on the common ground of Trinitarian dogma, each "believed that he was saying something better with his doctrine than others before him." [21]

In our search for the cause and meaning of the church divisions such an irenic view can mislead us as easily as the mutual calumnies in the hurly-burly of the fourth and fifth centuries. In both cases we may be inclined to find the cause in the people who participated, thinking that they separated or united according to the divergence or convergence of their personal impulses. This makes nonsense of the church's theological argument. It is in fact possible to give an accurate account of the dogmatic argument without so much as naming the participants. The modalistic Christology (c. 200) and the opposing dynamistic both have truth in them. The evaluation of this in no way depends on the names or personalities of the representatives. The same is true of the whole doctrinal controversy in the following century and on to that regarding Monotheletism. The only reason why the student of this doctrinal history needs to know the persons concerned is that in their writings he can trace the impulses inherent in the matter itself which move the argument along.

The Letters of Fellowship themselves are instructive examples of how the matter leads the persons and not the persons the matter. The participants do not join themselves together to dispose of some common matter. Rather the common matter, whether Nicaea or Anti-Nicaea, Chalcedon or Henoticon, is the a priori of their fellowship. It can happen that a newly established fellowship may soon fall apart again, as was the case after Nicaea's too slick papering over of actual differences. On the other hand a genuine accord, such as that between Severus and Julian of Halicarnassus, may break under the impact of some new question. In every case it is dogma that either makes or impedes the fellowship.

As soon as Letters of Fellowship or other church letters are limited to a specific compass, we have division among churches. The boundary is not the cause of the division but its consequences. The cause of the division is the dogmatic disjunction. This expresses the constitutive significance which dogma has for church fellowship. Dogma is confession. If there is no confessional concord, the unity of the church and so also church fellowship are, at the very least, in doubt. Breaking fellowship does not always immediately follow the outbreak of dogmatic differences. To be sure, little time was lost in excommunicating the heterodox, but the intention in putting them out of the church altogether was to keep the church undivided. Only when it became clear that this was not being achieved, that excluded bishops in fact remained at their posts or others continued in fellowship with them, only then did rupture of fellowship between one church and another become a reality.

How the practice matched the theory is another question. In the party strife after Nicaea and despite all the excommunications and all the diverging resolutions of provincial synods on all sides, men clung to the fiction of the unity of the established church. The pressure of the civil power gave support to this. It is always interested in the external unity of the church.[22] In the church itself there were always earnest misgivings as men contemplated the formal rupture of church fellowship. Basil applies the picture of the church as the body of Christ to the relation of churches with one another.[23] In the East he sees the church already divided; the heretics are in the majority. In this situation Basil uses this picture as the basis of his call to the West for help. Actually his application of the picture does not go beyond the churches who remain orthodox. So much, however, is clear that even when church fellowship is revoked it may not happen without reference to the body of Christ.[24]

There was never any doubt that the manifest heretic who refused instruction should be "cut out" (ἐκκόπτεσθαι in excommunication formulas). In the case of a bishop, however, does that mean his whole church too? In the regular administration of affairs each church grants or denies fellowship through its representative, the bishop.[25] We have, however, already observed Dionysius of Alexandria circumventing the bishop and writing directly to the congregation in Antioch. The justification for this is that the bishop there was in his eyes a manifest heretic. Fellowship between churches is not merely between bishops but rather between all the members of one church with those of another, and it can therefore remain intact even when the bishop is put out. Such fellowship is the prerequisite of welcome into another church, and this condition is guaranteed by issuing and mutually recognizing credentials. But the credentials are boundaries too. The boundary runs between orthodoxy and heterodoxy. The hierarchical unity of the episcopate and orthodoxy are both criteria of the unity of the church. However, when these two come into collision, orthodoxy has the unqualified preeminence. One may never have fellowship with a heterodox bishop even though everything else about him may be canonically impeccable. One may, however, have fellowship with an orthodox congregation even without, or indeed in opposition to, its heretical bishop.

On this side of the boundary between orthodoxy and heterodoxy there is doctrinal agreement (homodoxy), and this manifests itself in the exchange of Letters of Fellowship. The same is true on the other side of the boundary, where the terms orthodoxy and heterodoxy are merely transposed. There is of course more to church fellowship than the exchange of Letters of Fellowship, and yet, however else it may manifest itself, its expressions never transgress the boundary of doctrinal agreement.

Notes to Chapter 12

1. δι' ἐπιστολῶν ἐκκλησιαστικὸν δόγμα τοῖς πανταχόσε διετυποῦντο, *H. E.*, V, 23, 2: Stevenson, p. 148. τύπος (διετυποῦντο) indicates a certain pattern, *forma*, the beginning of the *literae formatae*. See ch. 10, n. 19. Also see Edward B. Pusey, *The Councils of the Church* (Oxford, 1857), p. 51.

2. Rudolph Sohm, *Kirchenrecht*, I, 361.

3. Evagrius says of Severus of Antioch (*H. E.*, IV, 4): μάλιστα ἐν ταῖς καλουμέναις ἐνθρονιστικαῖς συλλαβαῖς καὶ ταῖς τούτων ἀμοιβαίαις, ἃς διεπέμψατο τοῖς ἑκασταχοῦ πατριάρχαις. ἐνθρονιστικὴ is the announcement of a bishop's enthronement, and ἀμοιβαία obviously that of his reception.

4. τὰ γράμματα κοινωνικά, *H. E.,* VII, 30, 17. Cf. Stevenson, pp. 356 f.

5. *H. E.,* VII, 30, 19: Stevenson, p. 280.

6. For Alexander see Socrates, *H. E.,* I, 6. Theodoret, *Ep.* 87; similarly *Ep.* 62, 122; κοινωνικὰ γράμματα, *H. E.,* IV, 22, 27: Parmentier, p. 258, 10. Basil, *Ep.* 197, *in.;* 204, 7: *PG,* 32, 709; 753: Deferrari, III, 91; 173.

7. *Literae synodicae* (γράμματα συνοδικὰ) can also mean the convocation of a synod by the metropolitan. Kober, *Deposition,* p. 492.

8. The Africans to Spanish congregations in Cyprian, *Ep.* 67: Lacey, pp. 111 ff.; the Milan Council to Rome, Mansi, III, 664; a Synod of Antioch to Peter Mongo of Alexandria, Zacharias Rhetor, *H. E.,* V, 10 ff.: Hamilton and Brooks, pp. 126 ff.; Pusey, p. 276.

9. Hahn, pp. 310 ff.; *LCC,* III, 349 ff.; Bindley, pp. 108 ff., 212 ff.

10. *Ep.* 112: Schulze, IV, 1185

11. An "ecumenical" council can also send an *epistola synodica* to a specific address, as did that of Nicaea to the "brethren in Egypt, Libya, and Pentapolis" concerning the Meletian schism there. Socrates, *H. E.,* I, 9: Stevenson, pp. 368 ff.

12. Socrates, *H. E.,* I, 6: *PG,* 67, 45 a.

13. Philostorgius, II, 7

14. Ibid., IV, 11. When his encyclical of 475 "for the unity of the holy churches [plural] of God" had the reverse effect, the usurper Basiliscus had to send out after it a counterencyclical (ἀντεγκύκλιον). Evagrius, *H. E.,* III, 4, 7: Bidez-Parmentier, pp. 100 ff., 106 f.

15. Theodore the Lector, II, 41

16. *Ep.* 243, 4: *PG,* 32, 909; Deferrari, III, 447.

17. *Eps.* 90, 204, 243, 263, et passim. Pusey, pp. 273 f.

18. *Ep.* 69: Deferrari, II, 47

19. *Ep.* 82: Deferrari, II, 99

20. Zacharias Rhetor, *Hist. misc.,* IX, 21—26: Ahrens-Krueger, pp. 212—236; Hamilton and Brooks, pp. 271—295.

21. *H. E.,* I, 11: Bidez-Parmentier, p. 18, 16.

22. For the relationship between the Arians and the Meletians in Egypt and of the Arians toward one another see Sozomen, *H. E.,* II, 21. Cf. Greenslade, pp. 151 f.

23. *Ep.* 243, 1: *PG,* 32, 901 f.; Deferrari, III, 435 f.

24. The Henoticon of Emperor Zeno (482) desires "that the holiest churches be united and members join hands with members." The devil has ever been

intent on divisions "because he knows how the whole body of the church is weakened by discord." Evagrius, *H. E.*, III, 14: Bidez-Parmentier, p. 112, 4; H. Bettenson, *Documents of the Christian Church*, 2d ed., (London, 1963), p. 124.

25. The church in the West knew the exclusion of a bishop from the fellowship of other bishops. Here the excluded bishop retained all his other rights and functions within his own diocese. The members of his diocese were affected insofar as his *literae formatae*, and so also the credentials he issued (Letters of Fellowship and Commendation), were not recognized by other bishops. When they therefore traveled outside their home diocese, they were, like their bishop, unable to receive Holy Communion. Leo the Great, for example, imposed this kind of exclusion on those bishops of the so-called Robber Council who were unwilling to acknowledge their fault (Kober, *Kirchenbann*, pp. 43 ff.). This sort of exclusion was unknown in the East.

Bibliography for Chapter 12

See bibliography for Chapter 10.

Bettenson, Henry. *Documents of the Christian Church*. 2d ed., London, 1963.

Diamantopoulos, A. N. *Basile le Grand et Rome*. This was inaccessible to me. Cf. B. Altaner, *Patrology*, trans. H. C. Graef (Edinburgh-London, 1960), p. 345, and the sharp critique in *Revue d'Histoire Ecclésiastique*, 1932, p. 740.

Ernst, V. "Basilius des Groszen Verkehr mit den Occidentalen," *Zeitschrift fuer Kirchengeschichte* (1896), XVI, 626 ff

Pusey, Edward B. *The Councils of the Church*. Oxford, 1857.

Rheinwald, F. H. *Die kirchliche Archaeologie* (1830), 99.

Schaefer, J. *Basilius des Groszen Beziehungen zum Abendlande. Beitrag zur Geschichte des 4. Jahrhunderts*, 1909

13

ALTAR FELLOWSHIP BETWEEN CHURCHES

The local congregation experiences the primary and most complete expression of its fellowship in the common service (p. 64). In the nature of things this enactment of fellowship is always limited. The services of the early church were never mass meetings. Besides, participation in the Eucharist was fundamentally limited by the exclusion of the heterodox, and even visitors in doctrinal agreement were admitted only on the basis of special credentials. Yet in its divine service each congregation assembles before and about its Lord, and He again gathers all local congregations into one single church (ecclesia). When the Didache prays for the gathering of the ecclesia "from the four winds," [1] it is speaking not of the local congregation but of the whole church. Even though they may be scattered, Christians are reminded by their suffering that they are one single "brotherhood in the world" (1 Peter 5:9). According to Justin's account the liturgy of his day contained the petition "for all others in all places." [2] Such a petition remains in all later liturgies. Intercession in the service is never confined to the local congregations. Selective petitions first came to be used when the custom emerged of praying for living or deceased individuals specifically mentioned by name. These names were recorded in the diptychs and read at the proper place in the liturgy. Since patriarchs and bishops were also specifically named, [3] it is clear that the distinction was accorded only to those in doctrinal agreement. In this way the diptychs become documents of fellowship between churches. If fellowship was broken off with anyone named in these documents, whether by dismissal from office or excommunication, his name was crossed out in the diptych. His readmission into fellowship brought with it also the restoration of his name to the diptych. [4]

Fellowship between churches found further expression in the special position accorded visiting clergy as distinct from visiting laymen. The clergy must also furnish credentials. Things are to some extent harder for them. They cannot simply set off in the same confidence of a ready welcome as a layman can. They are bound to the place where they were ordained, and they may be ordained only in the province in which they were baptized. The reason given for this by the Council of Elvira is that elsewhere men do not know how they walk.[5] From the rule that visiting clergy are to be honorably received (*Ap. Const.*, II, 58, 2) we may infer that from time to time clergymen were apt to go traveling far and near. At the bidding of his bishop, however, every presbyter and deacon had to return. If he disregarded the summons, he was permitted to receive the Holy Communion only as a layman (*Ap. Can.*, 15 [14]). Clergymen were often sent as messengers or to do a job commissioned by their church. The Synod of Laodicea even prescribed that the clergy be permitted to travel only on episcopal orders (Canon 42). In every case they were under the same obligation as laymen when it came to furnishing credentials. No clergyman was allowed to travel without a canonical document (κανονικὰ γράμματα, Canon 41). Clergy received Letters of Commendation (συστατικαὶ) and so enjoyed the standing of those for whom such documents were reserved by the Council of Chalcedon.[6] Later they needed a further dimissory letter from the bishop, as the bishop also did from the metropolitan.[7] The *Apostolic Canons* apparently do not quite trust these Letters of Commendation. They require that strange bishops, presbyters, and deacons be examined even though they may have Letters of Commendation. If they show themselves to be God-fearing preachers (κήρυκες τῆς εὐσεβείας), they are to be received. If not, their needs are to be supplied, but they are not to be admitted to the *koinonia* (Canon 34 [32]). This sounds quite like the *Didache*, only there it was a matter of wandering prophets, while here it is every cleric right up to the bishop.

There is a deeper reason for these special requirements imposed on traveling clergy. An essential of church fellowship is the Eucharistic *koinonia*. For the layman this is fulfilled in receiving *(metalepsis)* the Eucharist. For the cleric it means in addition the execution of his office in performing the liturgy. According to the Council of Arles (314) visiting bishops "who often come to a town" are to be given opportunity to "sacrifice." [8] However, in this matter one bishop should not put pressure on another.[9] The *Apostolic Constitutions* enjoin that a visiting presbyter is to be "received into [their] fellowship" (προσδεχέσθω κοινωνικῶς) by the presbyters, and similarly a deacon by the deacons. In the service a visiting bishop should sit with the local bishop, who should accord him equal honor. The local bishop should call on his visitor to address some words of instruction to the congregation because admonition from a stranger is very effective. He should also permit him to offer the Eucharist. If he modestly declines this, he ought to be induced at least to give the congregation the blessing (II, 58, 3 f.). The Synod of Neocaesarea (314—325) forbids only rural priests "to sacrifice, and to give the bread or the cup with prayer" in the city church while the bishop or city priests are absent. From this we may conclude that normally priests (presbyters) were permitted to perform their functions away from home (Canon 13). The Synod of Antioch (341) decrees that a cleric who transfers from his own parish into another and there attempts to settle down completely (παντελῶς) and stay for a long time may no longer officiate in the liturgy (λειτουργεῖν), above all (μάλιστα) if his bishop has summoned him home in vain (Canon 3). From this we see that during a short sojourn permitted by the bishop a cleric may also away from home perform the liturgy according to the rank of his office.[10]

The medieval canonists cannot be faulted for taking the right to "read Mass" or "celebrate" as belonging to bishops and priests by virtue of their office. This is in harmony with the general rule of the Council of Chalcedon that clergy enjoy the privileges of their office also in other congregations.[11] There is, however, more to it than that. When a layman goes to Communion in another congregation it is, so to speak, a private affair, but a clergyman away from home remains a member of the clergy of his own parish. His name continues there in the "catalog" or "canon." [12] In this way he is not just a private person, and his participation in the liturgy of another place is evidence of altar fellowship *(communicatio in sacris)* between the *churches*. This is also implicit in the invitation to a visiting bishop to address the congregation as set forth by the *Apostolic Constitutions*. This can happen only between those in doctrinal agreement, for it expresses unity in the teaching office.

The right to celebrate the Eucharist in another place can indeed be revoked. The 15th (14th) *Apostolic Canon* agrees, in part even verbally, with Canon 3 of Antioch which we have seen forbidding a cleric to officiate in the liturgy when he has been away a long time without the permission of his bishop. Here we find added at the end, "He shall there communicate as a layman." [13] There are also other reasons for thus reducing a cleric to receiving the Sacrament as a layman. According to the Council of Elvira a deacon who after his ordination is shown to be guilty of a previous mortal sin must as penance "receive lay Communion" for five years.[14] Basil similarly demands that a cleric guilty of mortal sin shall lose his rank of honor (βαθμός) but yet not be excluded from the *koinonia* of the laymen.[15] Here we find clergymen receiving different treatment from that given laymen excommunicated for mortal sin. The reason Basil gives for this is that the same offense ought not to be punished twice.[16] The punishment meet for a cleric is degradation, and that by itself is punishment enough. This is scarcely convincing, for if the cleric has greater privilege than a layman by virtue of his office, then when he is guilty his punishment ought also to be greater. Beside degradation he should also be excluded from the Sacrament altogether as a layman is. This does in fact happen in the case of heresy or apostasy. Then a cleric does not escape excommunication (*Ap. Can.*, 62, 61). The Council of Sardica accepted Hosius' proposal that bishops who exchange their bishoprics for property, honor, or power should not be deemed worthy of even so much as lay Communion, in grievous cases indeed not even "at the end," that is, at the point of death.[17]

Admission to lay Communion grants reconciliation to the cleric as it does also to the penitent layman. Cornelius of Rome (251—3) writes of a bishop who participated in the schismatic election of Novatian and who later repented. "Upon the entreaty of the whole congregation there present we partook of the Communion with him as with a layman" (*H. E.*,

VI, 43, 10). This bishop was clearly not permitted to celebrate the Sacrament or join in its administration, but he was permitted to receive it with the laity. His participation in the schism had automatically excluded him. Admission to lay Communion therefore meant readmission to church fellowship, even if not restoration to episcopal office. Even if a penitential period was imposed on a cleric in addition to his demotion, admission to lay Communion still meant reconciliation.[18] The fact that he was admitted only to lay Communion, whether after some completed penance or not, makes it clear that he was deprived of officiating in the liturgy and that this deprivation was intended as punishment.

Interconfessional relations are nowadays sometimes so arranged that where church fellowship is complete there is mutual welcoming of the laity to the Sacrament and of the clergy to its celebration, while where church fellowship is incomplete the laity may mutually receive the Sacrament but the clergy may not mutually celebrate it. Such gradations and distinctions in church fellowship have absolutely no connection with the regulations of the early church, except that a distinction as such is made between receiving the Sacrament and officiating at it. Church fellowship was not achieved in the early church by the reception of communicants or celebrants from elsewhere. In every case established church fellowship was the indispensable condition of any such reception. Either there was or there was not fellowship between two churches or two bishops, which practically amounted to the same thing. If there was, then the laity and clergy of the one might receive and celebrate the Sacrament in the other; if not, neither was possible. Deprivation of the right to celebrate was the consequence of deposition, degradation, suspension, and of course complete excommunication. It punished a clergyman for what had been unworthy of him. Never did the relations between two churches and their bishops provide for permitting the laity to receive the Sacrament while denying the clergy the privilege of officiating in it because church fellowship was somehow incomplete or because the congregations or their bishops were of different confessions or only in partial confessional agreement. There was either complete fellowship or none at all.

When the laity are granted the right to receive the Sacrament and the

ALTAR FELLOWSHIP BETWEEN CHURCHES

clergy to celebrate it in another church, we have the implementation of the *communicatio in sacris*. This takes place only in full church fellowship, of which agreement in doctrine and unity in confession are the basis and condition. Within these limits church fellowship, which includes altar fellowship, embraces the whole church. All the individual members of a local congregation participate also in the fellowship of the whole church. For this, however, they must be members of a specific parish (p. 133). Decisions regarding fellowship were corporate decisions (parish, province, patriarchate). We must defer for the present the question what members of a church are to do if they are not in agreement with the decisions made through their authorities. We must first further enlarge the picture of the altar fellowship between churches which is corporately granted or refused.

Irenaeus reminds Victor of Rome that his predecessors had "sent the Eucharist" also to "those of parishes" dating Easter differently from Rome.[19] Here it is not a matter of admitting individual traveling Christians to the Eucharist. Irenaeus is intent on proving the fellowship between the churches. This sending of the Eucharist, which can only mean the consecrated elements, is obviously intended to make possible that partaking "of the same loaf" which is the receiving *(metalepsis)* of the body of Christ. We are reminded of what Justin tells us about part of the consecrated elements being carried to the absent widows, orphans, sick, and imprisoned. From what Irenaeus says we may conclude that the Eucharist was sent even farther afield. He is quite right in looking upon this as evidence that the Roman bishops witnessed to the fellowship between the churches in this manner. The Synod of Laodicea later forbade this practice presumably because of possible abuse.[20] The cogency of the proof which Irenaeus draws from this practice of the Roman bishops remains intact.

Irenaeus adduces a further proof by pointing out that Anicetus of Rome "granted the Eucharist" to Polycarp of Smyrna when he visited Rome.[21] Polycarp was not in Rome incognito, that is, as a private person, but as bishop of his church. Anicetus' action therefore must be understood to bestow permission to celebrate the Sacrament. We see quite clearly what Irenaeus has in mind. What happened during Polycarp's visit is proof positive of enacted fellowship between the churches of Rome and Smyrna. Practiced altar fellowship is proof of the fellowship between the churches of Rome and Asia Minor. The obvious corollary of Irenaeus is that there can be no altar fellowship without church fellowship, and he could not have used this line of argument unless he was sure that Victor of Rome held the same view. The whole argument is built on the undoubted fact that by revoking fellowship with the churches of Asia Minor Victor also severed altar fellowship with them. This is taken for granted by Irenaeus, Victor, and the bishops who protest against the exclusion of the people of Asia Minor.

In the event of schism, altar fellowship automatically ceases. It is reported of Novatian that after he had himself elected as schismatic bishop in Rome, he demanded of every communicant, "Swear to me by the body and blood of Christ never to leave me and turn to Cornelius." A poor soul could only receive the Sacrament after he "had cursed himself" in this way. This report was written by Cornelius of Rome to Fabian of Antioch. Eusebius quotes this letter and judges this action of Novatian as the worst of all schismatic follies (*H. E.*, VI, 43, 18 f.). Such an oath demanded during the celebration of the Eucharist was scarcely to be approved — that is, if Novatian actually did demand it — and there are details furnished by Cornelius which suggest that his account is marred by malicious crudities allegedly supplied by eyewitnesses. However that may be, the unmistakable consequence of the schism was that a Christian could not receive the Sacrament in both the Roman episcopal churches, the Catholic and the Novatian. Cornelius, the Catholic bishop, took the same view, for he admitted a former follower of Novatian to Communion only after he had confessed and renounced the error of his Novatian ways.[22]

The schism was then still in its infancy. Later, when the Novatians had completed their independent organization, they were under no circumstances allowed to receive the Sacrament in a Catholic church. This is clear from the evidence of what was required before their request for reception into the Catholic Church was granted, and then only from case to case (p. 116). The Novatians on their side obviously did the same, and indeed more strictly.[23] The practice of both sides was completely consistent. In every schism both sides charged each other with "rending the body of Christ." Mutually to grant and practice Eucharistic *koinonia* would be a flat contradiction of this. Epiphanius saw the schism between Bishop Meletius of Lycopolis and Peter of Alexandria completed in this way that they "prayed separated from one another, and so also each performed the other holy services (ἱερουργίας) by himself." [24] Prayer and altar fellowship were broken. The Council of Nicaea tried to remove the schism. It prescribed, among other things, that the clergy installed by Meletius should, after bestowal of a new ordination, retain their rights to conduct the liturgy according to their rank.[25] Thus they were privileged to celebrate the Sacrament in Catholic congregations too. This privilege is a criterion of altar fellowship and is therefore one revoked during a schism. Schism begins with a break in altar fellowship *(communicatio in sacris)* and ends with its restoration.

In the great dogmatic controversies some time usually lapsed before the formal revocation of church fellowship. Each party was trying to win over the whole church. In the Arian controversies there was a sort of moratorium before the complete rupture between the churches. Arians and Nicaeans maintained a limited fellowship with one another. Only altar fellowship was suspended. We must look at this fact more closely later (p. 176). We see here that when the matter is ready for synodical decision, the consequences follow automatically. The heretics are excommunicated. But then the question arises, as we have already observed, whether the majority is strong enough to carry out this exclusion, whether bishops and clergy can in fact be removed from their office and prevented from conducting services and administering the sacraments.

When the emperor summoned an ecumenical council to Ephesus in 431, the parties did not even come and meet together. Majority and minority held separate meetings, and each attacked the legitimacy of the other. The controversy was about the teaching of Nestorius. Cyril lead the majority to declare Nestorius deposed. The latter submitted and immediately went into a monastery. Thus the matter might have rested with the rift apparently forestalled. However, John of Antioch and the other bishops of the minority did not submit when their opponents attempted to impose similar treatment on them. They replied in kind. The synod of the majority excluded them from church fellowship and added that until they confessed their error they were not to exercise any episcopal or priestly privileges.[26] Those thus condemned would not submit, and so the churches' rupture impended. The majority with the local bishop Memnon were successful in forcibly preventing the Antiochenes from holding services in one of the city churches. The Antiochenes demanded a similar interdict on the other side from the imperial commissioner, Candidian. He consented and declared, "It is my will that neither party celebrate the Sacrament so that no schism may arise in the holy orthodox church." [27] He was actually unable to have his way against Memnon and the city populace which supported him. However, what he wanted as the representative of the emperor is quite clear. The avowed purpose of the council was to prevent the doctrinal differences from splitting the church. What had happened already gave grounds for fearing the worst, that is, the exact opposite of the council's purpose. Both parties had already excommunicated each other. If the bishops of both sides celebrated the Sacrament separately, the split would be consummated. As soon as that happened, it would be obvious that their mutual excommunications had failed to remove the opponents from the church. Where the Eucharist is still celebrated, there there is still church. If each party can still celebrate the Eucharist even though excommunicated by the other, it remains possible for the emperor to decide in favor of one or the other, but he cannot do away with the fact that two churches now confront each other, each maintaining and the other denying that it is the body of Christ. The denial of altar fellowship has made the split of the church complete.

Fifty years later the battle raged about Chalcedon and Emperor Zeno's *Henoticon*, which was to suppress and replace the Chalcedonian dogma.[28] Rome stood for Chalcedon with implacable rigor, as Acacius of Constantinople did for the emperor. The other Eastern patriarchs also supported the *Henoticon*. In 483 Pope Felix III sent his legates

Vitalis and Misenus to Constantinople to set the emperor and Acacius to rights. There were also supporters of Chalcedon in the East and in the capital. For this reason as well the emperor and his patriarch were not inclined toward a break with Rome. They were, on the contrary, intent on maintaining the appearance of unity. The papal legates were actually ready to celebrate Holy Communion with the patriarch, and on this occasion the name of Peter Mongo was also read from the diptychs, a man whose heresy was notorious in Roman eyes. Their participation in the Eucharist demonstrated a church fellowship extending from Rome through Constantinople to the heretic in Alexandria. Altar fellowship *(communicatio in sacris)* is proof of church fellowship.[29]

The legates here acted contrary to their commission. For Pope Felix a supporter of the *Henoticon* was a heretic with whom church and altar fellowship were possible only if he recanted his heresy. A Roman synod deprived Vitalis and Misenus of their office and even excluded them from the "unspotted *koinonia.*" This was a standard term for Eucharistic *koinonia.*[30] Acacius, too, was then (484) pronounced deposed, excommunicated, and damned. This was the beginning of the first great schism between Rome and Constantinople. The legates Vitalis and Misenus were not personally charged with heresy. Their exclusion was in accordance with the canonical principle that bishops and clergy who communicate with schismatics are themselves excommunicated. They had practiced altar fellowship where church fellowship was in question. Consequently they also had to be excluded from the *koinonia* of the Roman church.[31]

One hundred years later, during the Persian War of Justin II, many Armenian refugees, episcopal and lay, came to Constantinople, led by their catholicos. At first they went to Communion with the orthodox Chalcedonian patriarch "without misgivings," that is, they did not consider that the Armenian Church had not accepted the dogma of Chalcedon. When the bishops who remained at home and other members of their church reproached them about this, they separated themselves and had Communion in their own services in a private house.[32] They even had no fellowship with the Monophysites there who were anti-Chalcedonians like themselves. Altar fellowship was possible only where there was confessional unity.

The Armenians whom Basil II (975—1025), the "Slayer of the Bulgarians," settled in the Balkans as a barrier against the Bulgarians were persuaded by the metropolitan of Sebaste to confess the doctrine of Chalcedon. As the Armenian historian puts it, "in accepting the Council of Chalcedon" they "renounced the unity of the Armenians." [33] That meant the end of fellowship with their home church and therefore also the end of altar fellowship.

Notes to Chapter 13

1. *Didache,* 10, 5: *LCC,* I, 176

2. *Apology,* I, 65: *LCC,* I, 285

3. Jungmann, *The Mass of the Roman Rite,* II (1951), 154 f., 245 f. (1959), 396 f., 445

4. After Chrysostom was deposed, the Western bishops broke fellowship with the East until the bishops there "had restored" his name "in the diptych of the dead bishops" (συνέταξαν, Theodoret, *H. E.,* V, 34, 10; *taxis* = *diptychon*). The struggles between East and West after Chalcedon saw the same names struck, restored, struck again, and so on — as fellowship was broken or restored.

5. Arles (314), Canons 2 and 21: *CCL,* 148, 9 and 11; Stevenson, pp. 322 ff. Nicaea, Canons 15 and 16: Bright, pp. xiii f., 55 ff.; Stevenson, p. 362. Antioch (341) with restriction, Canon 3. Cf. *Ap. Can.* 14 (13) and 15 (14), and the confession of Bishop Damasus of Rome, Canon 9: Hahn, p. 273. Cf. Chalcedon, Canon 20: Bright, pp. xlv, 207. But exceptions were always made — principally for bishops. Elvira, Canon 24.

6. As distinct from those in need who received only Letters of Peace. Chalcedon, Canon 13: Bright, pp. xliii, 191. Cf. above, p. 132. συστατικὰ appears also in *Ap. Can.,* 13 (12), and 34 (32); Sardica, Canon 9: H. Hess, *The Canons of the Council of Sardica* (Oxford, 1958), p. 132; Quinisextum, Canon 17.

7. The *congregation* in Lyons issued Irenaeus' Letter of Commendation to Bishop Eleutherius of Rome (*H. E.,* V, 4). On the other hand, the presbyter Clement of Alexandria was commended to the congregation of Antioch by the *bishop,* Alexander of Jerusalem (*H. E.,* VII, 11, 6). *Ap. Can.* 34 (32); Agde (506), Canon 38: Mansi, VIII, 321; *CCL,* 148, 208 (*epistola episcopi sui); Epaon (517): Mansi, VIII, 560 (antistitis sui).* These last two are from southern Gaul. At Agde the duty to furnish credentials was extended

also to monks. For the *literae dimissoriae* (ἀπολυτικαὶ) see Zonaras and Balsamon on Chalcedon, Canon 11: *PG*, 137, 425 ff.; Bright, pp. xlii, 185 ff. Upon occasion bishops and specially authorized clerics received Letters of Commendation from the governor or the emperor. Athanasius came to Palestine, "armed" (ὀχυρωθεὶς) with letters from Emperor Constantine, and Bishop Maximus of Jerusalem therefore did not hesitate to grant him the *koinonia* and the "honor" (ἀξία). Socrates, *H. E.*, II, 24.

8. Canon 19: *CCL*, 148, 13; Stevenson, p. 325.

9. Canon 17: *CCL*, 148, 12; Stevenson, p. 324.

10. Canon 13 (12) of the *Apostolic Canons* reads like a most curious pleonasm when it says that excommunication falls upon anyone who receives a clerical or lay person without a Letter of Commendation. Whoever is excommunicated can have no Commendation to submit and, alternatively, whoever submits a Commendation cannot be excommunicated. The meaning can only be that a Commendation must be required from every clerical or lay person in order to insure that he is not excommunicated. Canon 13 of Chalcedon leaves no doubt when it declares that no strange cleric or unknown person may officiate (λειτουργεῖν) without a Letter of Commendation (Bright, pp. xliii, 191)

11. Canon 5: Bright, pp. xli, 165 f.

12. No cleric may be "cataloged" (καταλέγεσθαι) in two towns (Chalcedon, Canon 10: Bright, pp. xlii, 183 f.). "Canon" in this sense occurs at the end of Canon 17 of Nicaea (Bright, p. xiv).

13. ὡς λαικὸς μέντοι ἐκεῖσε κοινωνείτω.

14. *Communionem laicam accipere*, Canon 76. Cf. Sardica, Canon 19: Hess, p. 86.

15. Canon 32: *PG*, 32, 727; Deferrari, III, 125. Cf. Canons 3 and 70: *PG*, 32, 673 and 801; Deferrari, III, 23 and 255

16. Nahum 1:9. Canon 3: *PG*, 32, 673; Deferrari, III, 23.

17. Canons 1 and 2: Hess, pp. 76 ff.

18. Elvira, Canon 76. *Ap. Can.*, 62 (61). Cf. Cyprian, *Ep.* 67, 6: Lacey, p. 116. Bishop Basilides lost his office because of his offenses, did penance, and then congratulated himself when it was granted that with him people might "communicate as with a layman" *(satis gratulans si sibi vel laico communicare contingeret)*.

19. *H. E.*, V, 24, 15: Stevenson, p. 150.

20. *Apology*, I, 65 and 67: *LCC*, I, 286 f. Laodicea, Canon 14. On the later practice of sending out the consecrated elements see Th. Schermann, *Die*

allgemeine Kirchenordnung, II, 419, 437. Cf. G. Dix, *A Detection of Aumbries* (London, 1942), pp. 16 ff.

21. *H. E.*, V, 24, 17: Stevenson, p. 150

22. *H. E.*, VI, 43, 10: Stevenson, p. 263.

23. Socrates, VII, 25: *PG*, 67, 796 c, d.

24. *Haer.*, 68, 3, 4: *GCS*, III, 143, 8. This point is certainly clear even though one may otherwise prefer the sources for this schism which diverge from Epiphanius. Cf. Greenslade, p. 53.

25. τὴν τιμὴν καὶ λειτουργίαν. Synodical Letter to the bishops of Egypt, etc. Socrates, I, 9: *PG*, 67, 80 a. There are a few insignificant variations in Theodoret, *H. E.*, I, 9: Parmentier, p. 40, 7; Stevenson, p. 369, 7; Greenslade, pp. 151 f.

26. *ACO*, I, 1 and 3, pp. 24, 30 and 25, 29: μηδεμίαν ἔχοντες ἄδειαν ὡς ἐξ αὐθεντίας ἱερατικῆς. . . . Cf. the circular letter to the bishops of all provinces etc., p. 27, 14. Evagrius, *H. E.*, I, 5: ἀποκρίνονται δὲ τῆς ἁγίας κοινωνίας καὶ πάσης αὐθεντίας ἱερατικῆς. The historian here plainly interprets the synodical ruling as exclusion from Eucharistic *koinonia* since the attribute "holy" would be quite extraordinary with *koinonia* in the more general sense of church fellowship. Cf. Bright, pp. 124 ff.; Bindley, pp. 138 f.

27. *ACO*, I, 4, p. 44, 3; *Ego autem neutram partem volo celebrare, ne forte aliquod schisma sanctae atque orthodoxae generetur ecclesiae.* The expression *celebrare* derives here from the formula *missarum celebrare collectam* which John of Antioch used in his grievance (p. 43, 31). Theodoret reports Candidian as saying, *Si non fueritis pacifici, non concedam uni parti congregari. Ep.* 169 (to Alexander of Hierapolis): Schulze, IV, 1346. We have both reports only in Latin translation.

28. Bettenson, *Documents*, pp. 123 ff. When Bishop Juvenal of Jerusalem returned home from Chalcedon, he faced the open rebellion of the Palestinian monks, who elected one of their own number as opposition bishop. Here there was a complete split within an episcopal church. Only imperial intervention restored the situation for Juvenal. E. Honigmann, "Juvenal of Jerusalem," *Dumbarton Oaks Papers*, 5 (1950), pp. 247 ff. R. V. Sellers, *The Council of Chalcedon* (London, 1953), p. 255, n. 1.

29. Evagrius, *H. E.*, III, 18—20: Bidez-Parmentier, p. 117. Liberatus, *Breviar.* c. 18: *PL*, 68, 1028. Theophanes, *Chronographia*, ed. C. de Boor, I, 132, 18.

30. Evagrius, *H. E.*, III, 21: τῆς ἀχράντου κοινωνίας ἐχωρίσθησαν. Cf. I, 13: Bidez-Parmentier, p. 21, 6: τὸ ἄχραντον ἱερουργήσαντες σῶμα, τῆς ζωοποιοῦ κοινωνίας ἀλλήλους μετέδοσαν. Also Quinisextum, Canons 23 and 51.

31. Ten years later Misenus was again received into church fellowship; Vitalis had already died. Fritz Hofmann, *Der Kampf der Paepste,* pp. 58 f.

32. John of Ephesus, *H. E.,* II, 23.

33. Stephen of Taron, *Armenische Geschichte,* trans. H. Gelzer and A. Burckhardt, 1907, p. 149. V. Inglisian passes over this occurrence in his otherwise very thorough and illuminating account of Chalcedon and the Armenian church, *"Chalkedon und die armenische Kirche,"* 1953.

From Stephen of Taron we have a letter to the metropolitan of Sebaste from the Armenian catholicos in which, after talking about the church's requiring the confession of sins, he says, "For what reason could people be allowed to forget this, and how can other rules be given to these your people? The offenses of the priests *(sic!)* are not laid bare, and they eat without discernment of the Lord's body and blood, regarding which Paul loudly proclaims, 'Let a man examine himself and thereafter eat of this bread and drink of the cup.' Only in observing this confession can the priest be examined and each directed to his proper place" (p. 182, 25). The problem here is not heterodoxy; that had already been dealt with exhaustively. It seems more likely a question of a relaxation in requiring confession.

Bibliography for Chapter 13

Bishop, E. "The Diptychs," appendix to R. H. Connolly, *The Liturgical Homilies of Narsai,* Cambridge, 1909, pp. 97—114.

Cabrol, F. "Diptyques," *Dict. d'Arch. Chret. et de Lit.* IV, 1045 ff.

Dix, G. *A Detection of Aumbries.* London, 1942.

———. *The Shape of the Liturgy,* Westminster, 1945, pp. 498 ff.

Grillmeier, A. and H. Bacht. *Das Konzil von Chalkedon,* 3 vols., 1951—54.

Hess, Hamilton. *The Canons of the Council of Sardica.* Oxford, 1958.

Hofmann, Fritz. "Der Kampf der Paepste um Konzil und Dogma von Chalkedon von Leo dem Grossen bis Hormisdas," *Das Konzil von Chalkedon,* II, 13—94.

Honigmann, E. "Juvenal of Jerusalem," *Dumbarton Oaks Papers,* 5 (1950).

Inglisian, Vahan. "Chalkedon und die armenische Kirche," *Das Konzil von Chalkedon,* II, 361—417.

Kober, F. *Die Suspension nach den Grundsaetzen des kanonischen Rechts,* 1862.

———. *Die Deposition und Degradation,* 1867.

Salig, C. A. *De diptychis veterum tam profanis quam sacris.* Halle, 1731.

Schermann, Th. *Die allgemeine Kirchenordnung,* II, *Fruehchristliche Liturgien,* 1915.

Sellers, Robert Victor. *The Council of Chalcedon.* London, 1953.

14

KEEPING ALTAR FELLOWSHIP INTACT

The great schisms (Sardica 343, Ephesus 431, between Rome and Constantinople 484) affected not only the disputing bishops but also their churches, not only patriarchs but whole patriarchates. Excommunication by an opponent did not remove a bishop from his church. He continued in his church in both office and fellowship. The case of the legates Vitalis and Misenus illustrates the basic principle that whoever communicates with a man who has been excluded excludes himself. The exclusion of such a man applies automatically to all the church members joined with him. The situation is the same as that in the second century when Victor of Rome in excommunicating Polycrates of Ephesus excommunicated his church and all those connected with him in Asia Minor.

All acknowledged that the fellowship of a church can no more be piecemeal than the church itself. Its integrity depends on the integrity of all members. No member may overstep the boundaries of fellowship without the approval of all members. Whoever communicates with a heretic, schismatic, or any man that for any reason is not within the fellowship thereby disqualifies himself from the fellowship. He is guilty of injuring the integrity of the whole. For this reason every member must hold to the Sacrament administered within the borders of the fellowship.

Archbishop Theophilus of Alexandria excommunicated his archpresbyter Peter and the likeminded presbyter Isidore because Peter had admitted to Communion a Manichean lady who had not previously renounced her heresy. That was in itself perfectly legitimate, but, claimed Isidore, the archbishop had previously given his approval. Isidore and the four "tall brothers" (Egyptian monks who admittedly had other reasons

for opposing Theophilus) went to Constantinople and sought intervention on behalf of those who they felt had been wrongfully excommunicated. The patriarch, John Chrysostom, received them honorably, and
nothing was put in the way of their participation in the divine services
(τῶν εὐχῶν). He would not, however, admit them to altar fellowship
until their case was investigated. All this was reported to Theophilus,
and he made the charge that Chrysostom had also admitted them to the
Sacrament, though in fact this was not so. He used the occasion against
Chrysostom and in so doing aided his opponents at court who finally
secured his dismissal.[1]

However we may judge the case, we observe how a single instance,
the admission of a Manichean to the Sacrament, started a chain reaction.
The archpresbyter was excommunicated for it. If this was right, then the
"tall brothers" also had to be excommunicated for they continued in fellowship with him as before. Chrysostom was above reproach in withhold-
ing the Sacrament from them, but he brought suspicion upon himself
in merely suspending altar fellowship, for he thereby indicated the need
for revision in the original instance. The Alexandrian Theophilus seized
the occasion to launch an attack in the interpatriarchal struggle. There
is a great deal more to this struggle that we cannot take note of here,[2]
but even if Theophilus did perhaps only use this instance as a pretext,
the whole series of events is in any case indicative of the sacramental practice of the early church.

There was universal recognition of the basic principle that inadmissible altar fellowship injures the integrity of church fellowship. The schism
within the Novatian church began when Sabbatius separated himself
from the Novatian congregation in Constantinople because unqualified
persons, he charged, were there admitted to the Sacrament.[3] The modern
theory that anybody may be admitted "as a guest" to the Sacrament in
a church of a differing confession, that people may communicate to and
fro in spite of the absence of full church fellowship is unknown in the
early church, indeed unthinkable.

Men of his fellowship found it unpardonable that Paul the Black
(Monophysite patriarch of Antioch) should once or twice communicate

with the Synodites (those who adhered to the Synod [Council] of Chalcedon). This was one of the reasons why the Egyptian Monophysites refused him church fellowship, and it contributed finally to his deposition.[4]

Perpetual vigilance was necessary for the preservation of the integrity of altar fellowship. It must be borne in mind that churches of different confessions or churches that were divided for other reasons often had their congregations in the same town or province. Their members lived next to each other. In the big cities the traffic to and fro between the groups appears scarcely susceptible of control, as Dionysius of Alexandria indicates already in the third century.[5] First impressions of the great divisions of the church are therefore subject to correction or revision. A first glimpse of the situation shows how the divisions caused by the divergences of bishops extended to their dioceses and so to all the members of their churches. Accordingly, it should be possible to indicate the boundaries of the parties on a multicolored map. Viewed this way, however, the break in altar fellowship which accompanied the withdrawal of church fellowship was of no great practical consequence. Within the geographically limited area, which in the case of the schism of 484 included the entire West, the break in altar fellowship had no effect whatever. Only a few traveling clergy and lay people who crossed the geographical boundary felt the effects. Their bishops' Letters of Commendation and Letters of Peace were not recognized beyond the border. The break in altar fellowship appeared to be controlled from above, and travelers appeared to be mere innocent victims of divisions in which they were not personally involved.

This picture changes as soon as we observe how the theological controversies resounded in the depth and breadth of the congregations (p. 145). It was impossible to contain or control the power to convince or mislead inherent in theological declarations and in the convictions which moved the churches. So long as those in the majority had not yet yielded to the temptation to secure their position by military force, there was nothing to keep minorities from organizing themselves within the same town or province. Thus already before Nicaea the Valentinians,

Montanists, and Novatians organized themselves into congregations within the area of the majority church and maintained themselves for centuries. These organizations were not produced from above but arose spontaneously from below. Whoever joined them did so in entire personal freedom. Even after Nicaea numerous small groups organized themselves in the same way. The big divisions differ in being directed from above to the extent that the regular church authorities — bishops, synods, and patriarchs — played a leading role. This does not by any means prove that the congregations and their members paid no attention to decisions about church and altar fellowship as things that just went on over their heads. The Arian moratorium is an example of how things really went.

According to the report of Philostorgius, the Arians, in spite of their doctrinal opposition to the "confessors of the *homoousios*" (the orthodox Nicaeans), participated in their "prayers, hymns, deliberations, and almost everything else except in the mystical sacrifice," that is, in all but the Eucharist. This relatively peaceful situation was brought to an end by Aetius, who persuaded his kindred spirits to organize a separate congregation (III, 14). From Sozomen we also hear that under Constantine the Arians did not as yet organize separate congregations. All assembled in fellowship together. The exceptions were the heretics and schismatics from before Nicaea — the Novatians, Phrygians (Montanists), Valentinians, Marcionites, and Paulianists (II, 32). Sozomen finds the reason for this in the emperor's general prohibition of conventicles, which commanded all Christians to use the same places of worship. Both reports show how the doctrinal differences reached into the local congregations. The peaceful situation described by Philostorgius was limited to a certain area, and Sozomen's account of the prohibition of conventicles to the time of Constantine. After Athanasius' first return from exile (339) tumult broke out between the opposing parties in Alexandria and elsewhere.[6]

Philostorgius dates the complete separation of congregations as beginning with the activity of Aetius in the middle fifties. It is important to him, however, to point out that already before that time his Arian brethren were by no means in full fellowship with the Nicaeans. They attended the divine services but did not partake of the Sacrament. This can only have been the situation where the Arians were in the minority. Where their own bishops held sway, as in Constantinople, there could be no doubt about their participation in the Sacrament. The question arises whether, in the places to which the report applies, the Arians refrained from participation of their own free choice or whether they were not rather excluded from the Eucharist by the orthodox majority or its clergy. If the latter is the case, then the treatment they received was that prescribed for the lapsed at Nicaea. This was the last stage before full reinstatement: "participating with the congregation in the prayers but excluded from the Sacrifice," that is, having a part in the rest of the divine service but not in the Sacrament.[7] This treatment prescribed for the lapsed cannot, however, have been the model, because it was a penitential procedure to which the Arians at that time could certainly not have been willing to accede. Contemporary church orders convince us that participation in the divine services by people who were nevertheless excluded from altar fellowship must be considered an abnormal situation. Since the case of joint worship reported by Philostorgius is to show freedom of action on the part of his confessional brethren, and since we hear of common deliberations (βουλεύματα), it seems probable that the abnormal arrangement arose by mutual consent.

This arrrangement can only have been considered provisional. It would have been utterly impossible when the congregations were quite independent as at the time of Paul. Every congregation was then in the position to judge false teachers as such and was empowered and bound to exclude them from fellowship immediately and completely. However, when the bishops took the whole responsibility for doctrine into their own hands, and when questions of doctrine came to be decided finally by synods, the congregations simply had to wait. The ability of local congregations to deal with heretics, as pictured above from the directions given in the New Testament, presupposes that an authoritative decision has been made regarding the heresy and its impermissibility within the fellowship of the church. This presupposition is still lacking in the stage of the doctrinal controversy described by Philostorgius (III, 14).

In spite of all the excommunicating, all parties clung to the fiction of the unity of the imperial church until the Council of Sardica in 343. Here the formal secession of the Eusebians, who opposed Nicaea, took place, and another 15 years went by before Aetius and Eunomius organized a separate church from Constantinople by the ordination of bishops for Asia Minor.[8]

The abnormal situation we have considered existed in a time when there was not yet a final and authoritative decision about the exclusion of the one or the other party. For this very reason it is significant far beyond itself. We are not told whether the same conduct of the Arians in different places was centrally directed or whether it was local and spontaneous. Central direction is conceivable, but in the absence of any acknowledged jurisdiction by Arian bishops beyond their own parishes it would be quite without effect, unless, of course, such direction won acceptance for itself in the scattered groups. In each case these arrangements presuppose judgment and understanding on the part of the members of the congregations. The doctrinal differences were understood in the congregations. They were understood as confessional differences which called for the personal decision of each member of the church. Some accepted the doctrine of the homoousia of the Son with the Father; others did not. These, the Arians, concluded that because of the lack of confessional unity they could not communicate together. That the Homoousians thought the same way is self-evident from all that we hear of Athanasius and the men in agreement with him.[9]

The significance of this provisional arrangement for the whole early church becomes most clear when it is compared with later attempts at unification in which the dissenters were to be forced to join in a common Communion (below, Chap. 15). In this latter case as in the former there is the same recognition of the lack of confessional unity and the same desire to reestablish the unity in the imperial church. In the attempt to unite the church by force, the Sacrament seemed to be the appropriate means. Get everybody to go to the Sacrament together, and unity becomes obvious — that is, you have a demonstration of it, even though in fact it does not exist. People could only come upon this thought if they saw the fellowship principle of the Sacrament in the mere act of the participants' joining in a communal meal and if they fancied themselves in complete control of the Sacrament as a means at their disposal for achieving the unification they desired. But it takes a strong imagination to credit so much theological reflection to people who try to achieve unity by the use of force.

In the case of the arrangement with the Arians both parties knew that they were not in confessional unity. They also wished to reestablish this full unity. They would otherwise not have engaged in the local deliberations with the Nicaean congregations. They could not, however, communicate together, for church unity is not the goal in celebrating the Sacrament together but the indispensable prerequisite. In this they are at one with the whole early church insofar as the understanding of the Sacrament is guided by theological considerations. The fellowship of the Sacrament is in partaking *(metalepsis)* of the body of Christ, something with which men may not do as they please. This fact must be respected by men, and by it they are to be guided. For this reason all who would partake of the Sacrament must first remove every dissension (above, p. 81). So long as there is anything that divides them, they may not communicate together. Any disunity carried into the celebration of the Communion does injury to the body of Christ.

This applies to all personal dissensions. The celebration together of the Sacrament is the seal of the most close and complete relationship between men. For this very reason conscientious Christians will refuse to receive it so long as their hearts feel dissension. We have seen how the Egyptian monks excommunicated Simeon Stylites (above p. 153). The counterpart to that is the action of Domnus (II) of Antioch. He personally sought out Simeon Stylites, and his impression of the man so moved him that he "earnestly desired the yet greater mystery." [10] Thereupon they together performed the consecration and gave one another the Sacrament. This was surely no less extraordinary for a man at the peak of the hierarchy than for a hermit. Both discovered that nothing stood between them. They sealed their unity with the Holy Communion in the open field. Jerome, too, reminded his former friend Rufinus how once at the Church of the Resurrection in Jerusalem, having sacrificed the Lamb *(immolato agno)*, they shook hands together at the Eucharistic sacrifice.[11] This memory served only to deepen the contrast with the bitter dissension that had since divided them and now made their communicating together simply impossible.

As little as in a case of personal dissension — and if gradations were at all permissible here, one would have to say even less than in it — can there be altar fellowship between those confessionally disunited. This is the basis of the Arian moratorium. The Armenians who came to Constantinople and at first offended against this principle were convinced, as we saw, of its correctness by their home church.

The doctrinal controversies were often accompanied by personal invective. The man and what he stood for were not held separate. This, however, was not necessarily the case. The relationship between the Arians and Nicaeans as described by Philostorgius is a splendid example of the opposite. There are many others. Zacharias Rhetor relates how first in Alexandria and later in Berytus he studied law together with Severus, who later became the Monophysite patriarch. At the same time he tried little by little to win him for the church's doctrine. In Berytus they formed a congenial group of students who worshiped in various churches and also prayed together — the original *Studentengemeinde*. When, however, Severus agreed to receive Baptism and asked Zacharias to be his sponsor, he declined the invitation. His reason: "I do not communicate with the bishops of Phoenicia but with the holy fathers of Egypt and Palestine." [12] This was at the time of the *Henoticon* controversy, and since the first of the "holy fathers" he names is Peter the Iberian, he is here identifying himself as a Monophysite. "The bishops of Phoenicia" and among them the bishop of Berytus apparently held to Chalcedon at this time.[13] Zacharias' conduct is the same as that of the Arians at the time of the moratorium. Although the group of students was certainly not made up only of Monophysites, they had theological discussions together, prayed together, and, the Monophysites included, went together to the divine services in the churches of the city. The baptism of Severus would be coupled with the Eucharist, and this final consummation of unity Zacharias had to decline because he was not in doctrinal accord with the bishop of the city.

To the early church a man was orthodox or heterodox according to his confession. He was the one or the other according to that confession with which he was "in fellowship." The fellowship in which he stood, the church to which he belonged, was shown by where he received the Sacrament. When the Princess Sophia received the Sacrament from a Monophysite priest before the enthronement of her husband (Justin II), it was clear to everyone that she wanted to have no fellowship with the Synodites (Chalcedonians). The reversal of this is reported about her by John of Ephesus (*H. E.*, II, 10). "She came into fellowship with the Synodites" as soon as she began "to communicate with the Synod." By his partaking of the Sacrament in a church a Christian declares that the confession of that church is his confession. Since a man cannot at the same time hold two differing confessions, he cannot communicate in two churches of differing confessions. If anyone does this nevertheless, he denies his own confession or has none at all.

Notes to Chapter 14

1. Socrates, *H. E.*, VI, 9; Sozomen, *H. E.*, VIII, 12 f. Cf. J. F. D'Alton, *Selections from St. John Chrysostom* (London, 1940), pp. 19 ff. Cf. above p. 121.

2. We find no mention of the incident at the Synod of the Oak in 403. Here Theophilus presided, and the deposition of Chrysostom was pronounced. The monks had for the most part made their peace with Theophilus in the meantime. A fragmentary report of the synod can be found in Photius, *Bibl. Cod.*, 59. B. J. Kidd, *A History of the Church to 461* (London, 1922), II, 437 ff. Bright, p. 45.

3. Socrates, *H. E.*, V, 21; Sozomen, *H. E.*, VII, 17: *PG*, 67, 621 c; 1469 a.

4. John of Ephesus, also called John of Asia, *H. E.*, IV, 15 f. Timothy the Presbyter, *PG*, 86, 41 c. Th. Hermann, *Patriarch Paul*, pp. 278 f. E. Honigmann, *Évêques et Évêchés Monophysites*, pp. 199 f.

5. *H. E.*, VII, 7, 4. See above pp. 129, 141.

6. Athanasius, *Epistola Encyclica*, 4 f.; *Apologia contra Arianos* 30 and 33: *PG*, 25, 232; 300; 304. Gwatkin, pp. 138 f.

7. Canon 11: χωρὶς προσφορᾶς κοινωνήσουσι τῷ λαῷ τῶν προσευχῶν· See above p. 96, n. 34. Bright, pp. xii, 44 f.

8. Philostorgius, *H. E.,* VIII, 2. More precisely it was the separation of the Eunomians (Anomoeans) from the mediating Arians who had control at court under Constantius. Cf. Eudoxius of Constantinople in chap. 15. M. Albertz, "Zur Geschichte der jung-arianischen Kirchengemeinschaft," *Theologische Studien und Kritiken,* 82 (1909), 205 ff.

9. The extant fragments of Philostorgius do not tell us where and how the Arians communicated during the moratorium. It is hardly to be supposed that they would forgo the Eucharist during these years. Perhaps it was celebrated in their homes. Bishop Eustathius of Sebaste is reported as advising certain persons to celebrate the Communion in their own home. The reasons, however, were different in this case. Socrates, *H. E.,* II, 43: *PG,* 67, 353 a. The Synod of Gangra (c. 343), which dealt with Eustathius and his followers, condemned his advice (Canons 6, 11). Later at the first Council of Toledo (c. 400) excommunication was decreed upon all who participated only in the divine services but never in the Sacrament (Canon 13: Mansi, III, 1000). The arrangement of a separate celebration of the Sacrament normally meant secession from the former church fellowship. In Pseudo-Leontius (*De sectis,* act. VI, 6: *PG,* 86, 1232d) in a discussion of the separation of the Agnoetae from the Theodosians we find, καὶ ἐκκλησίαν ἰδίαν ποιήσαντες καθ᾽ ἑαυτοὺς ἐκοινώνουν. A division of the imperial church was, however, just what the Arians wished to avoid at that time. Where they in fact partook of the Sacrament remains obscure.

10. Evagrius, *H. E.,* I, 13: Bidez-Parmentier, p. 21, 5: τῶν μυστικωτέρων ἐγλίχετο.

11. Jerome, *Apologia adv. libros Rufini,* III, 33: *PL,* 23, 563 b.

12. As given by M. A. Kugener, *Vie de Sévère, par Zacharie le Scholastique: PO,* II, 1, p. 78, 6

13. This is contradicted by Zacharias Rhetor when he tells us (*H. E.,* IV, 9) that Bishop Eustathius of Berytus associated with the Monophysite bishop Timothy Aelurus, who was exiled from Alexandria. On the other hand, compare the dates given by Gustav Krueger (p. 317) in the Ahrens-Krueger translation at p. 34, 22: Mansi, VII, 557: *PG,* 85, 1803. Hamilton and Brooks, ET p. 127. Severus was baptized in Tripoli but nevertheless joined the Monophysite fellowship together with others from the Berytus circle of friends.

Bibliography for Chapter 14

Albertz, M. "Zur Geschichte der jung-arianischen Kirchengemeinschaft," *Theologische Studien und Kritiken,* 82 (1909), 205 ff.

D'Alton, J. F. *Selections from St. John Chrysostom.* London, 1940.

Gwatkin, H. M. *Studies in Arianism.* 2d ed., Cambridge, 1900.

Hermann, Th. "Patriarch Paul von Antiochien und das alexandrinische Schisma vom Jahre 375," *ZNTW,* 27 (1928), 263 ff.

Honigmann, E. *Évêques et Évêchés Monophysites,* 1951.

Kidd, B. J. *A History of the Church to 461.* London, 1922.

Schwartz, Ed. "Palladiana," *ZNTW,* 36 (1937), pp. 168 ff. On Theophilus and Chrysostom.

15

ATTEMPTS AT UNION

Our account of church fellowship would not be complete without mention of the attempts at union in the early church. These were being made constantly, for the early church also genuinely suffered under its divisions. Only after the christianized police were at its disposal did it learn that subjugation of the weaker party provided the easiest way of removing divisions. Even so there were always attempts by other means to bind the broken ties together again, to compose confessional differences, and to overcome schisms. It was never sheer delight in disharmony that prompted even the heretics and schismatics to disturb the peace. It does indeed sound like wanton malice when Marcion tells the Roman presbyters who refused to receive him into the Roman congregation, "I shall split your church and throw a schism into it forever." [1] Yet even this arch-heretic had his objective reasons, as is recognized by his opponents in the labor they expended to refute them. He was in fact put out not as a peacebreaker but as a false teacher. The grounds given for excommunication or the revoking of church fellowship were always objective. Men of course did not have to wait for the perspicacity of modern historians to discover that these grounds could also serve as a cloak for the rivalry of church politicians, lust for power, contrary pigheadedness, or political opportunism. Contemporaries saw this already. Our question is whether things were different in the attempts at union.

From Constantine to Heraclius, Caesar almost always had his finger in the pie. Most often he also had the initiative. However, this does not of itself bring under condemnation either the successful or the unsuccessful union endeavors. It was self-evident that Caesar's politics would always include a keen interest in the church's internal harmony. Scarcely any basic objection could be raised by the church, not even, or rather, especially not, when this interest was for purely political reasons. The imperial synods, outstanding evidence of an "ecumenical" will to achieve concord, were summoned by the emperors and also actively supported by them in the disposal of their business. Even if the Councils of Nicaea and Chalcedon did in fact make their goals more remote by evoking a fuller development of the antitheses, it can hardly be said that it would therefore have been better for the church if they had never taken place.

We may note two successful efforts at union instigated by the emperor. In 433 the Alexandrians and the Antiochenes were prepared to accept a common confession, although two years earlier in Ephesus they were unable to agree (above p. 167). In 633 the Monophysites in Alexandria achieved doctrinal agreement with the orthodox of the established church. Both of these to be sure lasted only a short time, and there is some doubt whether everything was done quite above board. Nevertheless, they went at their task in the right way, or at least certainly not in an unchurchly way. Confessional differences can only be healed by confessional agreement.

A further example is the effort of the imperial patrician Mundar bar Charet [2] to reconcile the Monophysite parties (Jacobites and Paulites [3]) whose embittered dispute divided the whole Monophysite church in Syria and Egypt. Here, too, there was some political prompting. Mundar was head (πρῶτος φύλαρχος, chief of the chiefs of the tribes) of the Arabian tribes owing allegiance to Rome. They were all Monophysites, and he represented them before the emperor. The church rift weakened their internal political position, and so also his own. He would naturally do everything to remove the split. He himself, however, was also a Monophysite and as such an interested party in the church division. He could conceivably have taken sides and have used his political power for the party he favored. This he did not do. The strife in this case began not with doctrinal differences but with allegedly uncanonical ordinations. The split was manifested in the parties' not going to Holy Communion together.[4] Mundar did not go beyond repeatedly admonishing them to be reconciled, because both parties were "believers." [5] During his stay

in Constantinople in 580 he succeeded in bringing the leaders of the
Monophysite parties (now become three) to confer together. The result
was a peace treaty subscribed by all which urged bishops, clergy, monks,
and laymen to go to Communion with one another without objection.[6]

This union also did not last, but what interests us is the way in which
it was achieved. The Saracen prince acted as an honest intermediary.
He took no position in the controversy, or only so much as to regard it
as a matter not divisive of church fellowship. In the language of Protestant ecclesiastical jurists he was the "chief member of the church"
(praecipuum membrum ecclesiae). The parties therefore could not simply
ignore his voice, and yet he allowed them complete freedom to follow the
argument to an objective conclusion. He neither used threats nor be-
stowed any ribbons. In his many efforts toward unity there is never any
mention of his using the instruments of political pressure which were
at his disposal as head of the Arab tribes and also as imperial patrician.[7]
His role in this Monophysite union did not exceed that of the emperor
in those of 433 and 633. It was no more than formal mediation with
no desire to usurp the parties' right to decide according to churchly considerations. Justinian's efforts at union in 532 also remained within these
bounds. In that year the representatives of the Monophysites and of
Chalcedonian orthodoxy came together at his instigation for a free theological conference in the capital. Although they did not agree as he
wished they would, he declined to use force.

In contrast to these examples of Caesar's self-restraint, we must consider some others. In 369 the Emperor Valens, himself an Arian, came
to Tomis on the Black Sea. He visited the church there with his retinue
and summarily attempted to persuade their Bishop Brettanion "to communicate with those of the opposing confession" (i. e., the Arian).[8]
Brettanion, however, "bravely declared the dogma of the Nicaeans before
that man of power." He left the emperor standing and betook himself
with the supporting throng into another church The emperor obviously
expected that he or at least his Arian retinue would be admitted to Communion there and then. Embarrassed before the whole town, he had the
bishop arrested and exiled. A little later he had to have him brought
back again.

After telling of the outrageous demand the emperor made of the bishop, Sozomen adds "as he was accustomed to do." [9] There was method in this. Valens, like the Arab prince, took the view that the differences were not divisive. No one can deny his right to hold such an opinion. Unlike Mundar, however, he took sides in the church dispute, and that with the Arians. Yet even so when he expected of the Nicene bishop that they go to Communion together, he was not demanding that the bishop become an Arian. He was, however, demanding this concession, that it makes no difference whether you affirm or deny what the confession of Nicaea says of the Son's being of one substance with the Father. Despite the confessional disagreement he yet demanded church fellowship. But because he knew that he would not arrive at this concession by way of a theological agreement, he demanded that altar fellowship be granted as an act indicating a settlement. Altar fellowship is church fellowship. This would have been a union "without prejudice to the confessional situation." To Bishop Brettanion it would have been confessional treason.

Sozomen is undoubtedly right in seeing this instance as characteristic of Valens' methods. Theodoret tells of the Goths who made a treaty with Valens in order to get Roman land to settle on. Originally they were of the "apostolic" faith. The Arian Bishop Eudoxius, however, used the occasion to win them for the *koinonia* with the Arian Emperor Valens. His winning line was that ambition had been the whole cause of the doctrinal dispute and that there was really no doctrinal difference between them. Their own Bishop Ulphilas, Theodoret tells us, also persuaded them with the same arguments to go to Communion with Eudoxius and Valens.[10]

Now this could simply not have happened in this way. The Goths never held a confession different from that of their Bishop Ulphilas, and he was an Arian from the very beginning. Socrates and Sozomen maintain the contrary, but he was made "bishop of the Christians in the land of the Goths" by the Arian Eusebius of Nicomedia.[11] If he was an Arian before the parley with Valens, so were also his Goths. They did not need to be talked into it. Now Sozomen also reports that Communion with the emperor played a role in the political negotiations.[12] This piece of information, in which Sozoman is in agreement with Theodoret, need not be wrong simply because it speaks of Ulphilas as becoming an Arian himself at this very occasion and not before. If we take into account the whole internal state of the empire, it is altogether credible that the parties to this treaty also made promises to each other in the field of confessional politics. If this was the case, we may at least accept the fact from Theodoret's account that the imperial negotiators minimized the doctrinal differences. This would perfectly match the intentions of their master and make intelligible the methods he used to achieve union.

In this Valens is said to have followed the advice of the philosopher Themistios, who, according to Socrates, admonished him that he need not marvel at the dogmatic disunity of the Christians. This is trifling, he pointed out, in comparison with the mass of different dogmas among the Greeks. They have more than thirty. From this we may conclude that God wishes to be honored in various ways, and His majesty is indeed the more to be feared since it is obviously no easy matter to apprehend Him.[13] This advice was not without some effect on the emperor. He did deal more gently with the clergy; banishment replaced death. Valens may possibly have heeded this instruction of the philosopher. This would explain his theory of union but not its execution. He was not always comparatively gentle as in Tomis. When it suited him, he did not first negotiate but simply disposed of his church opponents quite brutally. Another time he could again make offers of union.

When the imperial prefect, Modestus, was in Edessa in 372, he assembled the orthodox presbyters and deacons and had them choose, as the orthodox historian puts it, either "to go to Communion with the wolf" or into exile. At first he spoke winsomely with wily tongue, then gradually more threateningly, until finally he went at an old cleric with "I have commanded you to communicate with those with whom the emperor communicates." He had already once used the imperative "Communicate with the emperor!"[14] No mention is made of composing their doctrinal differences. Neither is there any call to be converted to Arianism. The criterion of the commanded church fellowship is neither Arius nor Nicaea but the emperor. Communicate with the emperor, and everything will be all right! The protesting clergy were banished. Theodoret calls it "going to Communion with the wolf"; it was a shotgun union indeed.

In contrast to Valens, his brother Valentinian I, of Nicene persuasion, did not interfere in the church strife. The Emperor Gratian marks the turning point and Theodosius the final victory of Nicene orthodoxy in the imperial church and the unleashing of civil power to subjugate all dissenters. We are interested here only in the effort at union which Theodosius made before the promulgation in 383 of the harsher civil laws against all heresies. His plan was to call the leaders of the parties together to discuss the controverted dogmatic questions. He hoped in this way to achieve confessional unity for all.[15] This was the way toward union followed later by Justinian in 532 and by Mundar. Even when it was not successful, this method did not look outside the church for a solution. The emperor, however, was talked out of his plan by the orthodox Nectarius, bishop of Constantinople. At his elbow he in turn had as his counselor Novatian Bishop Agelios. It is not difficult to see why these two gentlemen did not think much of a theological conference. Neither of them knew much theology. Agelios had been bishop since Constantine's day and was therefore, as he himself confesses, not exactly young any more. It was only two years since Nectarius had jumped over into his church job while climbing up the civil servants' ladder.[16] On the other hand, Sisinnios was very much at home in theology and history. He was lector in Agelios' congregation and later bishop of the Novatians. He had better advice to offer. The spokesmen of the other parties should be called upon to answer one question: whether they were ready to acknowledge the testimony of the fathers before Nicaea as it related to the disputed dogmas. If they refused to do this, they would fall into disrepute with all the people. If they were willing, one could still over-throw them with the help of these old authorities.[17]

The emperor's intention to achieve union is here turned upside down. Unity is no longer striven for; the other parties are merely to be put to public confusion. The object is to draw away their following. The offer of union is now blotched with dishonor. Theodosius nevertheless

followed this advice. The other parties could not agree on an answer
to the question put to them. Thereupon the emperor summoned the
spokesmen of the Arians, Eunomians, Macedonians, and also Nectarius
as representative of the orthodox and Agelios for the Novatians. They
must present a written confession and have no more discussion.[18] Orthodox Nectarius is obliged to do the same in order to keep up an appearance
of a serious intention for a union. At the next meeting the emperor received the documents as they were handed in and then withdrew to compare them. Thereupon he announced his verdict. He tore up all the
confessions save only the orthodox one because they did not agree with it.
The way was open for a new union technique. In the future, unification
would be achieved by subjugation. The Novatians alone were exempted
from the heresy laws; as always, so now also, they steadfastly held the
dogma of Nicaea.

The important thing here is not that Caesar took sides in a church
dispute. That happened often enough. Here with a show of impartiality
and an apparent desire for unity Caesar was no longer content to be
a straightforward intermediary but moved into the role of arbiter of
doctrine. The next example of this sort is the conference with the Donatists in Carthage in 411. Here the instrument of coercion was the imperial commissioner. As arbiter he had the final decision, and that naturally fell as everybody knew it would long before. But this time the
spokesman of orthodoxy was not Nectarius, about whom Tillemont can
find nothing more honorable to say than that the Arians set his house
on fire. Here we have Augustine. He indeed tried long to achieve the
basis for the restoration of church fellowship with the Donatists by means
of theological instruction and conferences between the parties. The Council of Carthage, in which he also took part, did not refuse the name of
brother and still looked toward the final goal of a brotherly agreement.[19]
However, it also looked forward to Caesar's help in bringing things to
a decisive conclusion. The fact that the Donatists were here prepared
for the radical application of the heresy laws by being branded heretics
instead of schismatics is a large question all by itself. What concerns us
here is that in a church conference which is at least ostensibly intent on

unity Caesar's representative does not merely perform the task of intermediary but is acknowledged as arbiter and that a man like Augustine
finds this all perfectly in order. He deserts the way of the church which
he himself formerly followed and has recourse to something outside the
church.

Caesar cannot be made to bear all the blame for his incursions into
what was essentially church business, particularly when he received
prompting and theological applause from the church. Even so Valens
and Theodosius did take the initiative in their endeavors at union, and
with Valens it is certainly scarcely possible to show that he was prompted
by churchly concern. His theological adviser Eudoxius was no fanatic
but rather an honorable, fair-minded, somewhat timorous, but certainly
very adroit man. Eudoxius was most reluctant to part company with the
radical Arians, while the thought of union with the Homoousians left
him quite cold.[20]

His predecessor Macedonius, who was bishop of Constantinople off
and on from 342 to 360, shows us what union techniques a bishop of the
imperial church was capable of. Anti-Nicene Constantius was emperor;
the court party rigorously Arian. The years 359 and 360 saw the high-
water mark of Arian domination in the East. Theologically Macedonius
belonged to the Homoiousians, who were at first a middle party and then
a few years later joined completely with the Old Nicaeans (Homoousians). Obviously he could not stay long in the capital under Constantius without giving at least some unmistakable expression of his anti-
Nicene mind. This he did by setting upon the orthodox Nicaeans within
his reach.[21] He singled out particularly the Novatians as victims for his
purpose. They also loyally confessed Nicaea. They had prominent
members, and this was doubtless not the smallest reason for the esteem
which they enjoyed in the capital. Macedonius would do away with this
scandal. The undertaking would also not be without its rewards, for the
Novatians had three churches in Constantinople alone. These were also
used in their necessity by the Nicaeans who were here only a handful
although elsewhere the majority.[22] They were indeed so close to one
another that full church fellowship seemed likely. The Novatians, how-

ever, declined this, for as of old they still firmly held that mortal sinners may not be absolved.

Macedonius also wished to win them for *his* fellowship. But how? They would not be made amenable by having their churches torn down or because their Bishop Agelios left the city on account of the troubles. Macedonius simply demanded that they receive Communion with him.[23] Men held in high esteem were imprisoned and manhandled in an effort to make them willing. When all the ill-treatment proved fruitless, they had their mouths propped open with a piece of wood and the elements (τὰ μυστήρια) were stuffed in. Although there were further brutalities practiced also on women and children, these, according to Socrates, were felt to be the very worst. But what was that in comparison with the success achieved? The union had been achieved; Novatians had communicated with the Catholic Bishop Macedonius. Altar fellowship is church fellowship.

Imperial church politics were indeed not absent here, but the full responsibility rested on the called representatives of the church. The principles of Valens' union technique were here taken for granted. Macedonius simply applied them without any scruple or restraint. Both of them used as their basis the premise unquestioned in the early church that where Holy Communion is celebrated, there is church fellowship. This principle was established beyond all doubt and rooted in the life and experience of the early church. If a man is not in harmony with the confession of a church, he may not receive Communion when the Sacrament is celebrated there. Positively put, where men go to Communion together, there is confessional unity. Corroboration of this is given by the Old Arians at the time of the moratorium and by those unions which first achieved confessional unity before the parties received the Sacrament together. In the way that Macedonius and Valens went at church union, confessional disunity or whatever else might divide them (e. g., Novatianism) was pushed aside as irrelevant. They demanded only that everybody go to Communion together. For church-political reasons they adopted the pretense of a principle rooted in the life and experience of the church. By receiving Communion together they were ready to put up a show of unity which did not exist.

Another characteristic of this method is the use of force. There is only a difference of degree between stuffing the host down the throat and the use of the police force. Although he quotes a reliable authority, Socrates' picture of the foul deeds perpetrated upon the Novatians may at first seem overdrawn. Macedonius, however, was not alone in this method of doing things; he had followers. John of Ephesus reports the same of Patriarch John III (Scholasticus, of Sarmin). This man's whole campaign against the Monophysites was conducted under cover of a call to union. Here also union was to be achieved by ignoring the confessional contradictions and by the Monophysites' participation in the Communion of the Synodites (Chalcedonians). Nothing was left untried for achieving this purpose. Enticement gave way to threat, and threat to compulsion. Synodite priests were assigned to Monophysite monasteries so that the inmates would have no other choice but to receive the Sacrament from them. Here also opposition was broken by force. The Eucharist was forcibly put into the mouths of those who would not submit.[24] The women's convents were quite defenseless against such methods. The Monophysite churches were torn down, their services broken up, and their Eucharist trodden underfoot. Bishops and clergy were imprisoned. Plundering and maltreatment of every kind seemed to follow almost naturally. There is no reason to doubt the report of these occurrences. John of Ephesus lived through these years in Constantinople and was himself one of those imprisoned.

The man responsible here was beyond all doubt the orthodox patriarch. His successor, Eutychius, was not much of an improvement. Emperor Justin II mediated more than once when the Monophysites were being dealt with. His successor, Tiberius II, had no taste whatever for the violence used in the church. All that went on there might be put under the watchword supplied by Augustine, "Compel them to come in." Heretics must be driven into the Catholic Church. Here was a theological sedative to ease any conscience disturbed by Caesar's heresy laws.

A noteworthy feature in Constantinople was the manner in which the intention to use force was cloaked under an offer of union. The reason for the resort to force was ostensibly not the heresy of the Monophysites but their opposition to the union and so also to the common Communion. The Monophysite bishops were so plagued by the constant reproach that they were hindering union — a charge heard even in their own congregations — that they were finally prepared to communicate with the Synodites a couple of times. They sought salve for their consciences in this that when they came to participate in the Eucharist of their opponents they made it clear that they did not participate in their confession by cursing the Council of Chalcedon with a loud voice.[25] Such was the *koinonia* of the body of Christ when disagreements were not removed beforehand. It was not the refusal of altar fellowship but the coercion of consciences which drove men to it that here made the Lord's Supper a "Supper of dissension." This expression as it is quite often used nowadays comes close to standing the whole matter on its head.

All of the early church was by no means guilty of getting at union in this way. We have seen what care was exercised so that there should be nothing dividing those who partook of the Eucharist together, neither anything personal nor certainly anything confessional. Old Arians, Novatians, and Monophysites were here in complete agreement with the orthodox.[26] But how was it possible to ride roughshod over this conviction and establish coerced unions, which incidentally soon collapsed? The coercing Bishops Macedonius and John Scholasticus (and others who could be named), although they were the called representatives of the church, were after all acting in collusion with Caesar. In the case of Valens the initiative was Caesar's own. Even in those union endeavors we looked at first, in which force was not employed, politics were not entirely absent. Could it be that the way the church split up called for Caesar's intervention for the sake of the church and that in doing this Caesar simply made a few mistakes? Was the early church actually incapable, perhaps because of its excessive orthodoxy, of overcoming its divisions without Caesar's help in arranging unions?

It was simply not so. There is the example before Constantine of Dionysius of Alexandria, whose office held the highest ecclesiastical power over all Egypt (247—265). After the death of the Egyptian Bishop Nepos his chiliastic doctrine led to "schisms and the defection of whole

churches." So Dionysius himself reports in his account of what follows
(*H. E.,* VII, 24, 6). The teaching of these people reminds one of that
of the Adventists and similar groups in our day. Their favorite book
was the Revelation of St. John. Prominent among them were men who
knew the Bible inside out; there are numerous parallels to the Jehovah's
Witnesses of today (*H. E.,* VII, 24, 5). How did the presiding bishop
from Alexandria bring this breakaway under control? He could not yet
say with Augustine, "Compel them to come in," for the police were not
yet at the church's disposal. He did what one has a right to expect of
a true chief shepherd. He himself went to see the schismatics and heretics, gathered their presbyters and teachers together, and talked things
over with them. "For three days I sat with them from early in the morn-
ing until evening, seeking to correct what had been written [by Nepos]"
(*H. E.,* VII, 24, 7). It was all most orderly and brotherly. Precise questions were put and answers given. No one got pigheaded. Each took the
other's criticism seriously and sought to learn. The result was complete
agreement. The schism was healed.

In this instance there were a number of especially propitious secondary
factors. The schism was new and local. The false teachers were reason-
able people. All the patience and wisdom of that truly spiritual man
Dionysius would scarcely suffice with the Jehovah's Witnesses of today.
Things would likely not have gone so smoothly if his opponent had been
another presiding bishop. There were not only polemics in the church
before Constantine but rivalries too. When fraternal relations were restored, and this was the rule in the church of the majority, it was not
without jealous safeguards for personal spheres and powers. Yet even
so there was as little need then as in the schism of the Egyptian Adventists
for either Caesar's initiative or help toward unity. Even after Constantine, when Caesar's hand was only too evident in church affairs, the
Homoousians and the Homoiousians came to agreement without any
help from him. This unity they achieved was of supreme importance and
fraught with enormous consequences for the future of the church. It
began with the Synod of Alexandria in 362, that is, at the time when
Caesar in the person of Julian the Apostate (361—363) had again with-

drawn entirely from the affairs of the church, given complete freedom to all sects, heresies, and schisms, and left the church to her own resources in dealing with her divisions.[27]

From this it would seem that there is need of some correction in the widely held view of history which sees the orthodox teachers of the church as murderous men who knew only how to wound the body of Christ with their everlasting hairsplitting, while Caesar on the other hand was the merciful Samaritan who put things together again with his unionizing skill and disregard of the cost incurred (Luke 10:35). The first is simply not true, and the second can only show some semblance of truth if we look with only a political or church-political eye. Caesar's efforts to unify the church are far from inconsequential. When he was content to play the role of straightforward intermediary like Mundar, great service was rendered the church which it could accept without denying itself and its mission. Matters changed when Caesar moved into the role of arbiter. This meant in practice that the hope of coming to agreement within the church was sacrificed for a settlement by force. The favored party (now more and more called Catholic in a confessional sense) in this way came into the monopoly formerly enjoyed by the heathen state religion. All other Christians were thus put into the position of the church in the times of the persecutions before Constantine. The use of force against Christians before Constantine was stigmatized and abominated as characteristic of a heathen understanding of the state. Now it was not only conceded to Caesar but even made his Christian duty by the privileged church party because, or insofar as, force was not applied to itself, and because and insofar as the use of force was found to be advantageous.

The orthodox party was not alone in this, although they won the final victory with Theodosius. Things were no better under the Arian emperors. In the following century in the East we find the new parties taking turnabout in the seat of power and privilege. It is not our business to blame the one or commiserate with the other, but rather to weigh the profound perversion of the church which took place here. Caesar's frontal attacks on the church have done it less harm than his help in putting his instruments of power at the church's disposal. The lust for power did not here make its first entry into the church — it was at work there already long since — but it was here enormously propagated. Worst of all, it was called up from its former shameful dark allies and brazenly invested with sacred honor. It was even enlisted in the service of theological persuasion. Whoever has the power has the truth. The weak are branded by God Himself. And so we have arrived at the opposite of that Gospel with which the church first took its way into the world. It has here lost sight of what God has in mind for it and for the things of this earth.

The efforts at union by coercion belong in the same bundle with the methods employed in getting rid of those who enjoyed neither privilege nor concession. We have seen how they would both so arrange the church that disunity would be no more, a consummation which since the days of the apostles has been incessantly striven for with zealous concern and profound theological labor. There was disagreement about what was essential to the unity of the church and in what points differences are tolerable. Irenaeus did not see eye to eye here with Victor of Rome. One thing there was no disagreement about, at least before the onset of coercive unions, and that was that of all criteria confessional unity came first. No church fellowship could be countenanced where there was disunity in confessing the faith. Wherever there is disagreement, the Word is to be employed in refuting, teaching, and persuading, but wherever it falls short of its uniting goal, there can be no Holy Communion together. At times exclusions are necessary. Exclusion is a bitter thing for both sides, but it is not necessarily a resort to force. Even when full schism emerges, both parties can yet live outwardly at peace with each other. This does not necessarily indicate indifference, nor does it call for the "modern concept of tolerance."

We have already observed the temporary friendship in Constantinople between the Novatians and the Catholic Homoousians. It was so close that "they were minded to die for one another." [28] This was at the time when both groups suffered persecution from Macedonius. The early church did not lack similar instances. What was possible when they shared adversity did not have to become impossible when it ceased. A generation later both groups confronted one another in the persons of Novatian Bishop Sisinnios and John Chrysostom, patriarch of the orthodox Homoousian state church. The days of common adversity were long past, the friendship had grown quite cool. Their conversation was as follows:

Chrysostom: The city cannot have two bishops.

Sisinnios: Indeed, it does not.

Chrysostom (angrily): Obviously you want to be the only bishop.

Sisinnios: I do not say that but merely that for you alone I am not bishop, who am bishop for the rest.

Chrysostom (outraged): I shall see to it that you stop preaching, you heretic.

Sisinnios (disarmingly): I should only have to thank you for relieving me of that burden.

Chrysostom (quite relenting, διαμαλαχθείς) : I should certainly not like to put an end to your preaching if you find speaking such a burden.[29]

At the beginning of the conversation we see a prince of the church asserting his power. At the end we find humor achieving the same success for confessional peace as was achieved earlier by shared adversity.

We see that schism by no means required the privileged party to demolish the others' churches, as Cyril of Alexandria later did with the Novatian church there. Some even thought mortal blows and murder were then called for.[30] There was just as little necessity to preserve the integrity of the church by having heretics deprived of their civil rights or having the police banish them from the sight of the faithful. To recognize this, however, the church needed to remember that it is "not of this world." Yet in actual fact the privileged party of the church sang hymns of praise to Caesar's coercive measures. Nevertheless, in spite of all this, that way of dealing with heretics which accords with the spiritual nature of the church was not lost. It was the much-trodden way in the theological controversies and also the synods, however much else may have been unspiritual about them, as they strove to restore the lost or damaged unity in the confession of the faith.

The direst poisoning of the church came in the efforts at union by coercion when it took force into itself. Unspiritual means were brought into the service of a perverted goal: extortion of an acknowledgment of being at one so that the existing disunity might be covered over. In all the storms and struggles which the church endured, Christians yet knew that in the celebration of the Holy Communion they were gathered together with those at one with them in the faith. Here was a refuge and fortress defended against disunity's incursions. The call sounded forth in the liturgy that before receiving the Sacrament together anything that divided them must be removed, and this they did. We have seen how the Old Arians and Nicaeans went to Communion separately, not in order to destroy the peace but for the sake of peace. Nothing demonstrates the perversity of those union measures more clearly than their breaking into this last sanctuary of unity. Men were driven to Communion together not in spite of the fact that they were disunited in the confession of the faith but actually because of it. When men are pressed into altar fellowship, it is in order to cover up disunity. There is no essential difference between stuffing the host into a man's mouth and applying some other kind of pressure, as was done to those Monophysite bishops. It was just at the joint Communion, to which those harassed bishops in a weak moment allowed themselves to be driven, that the sham became quite transparent. They might curse the confession of fellow communicants to their hearts' content and with a loud voice, but the man promoting the union was quite satisfied if only they communicated with them.

It is therefore patently untrue to say that the efforts at union in the early church were less afflicted with doubtful motives and methods than their doctrinal controversies. They also teach clearly that not every establishment of church or altar fellowship can be regarded as a fulfillment of Christ's prayer "that they all may be one." In some of these His last will and testament, Christianity's holy of holies, Holy Communion, is misused and profaned. The sort of union endeavors which do this are the saddest items in this discussion of Holy Communion and church fellowship. We could not ignore them in this connection, but — and that needs to be said again — we may not use them to condemn the whole early church. They were an irreconcilable contradiction both of its theological understanding of the *koinonia* of the body of Christ, as also of the way in which the Holy Communion was customarily observed. For this reason also such efforts at union came to nothing.

Notes to Chapter 15

1. Epiphanius, *Heresies,* 42, 2.

2. Alamundaros in the Greek historians, a Ghassanid to be distinguished from the various Lachmids of the same name on the Persian side.

3. After Paul the Black. Cf. W. Elert, *Der Ausgang der altkirchlichen Christologie,* 1957, pp. 214, 220, 304.

4. John of Ephesus, *H. E.,* IV, 36

5. Ibid., IV, 39; cf. 21 and 36.

6. Ibid., IV, 40.

7. In 580 Mundar stood at the height of his power. His Arab tribes were desperately needed in the war against the Persians. They were to bear the brunt of the war. Emperor Tiberius II poured honors upon him when he visited the capital. He was even granted the king's crown. Mundar secured the emperor's promise to stop the "persecution of the Christians," as John of Ephesus puts it, that is, the suppression of the Monophysites (IV, 42). The promise was not kept for very long. His Monophysitism was naturally a very sore point with the orthodox of the imperial church. Shortly afterwards he was said to bear the blame for the defeat of the Comes Mauricius on the Euphrates. He was arrested and exiled to Sicily. Evagrius, *H. E.,* VI, 2: Bidez-Parmentier, p. 223, 18

8. Sozomen, *H. E.,* VI, 21

9. *PG* 67, 1345 a.

10. Theodoret, *H. E.,* IV, 37: Parmentier, p. 273.

11. Philostorgius, *H. E.,* II, 5. According to Socrates (II, 41 *fin.*) he is at any rate said to have defected to Arianism already at the Synod of Constantinople in 360.

12. Sozomen, *H. E.,* VI, 37.

13. Socrates, *H. E.,* IV, 32; Sozomen, *H. E.,* VI, 37.

14. Theodoret, *H. E.*, IV, 18: Parmentier, pp. 239 ff. Socrates (IV, 18) and Sozomen (VI, 18) also report the emperor's visit to Edessa but know nothing of this that went on there. From the precise personal details which he gives, most notably of the later fate of Eusebius, the spokesman in the conversation with the prefect, and of Protogenes (Parmentier, pp. 242, 17 ff.), we may conclude that he is following some good source of his own.

15. So at least Sozomen writes (*H. E.*, VII, 12): ὑπέλαβε πάντας ὁμοδόξους ποιῆσαι: *PG*, 67, 1444b. It is not necessary to enter here upon the question whether, in view of what preceded, we are to regard Theodosius as here seriously contemplating an actual possibility. Cf. King, pp. 53 f.

16. It was Nectarius who did away with the penitential priests in Constantinople. See above, p. 119. Cf. King, p. 40.

17. Socrates, *H. E.*, V, 10; Sozomen, *H. E.*, VII, 12.

18. The Eunomians were represented by Eunomius himself. The confession he presented on this occasion is preserved for us entire and reproduced by Valesius in his *Annotations to Socrates, H. E.*, V, 10: *PG*, 67, 587 ff. Ulphilas, bishop of the Goths, seems also to have been invited to this religious affairs conference. Cf. H. Boehmer, *RE*, 21, 553. In any case, he arrived in Constantinople shortly before and composed a confession (Hahn, p. 270). However, he probably died before the emperor made his decision. In Justinian's army the Goths still had the privilege to be heretics.

19. Mansi, III, 794. Cf. Frend, pp. 258 f., 275 ff.; Greenslade, p. 147.

20. Socrates, *H. E.*, IV, 13; 12 *fin.* There were others who judged Eudoxius differently; here Philostorgius has been followed. *H. E.*, IV, 14. Cf. Gwatkin, pp. 179, 238.

21. The following account is from Socrates, *H. E.*, II, 38, and Sozomen, *H. E.*, IV, 20. Socrates has earlier reported (II, 27) Macedonius' violence against the Homoousians.

22. *PG*, 67, 328c.

23. μετέχειν τῆς κοινωνίας αὐτοῦ, *PG*, 325a.

24. John of Ephesus, *H. E.*, I, 10; cf. the whole first and second books.

25. Ibid., I, 22 and 24.

26. The same is true also of the Macedonians. These particular followers of Macedonius formed an independent organization after his death. Socrates reports that they "communicated indiscriminately" (or "made the *koinonia* into a matter of indifference," ἀδιάφορον ἕως τινὸς χρόνου τὴν κοινωνίαν ἐποιοῦντο, *H. E.*, V, 4). It was not long before they made the final break of fellowship with the Nicaeans. They were later lumped together with the

Pneumatomachi and thus fell foul of the civil heresy laws. The orthodox Patriarch Atticus of Constantinople nevertheless gave one of their bishops protection against coercion from the orthodox party (Socrates, *H. E.*, VII, 3).

27. "When Julian invited the Galileans to fight out their difference for themselves, the reconciliation made rapid progress. Bishop after bishop went over to the Athanasian side, creed after creed was remodelled on the Nicene, and everything bade fair for the restoration of peace." Gwatkin, p. 67.

28. Socrates, *H. E.*, II, 38: *PG,* 67, 328 c.

29. Ibid., VI, 22: *PG,* 729 b.

30. Ibid., VII, 7; Theodore the Lector, *H. E.*, II, 11.

Bibliography for Chapter 15

Berkhoff, H. *Kirche und Kaiser. Eine Untersuchung ueber die Entstehung der byzantinischen und theokratischen Staatsauffassung im 4. Jahrhundert,* trans. G. W. Lochner, 1947, from *De Kerk en de Keizer.*

Elert, Werner. *Der Ausgang der altkirchlichen Christologie,* 1957.

Giesecke, H. E. *Die Ostgermanen und der Arianismus,* 1939.

Goubert, P. "Les successeurs de Justinien et le Monophysisme," in Grillmeier and Bacht's *Das Konzil von Chalkedon,* II, 179 ff.

Gwatkin, H. M. *Studies in Arianism,* 2d ed., Cambridge, 1900.

Honigman, E. *Évêques et Évêchés Monophysites,* 1951.

Meinhold, P. "Pneumatomachen," in the article on Macedonius in *Realenzyklopaedie der klassischen Altertumswissenschaft,* ed. Pauly, Kroll, and Ziegler, XXI, 1066 ff

Ostrogorski, G. *Geschichte des byzantinischen Staates,* 2d ed., 1952.

Peterson, Erik. "Der Monotheismus als politisches Problem," *Theologische Traktate,* 1951, pp. 45 ff.

Schmidt, Kurt Dietrich. *Die Bekehrung der Ostgermanen zum Christentum. Der ostgermanische Arianismus,* 1939. For Ulphilas see pp. 231 ff.

Stauffer, Ethelbert. *Christ and the Caesars,* trans. K. and R. G. Smith, 1955.

Stein, E. *Geschichte des spaetroemischen Reiches I, vom roemischen zum byzantinischen Staate* (284—476), 1928.

——. *Histoire du Bas-Empire,* II (476—565), 1949.

Tillemont, Lenain de. *Mémoires pour servir a l'Histoire ecclésiastique des six premiers siècles,* Vol. X, 1730.

Communio in Early Church Usage

Modern scholars who have considered the Creed's *sanctorum* as referring to things have taken account of the possibility that the holy things may be the sacraments. They have therefore centered their attention on the question whether this meaning is found elsewhere in church and theological usage. There are actually examples. The most diligent collector of these has been Ferdinand Kattenbusch, who adduces Jean Mabillon's references and himself adds some instances from Augustine.[1] Whether we can take *sanctorum* as referring to things obviously depends on what is meant by *communio*. The original meaning of this term in the Creed can also be determined only from the usage of the era in which it was incorporated in the Creed.

Communio with the genitive of things means that several persons together have, possess, gain, or experience these things as well as the bond thereby made between them.[2] Modern scholars have here pointed to the occasional formula *communio sacramentorum*.[3] The Creed's *sanctorum communio* should therefore mean that we possess the sacraments together and are thereby bound to one another. In a confession of faith this would be a rather insignificant point to make. The situation is different when mention is made of a *communio* of the body and blood of Christ.[4] Here *communio* does not refer to a joint possession of things in the way other things are possessed but to a participation in them such as could have meaning only in a confession of faith. This is quite patently the case when the *communio* of the things lies in the future, as, for example, when Pseudo-Augustine adds to *sanctorum communio*: "*quia dona spiritus sancti in hac vita diversa sint in singulis, in aeternitate tamen erunt communia in universis.*"[5] We must still ask why the Creed does not make use of *communicatio* or *participatio* instead of *communio*, expressions which are otherwise very much at home in this context.[6] Nevertheless, *communio* without any mention of things is used to refer to the Lord's Supper.[7] When used thus, *sanctorum communio* would have to be understood as *communicatio (participatio)*. We may at least say, then, that there is nothing in the early Latin church's usage of *communio* which stands in the way of interpreting *sanctorum* as a neuter genitive.

On the other hand, what about *sanctorum* as referring to persons? *Communio* with a genitive of persons *(sanctorum* from *sancti)* does occur, but rather infrequently.[8] It is easy to see why. For a pregnant usage the genitive of persons is too imprecise. The *Corpus iuris civilis,* on the evidence of its index, uses only a genitive of things with *communio.* If the relation of persons to one another is to be expressed, precision is served by the use of the preposition *inter* or *cum.* Accordingly, we find, for example, the expressions *communio cum libertis* or *communio inter sanctos viros.*[9] Yet if on this score we once more examine Augustine's formula and those of the Middle Ages which define the church as a relationship of persons (pp. 6 ff.), we cannot charge them with imprecision. It indeed makes considerable difference whether the members of the church are described as *christiani* or *fideles,* as *praedestinati* or *catholici,* whether the *sancti* are saints in the specific Catholic sense,[10] or whether the *defuncti* are also included. Behind these definitions lie completely different conceptions of the church. On the other hand, the accompanying terms *(congregatio, societas, collectio, respublica, consortium, universitas, communitas)* are genuine group concepts which render unnecessary any prepositions to indicate the relation between the members. They can all be understood as referring to groups and were in fact so understood.

It is different with *communio.* In legal usage we never find it referring to a group of people. For this we find *universitas* or *corpus;* for groups, *collegium, sodalitas, societas,* or similar terms. Elsewhere, too, in profane usage, as far as I can see, *communio* is never used for a group or association of persons.[11] Theological usage often employs the word in connection with the church, but as an attribute and not a synonym.[12] *Communio* here indicates a relation, the relation of fellowship effected by the church among its members through the faith, the confession, and obviously also the sacraments.[13] This use of the term can be narrowed down for the purposes of ecclesiastical law. It can then mean the church fellowship among bishops who recognize one another's orthodoxy and legitimacy, but never the association of bishops as such. Occasionally it may also refer to the fellowship of the clergy.[14] That single place in Augustine where he uses *communio sanctorum* must be interpreted in the light of all this (p. 6). The Catholic Church has excluded the Patripassionists *a communione sanctorum*. Even here it cannot be denied that he may be referring not to *sancti* but to *sancta*, that is the sacraments. When he thinks of the church corporately he calls it, as we saw earlier, *congregatio, societas,* or *populus sanctorum*. From the time of Constantine the clergy were a recognized corporate body. Constantine's basic edict of 320 in this matter does not, however, refer to this as *communio* but as *clericorum consortium, numerus,* or *corpus*.[15]

We must then also conclude that the *communio* of the Creed does not stand in the way of *sanctorum* as a genitive of persons either. Yet according to the usage of the period in which it was taken into the Creed it cannot be corporately understood, that is, it cannot mean that the church is the *corpus* of the *sancti*. What does it mean then? If the men who incorporated this formula into the Creed were actually thinking of holy persons, they would have done the church great service if they had expressed themselves a little more precisely. If they intended a man to confess that he knew himself to be in the *communio* of holy persons, then the formula would have to be *credo communionem* cum *sanctis*. If they intended a man to confess his belief only in the existence of this *communio,* then it would have to be *credo communionem* inter *sanctos*. But they did neither. On top of this if we do in fact have here a genitive of persons, then we are confronted by a variety of ideas about what is meant by *sancti*. What is more, *sanctorum* may very well be the genitive of *sancta*. The Latin creedal formula *sanctorum communio* is not only capable of two interpretations but of three, four, or even more. Its original meaning is completely uncertain.

Notes to Excursus I

1. *Das apostolische Symbol,* II (1900), 936.

2. Cicero, *Tusculanae disputationes,* 5, 5: *communio literarum et vocum;* Tacitus, *Annales,* 12, 19: *victoriae;* Tertullian, *Adversus Marcionem,* 1, 7: *nominum;* 5, 4: *rerum; De testimonio animae,* 5: *corporalium passionum;* Augustine, *De civitate Dei,* 14, 11: *peccati;* Hilary of Poitiers, *In Psalmum* 132, 2: *terrenarum domorum.*

3. Augustine, *De civ.,* 1, 35; Leo the Great, *Sermones,* 42, 5; 58, 3.

4. Augustine, *Sermones,* 172, 2: *in corporis et sanguinis Christi communione defuncti;* Hilary of Poitiers. *In Ps.* 64, 14: *per communionem sancti corporis.*

5. *Serm.,* 240, 1: *Op.,* Vb, 2189.

6. Tertullian, *Apologeticum,* 39: *a communicatione orationis et conventus et omnis commercii relegetur;* Cyprian, *Ep.* 19, 2; Augustine, *De civ.,* 20, 9: *in communicationem corporis Christi; De catechizandis rudibus,* 8: *sacramentorum participatio; De baptismo contra Donatistas,* 7, 93; *Serm.,* 117, 4: *ad participationem societatemque sanctorum.*

7. E. g., Elvira, Canons 4, 78: *communio dominica;* cf. p. 95.

8. Jerome, *Epistula* 82, 2: *communio patrum;* Cyprian, *Epistula* 69, 9: *malorum;* Hilary of Poitiers, *Ad Constantium,* 2, 2: *episcoporum;* Optatus of Milevis, *Contra Parmenianum Donatistam,* 5, 10: *fidelium;* Carthage III, Canon 42: *fratrum.* For further Donatist instances of *communio sanctorum* see above, p. 6, n. 3.

9. Scaevola, *Corpus iuris civilis, Digesta,* 31, 88, 6; Cicero, *De legibus,* I, 23: inter *quos est communio legis,* inter *eos communio iuris est.* Similarly Ennodius, *Epistola* 7, 28: inter *sanctos viros communio* (*CSEL,* VI, 194, 4); or Sulpicius Severus, *Chronica,* 2, 45: *ineundum* cum *his communionem* (*CSEL,* I, 98, 26). When he soon thereafter says *ut se . . . ab eorum communione secreverit,* we know what he means from the first formulation.

10. Many examples of this sense have been gathered from the early church by J. P. Kirsch in *Die Lehre von der Gemeinschaft der Heiligen im christlichen Altertum,* 1900.

11. For a treatment of *universitas, corpus,* and *collegium* in classical Roman law see Ludwig Schnorr von Carolsfeld, *Geschichte der juristischen Person,* I, 1933. In this apparently exhaustive collection of all the source material I found no instance of *communio* as a number of persons. All the other instances may be found in *Thesaurus Linguae Latinae,* III, 1960 ff.

12. Augustine, *In Ps.* 36, *Serm.* 3, 19: *communio universae ecclesiae;* Rufinus, *H. E.,* 5, 28, 19: *communio ecclesiastici corporis;* ibid., 6: *communio ecclesiae;*

Augustine, *Ep.* 43, 8: *communio christianae universitatis;* Possidius, *Vita Augustini* 14: *communio catholica;* the same in Augustine, *Ep.* 35, 4; Gregory the Great, *Ep.* 1, 14. Cf. E. Wolf, "Ecclesia Pressa," *Theologische Literaturzeitung,* 1947, p. 224.

13. Vincent of Lérins, *Commonitorium,* 3: *ab universalis fidei communione* (*FC,* VII, 271; Moxon, p. 12, 2). Phoebadius of Agen, *Liber contra Arianos,* 8: *illos tantum catholicos esse dicendi, qui in huius professionis communione concordant* (*PL,* 20, 18d); Elvira, Can. 34: *ab ecclesiae communione arceri.*

14. Augustine, *Contra Cresconium,* 3, 25: *ecclesiarum communio;* Hilary of Poitiers, *Ad Const.,* 2, 2: *episcopus ego sum in omnibus Gallicarum ecclesiarum atque episcoporum communione;* Carthage II, Can. 7: *episcopus tenens communionem catholicam;* Gregory the Great, *Ep.* 9, 176: *apostolicae sedis communionem;* of the clergy, Cyprian, *Ep.* 34, 1: *ad presbyteros et diaconos: quod . . . Gaio Didensi presbytero et diacono eius censuistis non communicandum . . . a communione nostra arceatur.*

15. *Codex Theodosianus,* XVI, 2, 3. Schnorr von Carolsfeld believes that *corpus* can here be understood as nothing more than estate *(Stand),* p. 157.

The Origin of the Formula *Sanctorum Communio*

The view formerly held which took Gaul as the home of *sanctorum communio* was called in question by the fact that it is already paraphrased by Niceta in his *Explanation of the Creed* (Ch. 10), though in the sequence *communio sanctorum*. Who is this Niceta? The only source which names him as the author (*Cod. Chisianus*, 14th cent.) describes him as the Bishop of Aquileia. There are various reasons why this designation will not do. Kattenbusch suggests that Niceta is one of the Gallic bishops he has brought to light. One cannot escape the suspicion that he does not wish to let anything prejudice his acceptance of the traditional view that the formula originated in Gaul. Nowadays there is general agreement that he is Niceta, Bishop of Remesiana, whom Gennadius mentions and to whom he ascribes the writing called *De symbolo* (*De vir. ill.*, 22). After Huempel's investigations we may take it as established that he is none other than the missionary Bishop Niceta of Remesiana mentioned by Jerome and a friend of Paulinus of Nola. Remesiana lies in the province of Dacia Mediterranea which we call Serbia.[1] His *Explanation* takes us therefore to the border region where the ecclesiastical and theological currents flow back and forth between East and West. Hence the possibility emerges that *sanctorum communio* has its home not in the West but in the East, and that therefore it is to be understood according to the Greek text. This is made more likely by the fact that G. Morin, A. E. Burn, and Theodor Zahn find in Niceta on other subjects, too, a fund of ideas which derive from the church in the East.

Niceta begins by defining the church as *sanctorum omnium congregatio* and then goes on to say that the patriarchs, prophets, apostles, martyrs, and all the just "who were, who are, and who will be, are one church, for they are sanctified by one faith and conversation, marked out by one Spirit, and are become one body." United with them also are the angels and the celestial powers and dominions. "Therefore in this one church believe that you will attain the communion of the holy things/persons. Know that this one catholic church is established in all lands of the world, to whose communion you are to hold fast." [2] Kattenbusch translates *communio sanctorum* "fellowship with the saints" and so gives the impression that *communio* and *congregatio* mean the same thing. The context, however, shows that they are not the same for Niceta. He merely says that the *communio sanctorum* is to be had only "in" the one catholic church as the *congregatio sanctorum*. No definition of *communio* is given. This can only mean that the writer takes for granted that the word is generally understood; it needs no further explanation. The context shows clearly that he is not the one who incorporated the phrase into the Creed. When this work was composed, some time had already elapsed since the Arian battles and the strife about the *homoousia* of the Holy Ghost, which ended for the orthodox church in 381. Clear indications of this are contained in the document. In 395 Niceta was already well known because of his missionary success. We know he died after 414. His *Explanation of the Creed* may have been written in the last decade of the fourth century. The formula *sanctorum communio* which it presupposes must therefore be earlier.

Kattenbusch believed that he had found the earliest instance of the phrase in the documents of the Council of Nimes (396).[3] This is at a time near to Niceta's writing even though there is a considerable difference between an appearance in a synodical resolution and reception into the Creed. Canon 1 of this Gallic national council is directed against "many who come from the farthest East," pose as presbyters and deacons, and with dubious maneuvers "give the *sanctorum communio* an appearance of simulated religion." Persons of this sort are not to be allowed to serve at the altar.[4] What does *sanctorum communio* mean here? Kattenbusch says participation in the Eucharist; Von Soden, participation in the sacraments, and he would use this to prove that *sanctorum* refers to the holy things *(sancta)*. R. Seeberg also envisages the celebration

THE ORIGIN OF THE FORMULA SANCTORUM COMMUNIO

of the Eucharist here but nevertheless feels that *sanctorum* refers to the saints, that is, the true Christians in contrast with the simulated religion of these other people. The formula, we see, is encumbered already at its first appearance in the West with the uncertainties of interpretation we have observed above. Our interpreters, however, agree about one thing: the formula here means participation in the Holy Communion. If this is so, then we have striking evidence that the formula was originally otherwise intended than the way it came to be conventionally understood in the West after its reception into the Creed.

The clerics who aroused suspicion in Gaul came from the East. Everything points to the fact that they belonged to one of the heretical groups against which antiheresy laws were promulgated in Constantinople. The application of these was more vigorous in the vicinity of the capital and less so in the more remote provinces. Hefele and Kattenbusch take these fugitives to be Manichaeans. However, it is difficult to imagine that Manichaeans would attempt to participate in the Eucharist of the Catholic Church in Gaul. They were more likely Apollinarians. The rescript of the Emperors Gratian, Valentinian, and Theodosius of 388 to the Praetorian Prefect Gynegius was directed against these, and already in this rescript — eight years before the Council of Nimes — we find the formula *communio sanctorum*.

> We command that the Apollinarians and other sectarians of diverse heresies be prohibited from all places, from the walls of cities, from the assembly of honorable people, and from the *communio sanctorum*. They shall not have the right to ordain clergy. They shall not be permitted to gather congregations either in public or in private churches.[5]

These sectarians are no longer entitled to appoint bishops. Those who have been their bishops are to lose their title and honor. Then comes *communio* again. Of the bishops it says, "They shall go to places which most effectively separate them from human *communio* as though by a wall."

In an earlier rescript of 383 the Apollinarians and other sectarians are forbidden to build congregations in city, country, or villa (XVI, 5, 12).

A further rescript of 384 decrees that all those who hold spiritual office among them are to be mercilessly driven out of every corner of the capital *(huius urbis)* where they lurk, and then adds, "In other places they may live separated completely from the assembly of good men" (XVI, 5, 13). The new rescript of 388 clearly shows an increase of severity in being directed against the laity also. There is nevertheless some lack of precision in its local stipulations. If the sectarians are excluded from all places, it is scarcely necessary to say that they are to be removed from the towns. They could indeed be forbidden, as in the rescript of 383, to form congregations in the country, but scarcely the right to live there, unless the authorities intended to throw them out of the empire, lock, stock, and barrel. We note that despite the increase of severity their continued existence is reckoned with, for they are again forbidden to build congregations and appoint clergy.

What is meant by this keeping them from the *communio sanctorum?* In the Theodosian *Book* XVI, which contains these heresy laws, *communio* is used in almost every conceivable way.[6] It is also used as meaning the Eucharist (*solemnitas dirae communionis,* 5, 12). According to the rescript of 388 all Apollinarians are to be excluded from the *communio sanctorum* but only bishops from the *humana communio.* The same fate is not decreed for all Apollinarians. They are to be kept "from all places." Yet account is taken of their continued existence, for they are not to form congregations, appoint clergy, or hold either public or private divine services. They are further to be kept from the *communio sanctorum.* To take this as "congregation" or "fellowship of saints" produces a sheer redundancy no matter whether it was later taken in the West to refer to the church or not. The law is indeed drawn in imperial Latin, but when it speaks of church matters it presupposes concepts of the Eastern church. If we therefore substitute the Eastern church's τῶν ἁγίων κοινωνία, there remains no doubt whatever what is meant here. The rescript orders that sectarians are nowhere to be admitted to the Holy Communion. The reason for making such a law is perfectly clear. We have only to consider what the Eucharist meant to every Christian in the early church to understand how the Apollinarians with all their own ser-

vices prohibited would seek to receive Communion in Catholic congregations. We need only recall the church regulations against such attempts
(above, p. 129). The synodical resolution of Nimes is to be thought
of as such a regulation.

With *communio sanctorum* appearing eight years before the Council
of Nimes in a rescript to the Praetorian Prefect in Constantinople, we
may now regard what was only a possibility in the case of Niceta as good
as proved. The phrase has its home in the East. Its father can as little
be the man who framed the civil law as the man who explained the Creed
in Dacia. Its use in a civil law means that it was understood without
need of any further explanation throughout the realm of that law.

The confession of Jerome which takes us back another decade (above,
p. 8) was first edited by Morin. It was he who then suggested that this
confession was required of Jerome during his stay between 374 and 379
in the wilderness of Chalcis southeast of Antioch (Jerome, *Ep.* 17).
Internal evidence confirms this suggestion both geographically and chron-
ologically. Its first parts contain characteristic elements of the type which
clearly distinguish the earliest Eastern baptismal confessions from those
of the West. It still lacks the Nicene *consubstantialis (homoousios)*, however, and there are peculiarities which we find in the particular tradition
of Antioch. Following Morin's important suggestion, Zahn pursued these
peculiarities further. He found one addition which is quite unknown
in the West but already present in Ignatius ("crucified under King
Herod").[7] What is said about the Holy Ghost clearly presupposes the
appearance of the Pneumatomachi, of whom we hear first in the letters
of Athanasius between 358 and 362.[8] This confession of Jerome is at
present the oldest witness to the date of the appearance of *sanctorum
communio*. It is a decade older than the imperial rescript of 388 and
almost two decades older than the resolutions of Nimes and Niceta's
Explanation of the Creed. We can no longer doubt that the phrase
originated in the East and that it is a translation from the Greek.

If our interpretation is correct, the imperial rescript of 388 means
exclusion from the Eucharist when it speaks of keeping men from the
communio sanctorum. We find a practical application of the phrase

in this sense in the synodical letter of Bishop Theophilus of Alexandria in 401 to the bishops of Palestine and Cyprus. This is preserved in translation in Jerome's letters. Here we read, "It was the endeavor of them all (the monks opposing Theophilus, cf. above, p. 174) to defend heresy under the name of Isidore, who for various reasons had been excluded (*separari*) from the *communio sanctorum*." [9] Isidore was a presbyter who had previously been used for important missions by his bishop. If we should follow today's customary understanding of *communio sanctorum*, we could, indeed would have to, take this *separari* to mean excommunication. The facts of the case simply make this impossible. This word is used of Isidore while the disciplinary measures intended against him are yet tentative.[10] Theophilus condemns his opponents for intriguing for Isidore's escape from these measures. Consequently *separari* cannot mean excommunication, nor yet deposition, but only suspension. *Separari* is therefore the translation not of καθαιρεῖσθαι but of ἀφορίζεσθαι (*Ap. Can.*, 25). The term can also not mean Isidore's condemnation to "lay Communion" (above, p. 163). The only possibility therefore is to take it as καθαιρεῖσθαι τῆς λειτουργίας (Antioch, 341, Canon 3), that is, the suspension from priestly administration of the κοινωνία τῶν ἁγίων. The comment that suspension had already been imposed by "many bishops" reflects the fact that clergy were given the right to celebrate elsewhere upon presentation of Letters of Commendation from their bishop (above, p. 161). It is impossible to make this synodical document refer to the *koinonia* of the saints. The only possible meaning is the holy things of the κοινωνία τῶν ἁγίων μυστηρίων. Jerome, too, could not have understood in any other way the term *communio sanctorum* in his translation.

In the East the meaning of τῶν ἁγίων κοινωνία is quite clear and simple. The usage of *sanctorum communio* in the West on the other hand is quite uncertain. There is ambiguity in both *communio* and *sanctorum*. We are confronted by a positive chameleon. This contrast itself points to the fact that the phrase traveled from East to West and not the other way. Its meaning could not have been in doubt for its authors. Uncertainty arose only when it migrated to a region where church, language, and ideology were different. To set forth the likely external circumstances of this journey would be to carry owls to Athens. The fathers of the Gallic national council at Nimes in 396 could not have been ignorant of the imperial rescript of 388. In both these instances the phrase merely puts in an appearance. In Niceta we find it first in the Creed. His first visit to Paulinus of Nola was in 398. Paulinus was from Bordeaux.[11] Jerome's confession derived from Antiochene circles also traveled to the West, as is shown by the Latin translation edited by Morin.

What of the baptismal confession of Antioch itself? From John Cassian, who was an ardent admirer of Chrysostom and in Constantinople until 403, we have a document in which he does battle against Nestorius "with his own weapons." In it he tells of "the text and faith of the Antioch confession." Around 415 he founded a monastery at Marseilles. However, since he is interested only in the Christological part, he breaks off after "He shall come again to judge the quick and the dead" with "etc." *(et reliqua).*[12] From this we cannot prove that *sanctorum communio* was not in the Third Article. The fragment of the Greek original drawn from the documents of the Synod of Ephesus similarly contains only a part of the Second Article.[13] The Third Article which is supplied is a piecing together of bits from a homily of Chrysostom.[14] There is no proof here either that *sanctorum communio* was lacking. On the basis of this evidence one could as legitimately prove that the Third Article did not mention the church as that it lacked *sanctorum communio.* Chrysostom only mentions those parts of the Creed which have something to do with the passage he is expounding (1 Cor. 15:29). Since we have no other sources for the baptismal confession used in Antioch, it is impossible to disprove that *sanctorum communio* had its home in the church of Antioch. It is, to say the least, rather improbable that the phrase took its way into the world from the eremite's wilderness of Chalcis. That we happen to find it there first to the southeast of Antioch is due to the fortuity of our sources.

Notes to Excursus II

1. Kattenbusch, *Das apostolische Symbol,* I, 123 ff.; II, 440 ff.; 930 ff. Ernst Huempel, "Niceta, Bischof von Remesiana," Erlangen Dissertation, 1895,

summarized in *RE*, XIV, 26 ff. The text of Niceta's *Explanation of the Creed* is in *PL*, 52, 865 ff.; *FC*, VII, 49 f. For a comparison with other manuscripts see C. P. Caspari, *Kirchenhistorische Anecdota*, 1883, pp. 355 ff. The text of the Apostles' Creed which Hahn gives (§ 40) as that which Niceta explains is only put together from the *Explanation* itself. Cf. A. E. Burn, *Niceta of Remesiana*, Cambridge, 1905; Kelly, pp. 388 ff.; *FC*, VII, 3 ff.

2. *Ergo in hac una ecclesia crede te* communionem *consecuturum esse sanctorum. Scito unam hanc esse ecclesiam catholicam in omni orbe terrae constitutam; Cuius communionem debes firmiter retinere.* Kattenbusch, II, 930.

3. Kattenbusch proposes the year 394 (II, 930) and in so doing follows Hefele (II, 57 ff.; ET, II, 406). Similarly F. Lauchert, R. Seeberg (*Dogmengeschichte*, II, 466), H. von Soden (*RGG*, II, 995) and others. According to its superscription the council took place during the consulate of Arcadius and Honorius. They were both consuls in 394 and in 396. Hefele decides in favor of 394 because if it were 396 we would expect *iterum*. This, however, is not conclusive. More compelling is the case for 396 in Duchesne's *Fastes épiscopaux de Gaule* (2d ed., 1907), I, 366.

4. Cf. above, p. 129. The text is corrupt. Lauchert gives it according to Hefele with the emendations proposed by Knust and Nolte. *In primis quia multi, de ultimis Orientis partibus venientes, presbyteros et diaconos se esse confingunt, ignota cum suscriptione apostholia (epistolia?) ignorantibus ingerentes, quidam (qui dum?) spem infidelium (specie fidelium?), sumptum stepemque captantur (captant?),* sanctorum communioni *speciae (speciem?) simulatae religionis inpraemunt (imprimunt?): placuit nobis, si qui fuerint eiusmodi, si tamen communis ecclesiae causa non fuerit, ad ministerium altarii non admittantur.* Perhaps we should read: sanctorum communioni specie simulatae religionis ingrediuntur (instead of *inpraemunt*), ". . . they push themselves into the *sanctorum communio*." Cf. *CCL*, 148, 50.

5. *Cod. Theod.*, XVI, 5, 14. Cf. King, p. 57.

6. *Catholicorum communio*, 5, 43; *unitas communionis, gratia communionis,* 5, 62; 7, 5; *criminis* (of heresy) *communio*, 5, 40; the Eunomians are deprived of *communio iuris*, 5, 46; all *ecclesiae* are to give up those *quos constabit communione Nectarii episcopi Const. ecclesiae . . . episcopos esse societatos; . . . ex communione et consortio probabilium sacerdotum,* 1, 3; *reverendissimorum sacrae legis antistitum communio*, 4, 6; *venerabilis papae communio*, 5, 62; *fidei communio*, 4, 6; *catholicae communionis cultus*, 5, 46. Cf. Excursus I.

7. *Smyrn.* 1, 2: *LCC*, I, 113. G. Morin, Un symbole inédit attribué a Saint

Jérôme, *Rev. Bénéd.*, 1904, pp. 1 ff. The text according to Codex 28 de St. Mihiel (9th century): *Credo in unum Deum Patrem omnipotentem, visibilium et invisibilium factorem. Credo in unum dominum Jhesum Christum Filium Dei, natum de Deo, lumen de lumine, omnipotentem de omnipotente, Deum verum de Deo vero, natum ante saecula, non factum, per quem facta sunt omnia in caelo et in terra. Qui propter nostram salutem descendit de caelo, conceptus est de Spirito Sancto, natus ex Maria virgine, passus est passione sub Pontio Pilato, sub Herode rege crucifixus, sepultus, descendit ad inferna, calcavit aculeum mortis, tertia die resurrexit, apparuit apostolis. Post haec ascendit ad caelos, sedet ad dexteram Dei Patris, inde venturus iudicare vivos et mortuos. Credo et in Spiritum Sanctum Deum non ingenitum neque genitum, non creatum neque factum, sed Patri et Filio coaeternum. Credo remissionem peccatorum in sancta ecclesia catholica,* sanctorum communionem, *carnis resurrectionem ad vitam aeternam. Amen.* Cf. Morin, *Rev. d'hist. et de litt. rel.*, 1904, pp. 209 ff.; Theodor Zahn, *Neue Kirchliche Zeitschrift*, 1905, pp. 249 ff.

We may note five of the seven distinctive marks of Eastern confessions as listed by Hahn, p. 127, n. 344: (1) . . . (2) ἕνα before θεόν, κύριον, and πνεῦμα ἅγιον (only the latter is missing here); (3) the description of God as the Creator of all, which is foreign to the original Western creeds; . . . (5) ἡμῶν lacking after κύριον; (6) a usually detailed characterization of the Son's original relationship to God and to the world, which is completely absent in Western creeds; (7) the specific emphasis that the Son left this original condition at His incarnation and this for our sakes and our salvation, etc.

8. Shapland, pp. 16 ff. P. Meinhold, "Pneumatomachi," Pauly-Kroll-Ziegler, *RE*, XXI, 1066 ff. The statement about the Holy Ghost is found almost literally also in a confession that was earlier ascribed to Phoebadius of Agen. More recently it has been ascribed to Gregory of Elvira (near Granada, d. 392). Cf. in Berthold Altaner, *Patrology* (Edinburgh-London: Nelson, 1960), p. 320, the reference to J. A. de Aldama, *El simbolo Toledano I* (Rome, 1934), which was not accessible to me. Here, according to Altaner, there is to be found an unedited *Fides Hieronymi*, pp. 148—50. If this should happen to be the *Fides Hieronymi* already edited by Morin, then its statement about the Holy Ghost would be connected by De Aldama with the neighborhood of Gregory of Elvira. [This supposition is not borne out by De Aldama, who did not think it attributable to Jerome. He describes it as anti-Arian, dates it c. 381, and says that it is not Spanish. It presupposes both the *Libellus Fidei* and the *Tome* of Damasus, but there is no

recognition of Constantinople (381). De Aldama, p. 88. According to Hahn's criteria it is not Eastern. Trans.]

9. Jerome, *Ep.* 92, 3: *CSEL,* II, 150, 20. For the chronology of the letters see G. Gruetzmacher, *Hieronymus,* II, 70

10. *CSEL,* II, 150, 16; 151, 2 ff

11. Huempel, *RE,* XIV, 27, 3.

12. *De incarn. Dom. c. Nest.* VI, 3, 2: *CSEL,* II, 327, 27; the quotation is repeated exactly at 329, 19.

13. Hahn, following Caspari, p. 141

14. Ibid., p. 142. Chrysostom, *In 1 Cor. hom.* 10: *PG,* 61, 349.

Koinonia and the Holy Things

The first question with *koinonia* as with *communio* is whether according to common usage an attached genitive is more naturally understood of things or of persons. Both are grammatically possible, but in actual usage the genitive of persons is rare. Seesemann has shown that this is also the case in non-Christian usage.[1] In one instance Cyril of Jerusalem contrasts the *koinonia* of demons with the *koinonia* of God. In all the liturgies *koinonia* occurs only twice with genitives of persons. Theodoret speaks of the *koinonia* of the king of the barbarians, and in another place of the *koinonia* of Damasus.[2] Such examples can be found only after diligent search, but the genitives of things present themselves in droves. We need not take into consideration here those instances which speak of *koinonia* with God or Christ, as also Paul's *koinonia* of the Spirit (2 Cor. 13:13; Phil. 2:1). A confession of this sort of *koinonia* would of course be very meaningful in the Creed, but τῶν ἁγίων could not be derived from a nominative parallel with the others.[3] Kirsch finds a place in Athanasius where he believes he descries the forerunner of the personally understood creedal formula. Athanasius here enjoins that we direct ourselves to the goal of the saints (τῶν ἁγίων) and fathers. He adds that we otherwise become aliens from the *koinonia* of these.[4] The critical genitive is "of these" (τούτων), and this refers to the "saints and fathers." This, however, does not prove anything more than what has been known all along: the genitive of persons is possible and the saints (ἅγιοι) can be such persons. That this passage is not a formalized expression is shown by the connections of saints with fathers and by the whole context.

The settled rule is much rather that a *koinonia* with persons or of persons with one another is expressed with prepositions (μετά, εἰς, πρός, as already in 1 John 1:3, 6, 7). In the Maurist text of the Latin translation of Athanasius we find one occurrence of *communio fidelium* ("the communion of the believers").[5] The translator obviously had no second thoughts about this, for the West, as we have seen, has many variations of *communio, communitas,* and *congregatio* with such personal genitives as *fidelium, sanctorum, catholicorum,* etc. (above, p. 6 f.). But Athanasius actually wrote not *koinonia* "of" the believers (τῶν πιστῶν), but "with" the believers (μετὰ τῶν πιστῶν). The correct translation would therefore be *communio* cum *fidelibus.* Athanasius, Clement of Alexandria and the other Greeks who frequently use *koinonia* employ prepositions so regularly that the bare genitive of persons either does not occur at all or only as a rare exception.[6] It would therefore be quite extraordinary if τῶν ἁγίων κοινωνία were intended to refer to ἅγιοι, that is, "holy persons."

The connection of *koinonia* with things is also expressed with prepositions.[7] Here, however, the bare genitive is no exception, and innumerable phrases using it are employed alongside the prepositional construction. There is indeed scarcely a single abstract term in Greek theology which is not used with *koinonia* in this way.[8] Even though the meaning of such genitives may have to be explained from case to case, there can be no denying that τῶν ἁγίων κοινωνία fits most naturally in this long list of "holy things" as another genitive of things. The formal parallels to it certainly are incomparably more numerous and compelling than if we take it as a genitive of persons. Accordingly, the neuter interpretation could be subject to doubt only if no other examples — or at least no other interpretations suitable to our context — could be found. But we do not have to search long for these. Our previous explanation (p. 9 f.) needs merely to be furnished with the support of a few more examples.

The expression τὰ ἅγια appears occasionally as the opposite of "the evil things" (τὰ πονηρά).[9] This suggests such a general meaning that it gives no help in understanding the τῶν ἁγίων of the Creed. The word, however, is no waif and has its accredited place in the language of Christian worship. It is adopted by the Epistle to the Hebrews from the

Septuagint.[10] Even if it then means no more than the Old Testament holy place and its antitype in heaven, the door is here yet opened for it to enter upon other cultic uses. Already in the *Didache* we find our Lord's words "Do not give what is holy to the dogs" applied to the Eucharist.[11] It is true, the emphasis here is on the condition of the recipient. We find the same in the conclusion of the Eucharistic formula, "If anyone is holy, let him come; if not, let him repent." [12] Yet the demand for the personal holiness of the recipient is based solely on the objective holiness of the Eucharist itself, "Do not give what is holy (τὸ ἅγιον) to the dogs." The holy thing, then, has its assured place in Christian worship, and that in explicit connection with the Eucharist.

We find the same thing again in the formula which preceded the distribution in the later Eastern liturgies: τὰ ἅγια τοῖς ἁγίοις.[13] The ἅγιον (holy thing) of our Lord's words has become τὰ ἅγια (the holy things), but there can be no doubt that they mean the same as those words in the *Didache*. Its place in the liturgy indicates that the formula τὰ ἅγια is dual in meaning, for only the consecrated elements can be meant. It is for these that the communicants are preparing themselves.[14] Here we manifestly have the regular liturgical use of τὰ ἅγια and at the same time its clear meaning. Still other instances of this meaning are available in plenty.[15] This understanding of τὰ ἅγια was from the liturgy familiar to every Christian of the Eastern church. There can hardly have been any who did not recall this Eucharistic meaning of the ἅγια when he heard the formula τῶν ἁγίων κοινωνία. The connection would be made immediately if he thought about it at all.

In a document wrongly ascribed to Basil the Great, Kattenbusch found a passage which speaks of the κοινωνία τῶν ἁγίων in the life eternal.[16] He maintains that the saints (ἅγιοι) are meant here. On the other hand, Caspari and Von Zezschwitz point out that Basil uses the expression εἰς κοινωνίαν ἁγίων παρέρχεσθαι.[17] This plainly speaks of the Eucharist, and therefore ἁγίων is neuter. Other examples of this have been given earlier. It is impossible to see how persons can be meant in the eschatological passage. In the imperial rescript of 388 there is no question that the formula *communio sanctorum* refers to anything else than the holy things, for the reference there is to the Sacrament. The same is true of Jerome's confession in view of the syntactical parallel of *remissio, communio,* and *resurrectio.* (Above, p. 8)

The formula of the Eastern liturgies τὰ ἅγια τοῖς ἁγίοις is all but unknown in the West.[18] The corollary of this may well be that the Latin translators of τῶν ἁγίων κοινωνία gave it from the outset a meaning other than it had in the place where it was born.

Notes to Excursus III

1. *Der Begriff Koinonia im Neuen Testament,* pp. 15 f.

2. Cyril of Jerusalem, *Cat. myst.,* IV, 7: Cross, pp. 28, 69. *Ap. Const.,* VI, 18, 8: φεύγετε τῆς κοινωνίας αὐτῶν; VIII, 15, 3: τῶν ἀσεβῶν. Theodoret, *H. E.,* IV, 37, 3; V, 2, 1: Parmentier, pp. 274, 278.

3. Origen, *De principiis,* I, 2: *GCS,* V, 57; *In Joh.,* VI, 22: *GCS,* IV, 132, 18. Irenaeus, *Haer.,* V, 9, 2. Timothy of Berytus, Lietzmann, *Apollinaris,* p. 285, 12, et passim.

4. J. P. Kirsch, *Die Lehre von der Gemeinschaft der Heiligen,* p. 221. Athanasius, *Epistula ad Dracontium,* 4: *PG,* 25, 528b.

5. *Apologia contra Arianos,* 49: *PG,* 25, 335 a.

6. Cf. the indexes and Guido Mueller, *Lexicon Athanasianum* (1952), κοινωνία, p. 765.

7. Origen, *Contra Celsum, GCS,* I, 366, 15: πρὸς τὸ θεῖον; 270, 18: πρὸς τὸ θειότερον. Cf. 2 Cor. 6:14: τίς κοινωνία φωτὶ πρὸς σκότος. *Ap. Const.,* VIII, 34, 12; II, 62, 1: οὐδεμία κοινωνία θεῷ πρὸς διάβολον. Cyril of Alexandria, *Thes.,* 34: *PG,* 75, 612a, of the *pneuma:* διὰ τῆς πρὸς ἑαυτὸ κοινωνίας. *Ap. Const.,* II, 14, 3: τὴν ἐν λόγῳ κοινωνίαν. Chrysostom, *In Act. hom.,* VII: *PG,* 60, 64: κοινωνία ἐν ταῖς εὐχαῖς, ἐν τῇ διδοσκαλίᾳ, ἐν τῇ πολιτείᾳ. Cf. *Didache,* IV, 7: ἐν τῷ ἀθανάτῳ κοινωνοὶ . . . ἐν τοῖς θνητοῖς.

8. Origen, *GCS,* I, 255, 9: σοφίας. *Ap. Const.,* IV, 12, 4: τῆς πίστεως (cf. Philemon 6). Clement of Alexandria, *Paedagogus,* I, Ch. VII, 56, 3: φιλίας; *Stromata,* II, Ch. IX, 41, 2: βίου (= ἀγάπη); IV, Ch. VI, 27, 2: ἀφθαρσίας. Gregory of Nyssa, *Oratio catechetica magna,* 37: Srawley, p. 142, 1: ἡ γὰρ πρὸς τὴν ζωὴν ἕνωσις τὴν τῆς ζωῆς κοινωνίαν ἔχει; 28: Srawley, p. 105, 14: κοινωνία βίου (between God and men); similarly *Ap. Const.,* II, 14, 5 (between just and unjust). Cyril of Jerusalem, *Cat. myst.,* II, 7: τοῦ βαπτίσματος; V, 20: τῶν ἁγίων μυστηρίων; II, 3: τῆς

πιότητος τοῦ Χριστοῦ (cf. συγκοινωνὸς, Rom. 11:17); II, 5: τοῦ ἄλγους. Chrysostom, *PG*, 49, 373: τῶν φρικτῶν μυστηρίων; cf. 50, 653. In Christological contexts, Gregory of Nyssa, *Orat. cat. mag.*: Srawley, p. 152, 1: τῆς θεότητος; *Adversus Apollinarem*, 24: *PG*, 45, 1176b: τῶν ἀνθρωπίνων παθημάτων. Nestorius, F. Loofs, *Nestoriana*, p. 291, 6: κοινωνία ὀνομάτων. The translation of *cum alterius communione* in Leo the Great's *Tome* is regularly μετὰ τῆς θατέρου κοινωνίας.

9. Serapion, *Euchologion*, VI, 1: Funk, II, 164, 14; Brightman, p. 101, 37.

10. Heb. 8:2; 9:12, 24 f.; 13:11; singular 9:1-3. Ignatius, *Ad Philadelphenos*, 9, 1: τὰ ἅγια τῶν ἁγίων (the holy of holies): *LCC*, I, 110.

11. *Didache* 9, 5: *LCC*, I, 175. Cf. above p. 77.

12. *Ibid.*, 10, 6: *LCC*, I, 176.

13. *Ap. Const.*, VIII, 13, 12. Cyril of Jerusalem, *Cat. myst.*, V, 19: Cross, pp. 37, 78. *Testament of Our Lord Jesus Christ* I, 23, J. Quasten, *Monum. Euch.*, V, 250, 28, J. Cooper and A. J. Maclean, ET (Edinburgh, 1902), p. 71. F. E. Brightman, *Liturgies Eastern and Western* (Oxford, 1896), I, 475, 480. Anastasius Sinaita, *De sancta synaxi*, *PG*, 89, 841. Cf. Origen, *In Leviticum homilia*, 13, 6: *GCS*, VI, 477, 12: *sancta enim sanctorum sunt*.

14. Cyril of Jerusalem, loc. cit.: Μετὰ ταῦτα λέγει ὁ ἱερεύς· "τὰ ἅγια τοῖς ἁγίοις." ἅγια τὰ προκείμενα, ἐπιφοίτησιν δεξάμενα ἁγίου πνεύματος· ἅγιοι καὶ ὑμεῖς, πνεύματος ἁγίου καταξιωθέντες. τὰ ἅγια οὖν τοῖς ἁγίοις κατάλληλα. εἶτα ὑμεῖς λέγετε· "εἷς ἅγιος, εἷς κύριος, Ἰησοῦς Χριστός." ἀληθῶς γὰρ εἷς ἅγιος, φύσει ἅγιος· ἡμεῖς δὲ καὶ ἅγιοι, ἀλλ' οὐ φύσει, ἀλλὰ μετοχῇ καὶ ἀσκήσει καὶ εὐχῇ.

15. Hippolytus' liturgy in E. Hennecke, *Neutestamentliche Apokryphen* (1924), pp. 576 f.; G. Dix, *The Apostolic Tradition* (London, 1937), pp. 9, n. 12; 78, n. §; 17, n. 11. Dionysius of Alexandria in Eusebius, *H. E.*, VII, 9, 4. Basil the Great, *Moralia*, 21, 4: *PG*, 31, 741. Eutychius of Constantinople, *De pasch. et euch.*, 3: *PG*, 86, 2396a. Cf. Dionysius the Pseudo-Areopagite, *Hier. eccl.*, I, 4. Perhaps already in Irenaeus, *Haer.*, I, 10, 3: τὰ ἔθνη συγκληρονόμα καὶ σύσσωμα καὶ συμμέτοχα τῶν ἁγίων: *LCC*, I, 361. It is most unlikely that "the saints" are referred to here, for the pattern passage cited (Eph. 3:6) has συμμέτοχα τῆς ἐπαγγελίας, evidently a genitive of things.

16. *Libri duo de baptismo*, I, 2, 17: *PG*, 31, 1556 c. *Das apostolische Symbol*, II, 931.

17. *Regulae brevius tractatae*, Question 309: *PG*, 31, 1301 c.

18. J. A. Jungmann, *The Mass of the Roman Rite* (New York, 1951), II, pp. 297, n. 29; 317, n. 33.

Index of Synods and Persons

SYNODS

Agde (506) 170
Alexandria (362) 196
—— (430) 125
Ancyra (314) 73, 97, 101, 104
—— (358) 103
Anti-Montanist 127
Antioch (268) 113, 128, 135, 140, 150
—— (341) 72, 103, 122, 131 f., 136, 162 f.
—— (485) 158
Arles (314) 79, 103 f., 130, 133, 162, 170
Carthage I (345—48) 132, 134
—— II (387—90) 101, 208
—— III (397) 104 f., 136, 207
—— IV (so-called) 105
—— VIII (403) 191
—— XI (407) 129, 135 f.
Chalcedon (451) 61, 112, 123, 132, 138, 141, 145, 154 f., 161 f., 168 f., 170 ff., 176, 181, 186, 195
Constantinople (360) 201
—— (381?) 116, 122
—— (5th Ecumenical, 553) 61, 94
—— (6th Ecumenical, 680—81, Trullanum I) 53, 61, 112
—— (Trullanum II [Quinisext], 692) 116, 170, 172

Elvira (306) 102 f., 109, 116, 122, 131, 133, 161, 163, 170 f., 207 f.
Epaon (517) 170
Ephesus (431) 167, 174, 215
—— (449) 159
Gangra (c. 343) 183
Laodicea (c. 360) 116 f., 123, 161 165
Lateran (Rome, 649) 61
Milan (680) 61, 158
Neocaesarea (314—25) 92, 101, 162
Nicaea (325) 79, 94, 101, 104, 123, 127 f., 140 ff., 153 ff., 158, 167, 170 f., 178, 181, 186, 188
Nimes (Nemausus, 396) 8, 129, 134, 210 f., 213, 215
Of the Oak (ad Quercum, 403) 182
Quinsext, see Constantinople (692)
Saragossa (380) 103
Sardica (c. 343) 61, 147, 163, 170 f., 174, 179
Seleucia (359) 61
Toledo I (400) 104, 183
—— VI (638) 61
—— XI (675) 61
Turin (401) 104

PERSONS

B. = BISHOP; P. = PATRIARCH; CONST. = CONSTANTINOPLE

Abelard 10 f., 13
Acacians 61
Acacius, P. of Const. 168 f.
Adamantius 26, 146
Aetius 153, 177, 179
Agatho I, Pope 112
Agelios, Novatian B. 190 f., 193

Agnoetae 183
Ahrens 158, 183
Alamundaros 201
Albert, F. 13
Albertz, M. 183 f.
Aldama, J. A. de 217 f.
Algermissen, K. 148